The Failure of Governance in Bell, California

The Failure of Governance in Bell, California

Big-Time Corruption in a Small Town

Thom Reilly

LEXINGTON BOOKS
Lanham • Boulder • New York • London

Published by Lexington Books
An imprint of The Rowman & Littlefield Publishing Group, Inc.
4501 Forbes Boulevard, Suite 200, Lanham, Maryland 20706
www.rowman.com

Unit A, Whitacre Mews, 26-34 Stannary Street, London SE11 4AB

British Library Cataloguing in Publication Information Available

Library of Congress Cataloging-in-Publication Data

Names: Reilly, Thom, 1960- author.
Title: The failure of governance in Bell, California : big-time corruption in
   a small town / Thomas F. Reilly.
Description: Lanham : Lexington Books, [2016] | Includes bibliographical
   references and index.
Identifiers: LCCN 2016010028 (print) | LCCN 2016016874 (ebook) | ISBN
   9781498512121 (cloth : alk. paper) | 9781498512138 (Electronic)
Subjects: LCSH: Bell (Calif.)--Politics and government. | Political
   corruption--California--Bell--History--21st century.
Classification: LCC JS593.B735 R45 2016 (print) | LCC JS593.B735 (ebook) |
   DDC 320.9794/93--dc23
LC record available at https://lccn.loc.gov/2016010028

Printed in the United States of America

In memory of Charlie

Contents

Foreword

"If men were angels, no government would be necessary."
—James Madison, *The Federalist Papers No. 51*[1]

The scandal that erupted in the small town of Bell, California, in 2010 was that rare local government crisis that for a time goes beyond a merely regional story to impact the national consciousness. Big-city scandals often go national, and small-city incidents can. But what was so special about Bell?

First, it was about something simple to understand: dollars, big dollars—specifically, outrageous compensation to a small number of officials. City Administrator Robert Rizzo, his assistant Angela Spaccia, the police chief, administrative services director, general services director, and a few others were enjoying salaries two to four times the normal rate, ranging from approximately $250,000 to over $700,000. City Councilmembers were making more than $100,000 in a city whose population size legally entitled them to annual pay of less than $5,000.

Second, these massive sums enjoyed by "public servants" were in stark contrast to Bell's dismal economic circumstances, which included extensive poverty, high taxes, and high unemployment. Bell's former leadership's attitude was nicely illustrated by a former mayor who responded to community anger by saying, "In a troubled city, the city council should get paid a little more."[2]

Third, former city officials' immediate reaction to revelations of the scandal expanded the outrage. "If that's a (salary) number people choke on," the city manager said, "maybe I'm in the wrong business. I could go into private business and make that money. This council has compensated me for the job I've done."[3] The residents clearly could expect no relief from their leaders.

The scandal extended well beyond excessive salaries of eight officials. It also featured a questionable employee loan program; unauthorized contributions to pension programs; excessive fees and taxes charged to local businesses; sweetheart deals made to acquire property; and a $100,000,000 bonding program that paid millions to favored contractors for projects with little return to the city.

Today, six years after this story first broke in the *Los Angeles Times*, closure has largely been accomplished. Our law firm volunteered to represent a local group *pro bono* in promoting a 2011 recall, which resulted in all the councilmembers being replaced.[4] The new city council brought in a new city manager, new management team and city attorney, who found themselves facing $78,000,000 in claims without any cash reserves.[5] Happily, within four years, all these claims were resolved and the city had $25,000,000 in the bank.

So, on one level, Bell has had its fifteen minutes of infamy. The so-called "Bell 8" have been punished, two *Los Angeles Times* reporters won the Pulitzer Prize, and the country has gone on to other crises. But this is the point for academic review to reflect on whether there is a larger meaning or lesson here for those of us who care about public service.

Throughout these years of strife, it has been a pleasure getting to know the author of this work, Dr. Thom Reilly. He has closely followed the scandal and its aftermath, whose meanings we have frequently discussed. Some questions may never be answered. To me, the most mysterious is whether Rizzo was mastermind or puppet. In the criminal proceedings, one side portrayed Rizzo as the mastermind and Spaccia the loyal follower; the other claimed that Rizzo was not smart enough to be the mastermind and that the schemes did not develop until Spaccia arrived on the scene.

It is perhaps the most puzzling human question to emerge from the scandal. Dr. Reilly provides interesting insights on this question, and lets the participants speak for themselves without ultimately answering it. Frankly, after all the depositions and testimony, I don't know who really could give a satisfactory answer.

Dr. Reilly's book instead ultimately focuses on important issues of public administration and policy—how should a government control itself? He identifies key factors contributing to the scandal, and focuses particularly on what Bell might tell us about the council-manager form of government. While this model emerged as a reform of the strong mayor ("machine/political") approach, Dr. Reilly concludes that in fact there is no evidence to confirm that there are systemic differences in the two systems in how they respond to powerful constituencies, levels of citizen participation, quality of services, or operational effectiveness. He suggests that the "adaptive city" has evolved with elements of both systems, and that Bell's situation may best be explained by concepts of "political monopoly," geographic contagion, the corrupting effects of fiscal systems that enable revenue extraction, and a professional public-sector ethics lens.

Dr. Reilly concludes that the Rizzo/Spaccia scheme led to a form of collective corruption. The key factors that should have prevented this are (a) community participation through voting and direct participation in government; (b) electoral process; (c) vulnerability of the manager and key directors to removal; (d) the role of the top legal official in assuring proper and legal process; (e) regular audits and reporting of financial information; (f) transparency and access of public to information and civic involvement of organizations; and (g) periodic public internal assessment of organizational performance.

To this, I would add that anything that goes on over a number of years creates the opportunity for people who should be asking questions to get comfortable and become excessively deferential to long-serving managers. While long-serving employees are not more susceptible to corruption than short-serving ones, long-serving ones do not earn the right to be free from examination.[6]

Of course, Bell ultimately is the story of how no set of checks and balances can protect the public from dedicated malfeasers, given enough time. Clearly all humans are not angels—notably including those working in government. It is fine to say that we need to develop ethical officials, as we should. Yet our ultimate hope is in reinforcing the check and balance systems that have proven, on the whole, to prevent Bell's experience from becoming the norm in public service.

I think the real story of Bell is not only how it happened, but also what happened in the years after the revelations. It is true that the *Los Angeles Times* reporters, "stumbled" into the story. Yet the 4th Estate proceeded to perform its constitutional duty, and from there all manner of institutions responded. The District Attorney began criminal proceedings. The state Attorney General began a lawsuit challenging the right of the indicted officials to govern the city. The State Controller performed an audit. The California Board of Accountancy imposed fines and placed the City's audit firm on two years' probation. The Department of Corporations investigated various grants. The State retirement system invalidated various pensions. The federal government, through the SEC and IRS, investigated various bond programs and took enforcement actions. And through the civil judicial system, the city invalidated improper actions and recovered $10,000,000 in damages and restitution. Though a trial court made a mistaken ruling, the Court of Appeals addressed the issue broadly in precedent-setting rulings.

Although it has taken years, and millions in legal fees, the system responded in a reasonably satisfactory manner from the viewpoint of Bell's citizens. They now have a fully functioning local government, and have a reserve in the bank as good or better as a percentage of budget than most

California cities. The "Bell 8" have been punished, and minimal Internet research should keep any of them from ever being in a position to repeat their performance.

So Bell gives us a clear situation to avoid, and Dr. Reilly's book identifies and analyzes key points along the city's pathway to ruin. It also tells us that—short of our becoming angels—that this will happen somewhere again. This is not to lose faith in the system. On the contrary, the genius of federalism and our marvelously layered government prizes citizen participation and ethical behavior and does not condone corruption. The system is, ultimately, self-correcting. With this foundation, we will undoubtedly continue to muddle through fulfilling the aphorism of Winston Churchill that democracy is flawed, with its only virtue that it is superior to all other forms of government.

Dave J. Aleshire
Partner, Aleshire & Wynder LLP

NOTES

1. James Madison, Federalist No. 51. The Structure of the Government Must Furnish the Proper Checks and Balances Between the Different Departments. February 6, 1788. Retrieved from: http://www.constitution.org/fed/federa51.htm.

2. Gottlieb, J. & Vives, R. "DA Investigating why Bell council members get nearly $100,000 a year for a part-time job." *Los Angeles Times*. June 24, 2010. Retrieved from: http://articles.latimes.com/2010/jun/24/local/la-me-0624-maywood-20100624.

3. Gottlieb, J. & Vives, R. " Is A City Manager Worth $800,000? *Los Angeles Times*. July 14, 2010. Retrieved from: http://www.latimes.com/local/la-me-bell-salary-20100715-story.html.

4. Oscar Hernandez, Teresa Jacobo, Luis Artiga, George Mirabel. City council member Lorenzo Velez was the only city official who was not served with recall papers. Unlike the other city councilmembers, Velez was not receiving a salary beyond $600 per month. In the wave of anger at incumbent city councilmembers, however, Velez lost his seat on the council in the March 8, 2011 election.

5. The City's audits had been performed for sixteen years by Mayer Hoffman McCann P.C., and its predecessor. They were fined $300,000 and placed on two years' probation by the California Board of Accountancy. These audits did not disclose any of the financial schemes and a state audit by the State Controller revealed numerous audit violations. At that point no financial audits were performed in 2010 and 2011, and ultimately the city had to spend almost $1,000,000 during four audits over a two-year period to reconstruct the City's financial condition.

6. The trial court held the city had an indemnity obligation to the corrupt officials which could have cost millions, but the Court of Appeals ruled in two cases that victimized public agencies can pursue claims against corrupt officials without the official turning around and claiming that the victimized public agency must indemnify the corrupt official, and essentially have to pay for its own recovery efforts. (*City of Bell v. Superior Court* (2013) 220 Cal.App.4th 236; *People ex rel. Harris v. Rizzo* (2013) 214 Cal.App.4th 921)

Acknowledgments

This book had a long gestation period and was made possible by the tremendous contributions of a number of individuals. During this period the ideas in this book were often presented to others, challenged, debated, and refined. I owe a great deal to several people who labored through drafts and offered insightful critiques and suggestions.

Dave Aleshire, Anthony Taylor, and Michael Kratzer provided access to the voluminous legal documents that were essential to this book. Their time spent with me in person and careful review of the manuscript ensured I not only got the story right but also avoided making unjustifiable assertions. Larry Leavitt, Chester Newland, Rory Reid, Steve Smith, and an anonymous reviewer also labored through drafts of the manuscript. Their invaluable comments and good sense helped to clarify and refine my thinking. A special thanks to John Kirlin who provided much needed intellectual guidance on the theoretical frameworks.

The research assistance provided by my graduate assistants—Judi Brown, Gregory Coordes, Larry Gulliford, and Kyrstyn Richardson—was invaluable. In particular, Gregory and Larry's research and writing contributed significantly to the book. Gregory was involved early with conceptualizing the manuscript and co-authored parts of the book. Edward Spyra and Lauren Reilly offered guidance and design on the book cover. Bill Hart, who provided editing for the book, often made me appear literate where I was not, and suggested innovative ways to summarize the vast amount of legal research that could be highly technical. Kathryn Tafelski, assistant editor for Lexington Books, was very gracious with her time responding to my numerous emails.

Special thanks to the city of Bell for allowing me to visit and learn about their community. I am very appreciative of the time that Fernando Chavarria,

James Corcoran, Jeff Gottlieb, Sean Hassert, Ali Saleh, Nestor Valencia, and Doug Willmore spent with me assisting in my understanding of what occurred in Bell.

Finally, I give a very special thanks to my partner Jim Moore. He has a gift for encouragement, for knowing when to react and when to listen, and for providing much needed moral support.

Key

Jerry Brown – Former A
Elected Governor in 2

Tom Brown – Fo
Criminal Divi
2005; repr
City of S
Mayo

Randy Adams – Bell Police Chief, 2009 to 2010; resigned when scandal broke. Previously served as chief in the California cities of Glendale and Ventura

Clifton Albright – Partner with Albright, Yee & Schmit; hired by Rizzo as a contract attorney in 2005. Represented the City of Southgate in the corruption case involving Mayor Albert (Big Al) Robles

Dave Aleshire – Formed public law firm of Aleshire & Wynder in 2003; represented BASTA in 2010; hired in 2011 as the first permanent Bell city attorney since the scandal broke

Luis Artiga – Baptist pastor appointed to the council in 2008, elected in 2009; the lone member of the "Bell 8" to be acquitted of corruption charges by the jury

Victor Bello – Appointed councilmember in 1998; wrote the district attorney in 2006 and 2009 about corruption concerns. Resigned from council in 2009 to become assistant food coordinator for the Food Bank while keeping his $100,000 salary. Found guilty of corruption in 2013

Harlan Braun – Defense Attorney for Angela Spaccia; prior cases included representing Officer Briseno, who was acquitted in the Rodney King beating case; attorney Vincent Bugliosi on a perjury charge in the Charles Manson trial; and Elizabeth Taylor's physician, Michael Gottlieb

ttorney General for California from 2007 to 2011.
12

rmer Assistant US Attorney, Central District of California,
ion from 1991 to1995; hired by Rizzo as a contract attorney in
sented Rizzo in his DUI case. In 2005, his firm settled with the
outhgate for $2 million related to the city's suit for overbilling in the
Albert Robles corruption case

John Chiang – California State Controller from 2007 to 2015. Elected California State Treasurer in 2012

George Cole – Elected to council as a reformer in 1984 during the California Bell Poker Casino scandal; became known as the "Godfather of Bell politics"; ran the Oldtimers Foundation; found guilty of corruption in 2013

Steve Cooley – Los Angeles District Attorney from 2000 to 2012; oversaw the prosecution of the Bell 8; described governance in Bell as "corruption on steroids"

James Corcoran – Bell police sergeant and whistleblower forced into retirement for his reporting of corruption; received $400,000 and reinstatement to the force in the settlement of his whistleblower lawsuit

Ralph Dau – Los Angeles County Superior Court Judge. Presided over the civil case the California Attorney General's Office filed against former Bell officials

David Demerjian - Deputy Los Angeles County District Attorney who headed the Public Integrity Division. Led the criminal investigation of the Bell corruption scandal and subsequent prosecution of the Bell 8.

Eric Eggena – Hired by Rizzo as a prosecutor and later became director of general services where he oversaw city code enforcement; had city aggressively target residents and businesses for the minor violations

Christina Garcia – Former mathematics teacher and co-founder of BASTA; elected to the California State Assembly representing the 58th district (southeastern Los Angeles county) in 2012 and 2014

Lourdes Garcia – Began working for Bell in 1991 and became director of administrative services in 2003; granted immunity from prosecution for her testimony; her position was eliminated in 2011

Jeff Gottlieb – *Los Angeles Times* reporter who shared the Pulitzer Prize for uncovering corruption in the Bell; received the George Polk and the Selden Ring awards; left *Los Angeles Times* in May 2015.

Maria Grimaldo – Los Angeles County District Attorney's Office investigator who interviewed Mirabal in February 2010 concerning the high salaries paid to councilmembers and other corruption by city officials

Sean Hassett – Los Angeles deputy district attorney who prosecuted the "Bell 8"

Oscar Hernandez – Elected mayor in 2006 and 2007 and served again in 2009; former farm worker with limited English skills and a formal education to the 6th grade; convicted of corruption in 2013

Max Huntsman – Deputy supervisor in the public integrity division at the L.A District Attorney's office. Lead prosecutor against Angela Spaccia. Currently L.A County's Inspector General overseeing jails

Teresa Jacobo – In 2001 became first Latina elected to the council; a native of Mexico and a real-estate agent, was convicted of corruption in 2013

Kathleen Kennedy – Los Angeles County Superior Court judge; oversaw the "Bell 8" corruption trial

Ed Lee – Contract Bell city attorney from 1993 to 2010 while managing partner with Best Best & Krieger; simultaneously served as city attorney for Maywood, Downey, and Covina; Bell received $2.5 million to settle its malpractice lawsuit against Lee and his former firm

Bruce Malkenhorst – City Administrator in Vernon for twenty-nine years; convicted in 2011 for misappropriation of funds

George Mirabal – Funeral director first elected to council 1986, then served as city clerk for a year; appointed to the council again in 1993; convicted of corruption in 2013

Gilbert Miranda – Senior investigator for the Los Angeles County District Attorney's Office who investigated Rizzo and other Bell officials related to corruption allegations

Alan Pennington – Consulting actuary with Wells Fargo in Tennessee who advised Rizzo and Spaccia on the Bell Supplemental Retirement Plan

John Pitts – Former Bell city administrator convicted in 1984 for accepting a bribe and hiding his ownership in the California Bell Poker casino

Ana Maria Quintana – Elected as Bell councilmember in 2011 and re-elected in 2013. Led opposition to litigation fees charged by city attorney's firm in 2013. Opposed the 2015 charter reform ballot

Roger Ramirez – Bell resident who filed a public records request in 2008 for salary of city officials; received incorrect information from city

Robert Rizzo – Bell city administrator from 1993 to 2010; pleaded no contest to sixty-nine counts of corruption, sentenced to twelve years in prison and $8.8 million in restitution

Albert Robles (Big Al) – Former Southgate mayor, councilman, treasurer, and deputy city manager; convicted in 2005 for corruption and sentenced to ten years in prison, reduced on appeal; released after time served

Ali Saleh – Co-founder of BASTA; ran unsuccessfully for council in 2009; elected mayor in 2011 after Bell council was recalled; re-elected in 2015

Sean Sheffield – Spaccia's son injured in a motorcycle accident; Spaccia took time off to care for him from September 2007 to June 2008, and set up Sean to serve as a pass through for payments to a Pacifica Alliance Group to conduct a survey even though Sean did no work

Angela Spaccia – Hired in 2003 as an assistant to Rizzo; became assistant chief administrative officer in 2009; convicted 2013 on eleven counts and sentenced to eleven years and eight months in prison and more than $8 million in restitution

James Spertus – Former federal prosecutor in the US Attorney's Office for the central division of California; Rizzo's attorney in his corruption trial

Dennis Tarango – Served as Bell planning director while operating companies that did business with the city; held partnership with Rizzo in a horseracing business called Golden Aggie Ranch, Inc.

Anthony Taylor – Partner with Aleshire & Wynder; hired in 2011 as Bell's lead civil litigator

Nestor Valencia – Ran unsuccessfully for council in 2007 and 2009; founded the Bell Resident Club in 2007; elected in 2011 during the recall of the council; re-elected in 2015 and has served one term as mayor

Rebecca Valdez – Former Bell city clerk from 2007 to 2011, hired by Rizzo at the age of seventeen; testified in the corruption trial under promise of immunity; left Bell for employment in the California city of Covina in October 2015

Lorenzo Velez – A heavy equipment operator from Los Angeles, appointed to the Bell council in 2009 to fill out the term of Victor Bello; salary of a little more than $8,000 made him only councilmember not collecting $100,000

Ruben Vives – *L.A. Times* reporter who helped uncover corruption in Bell that led to criminal charges against eight city officials; shared Pulitzer Prize for 2010 investigative series

Pete Werrlein – Former Bell mayor sentenced in 1984 to three years in prison and a $21,000 fine for holding hidden interests in the city's California Bell Poker casino. Rehired by Bell to restart the defunct casino in 1993, the same year Rizzo became city administrator

Doug Willmore – First permanent city administrator since the corruption scandal; resigned in 2015 to become city manager in Rancho Palos Verdes. Prior to serving in Bell, he was city manager for El Segundo where he was fired after proposing a tax hike on the Chevron oil refinery; settled a whistle-blower and anti-retaliation lawsuit for $300,000

Chronology

1810   Antonio Maria Lugo received Spanish land grant for Rancho San Antonio

1875   James George Bell established community of Bell Station Ranch on part of the former Rancho San Antonio

1898   Bell Station Ranch renamed Bell

1927   City of Bell Incorporated

1977   Oldtimers Foundation opens its doors in nearby city of Southgate

1978   California voters pass Proposition 13, which limits property taxes

1980   California Bell Poker Club Opens

1980   Robert Rizzo begins work in the city of Rancho Cucamonga

1982   Bethlehem Steel plant in neighboring Vernon closes

1984   Bell Mayor Pete Werrlein, City Administrator John Pitts, and Santa Monica attorney Kevin Kirwan convicted of corruption related to the poker club

1984   George Cole elected to the Bell City Council

1986   George Mirabal first serves as city councilman. The following year he serves as the city clerk and then is appointed to city council in 1993 after the death of incumbent Jay Price

1988   Rizzo hired as city manager for the City of Hesperia

1992   Rizzo departs Hesperia after city leaders pressure him to resign

1993   Rizzo hired as Bell City Administrator

1993   Bell hires former mayor and convicted felon Pete Werrlein as a consultant

1993   Bell hires Ed Lee as city attorney; Lee holds the position until his resignation in 2010

1995   Bell Jackpot Casino (formerly California Bell Club) closes its doors for the last time

1998   Victor Bello becomes city councilman

2001   Rizzo divorces first wife

2001   Teresa Jacobo appointed to city council as the first Latina to serve

2003   Bell hires Angela Spaccia

2003   Bell voters approve Measure A, $70 million in bonds to develop the Bell Sports Complex

2005   Rizzo purchases a luxurious ranch home in Washington state and begins breeding thoroughbreds

2005   Spaccia leaves her job to take care of her parents from November 2005 until April 2006

2005   A November 29 special election turns Bell into a charter city by a vote of 336 to 54, with less than 1 percent of the population voting and many questionable absentee ballots.

2005   Southgate sues Clifton Albright's and Tom Brown's law firms for overbilling in the corruption case of Southgate Mayor Albert Robles; Brown's firm settles and pays Southgate $2 million

2005   Rizzo hires Clifton Brown as a legal consultant

2006   Rizzo hires Tom Brown as a legal consultant

2006   Oscar Hernandez elected Bell mayor; reelected in 2007 and 2009

2006   Bello writes to district attorney about corruption, and does so again in 2009

2007   Rebecca Valdez appointed city clerk, after being first hired by Rizzo at age seventeen for clerical work

2007   Spaccia takes leave from September 2007 until June 2008 to take care of her son who was injured in an accident

2007   Bell raises its property tax to the second-highest rate in Los Angeles County

2008   Luis Artiga is appointed to the Bell City Council. Elected in 2009

2008   Spaccia's title is changed from assistant to the chief administrator to assistant chief administrator officer

2008   Roger Ramirez submits public records request to City Hall concerning high city salaries

2009   Bello resigns from the council to become assistant food coordinator for the Food Bank; keeps his $100,000 salary

2009   Lorenzo Velez is appointed to the council after Bello resigns. His salary of $8,000 made him the only councilman not collecting at least $100,000

2009   Randy Adams hired as police chief

2009   Bell Police Sgt. James Corcoran, acting on anonymous tips about corruption, contacts the FBI

2010   Spaccia becomes interim city manager for Maywood from February to August

2010   In February 2010, Mirabal is interviewed by Los Angeles County District Attorney's Office investigator in response to his 2009 letters. The DA's office learns of high salaries paid to councilmembers

2010   Rizzo is arrested for DUI on March 6 in Huntington Beach

2010   Learning that officials were looking into Bell's high public salaries, the *Los Angeles Times* starts its own investigation and initiates a public records request

2010   *Los Angeles Times* reporters Gottlieb and Vives have their Little Bear Park meeting with Bell officials on July 9 and publish an article headlined "Is a City Manager worth $800,000?"

2010   BASTA is formed on July 16

2010   The L.A. District Attorney's Office, State Attorney General's Office and State Controller begin investigating allegations of voter fraud, conflicts of interest, high salaries, and other areas of possible corruption

2010   Rizzo, Spaccia, and Adams resign on July 23.

2010   Bell City Council votes to decrease their salaries to $673 per month on July 27

2010   The California Attorney General's Office files a civil complaint on behalf of Bell against Rizzo, Spaccia, Hernandez, Cole, Bell, Mirabal, as well as former police chief Randy Adams on September 15

2010   The "Bell 8" are arrested and handcuffed one by one on September 22

2010   Councilman Artiga resigns his council seat on October 5

2011   In March, voters recall all the indicted councilmembers and elect
        replacements. The votes are certified by the county board of
        supervisors following emergency state legislation, and the new
        council is sworn in on April 7

2011   On July 28, David Aleshire and Anthony Taylor are hired as first
        permanent city attorneys since the scandal

2012   Doug Willmore is hired on June 1 as the first permanent city
        manager administrator since Rizzo left in 2010

2013   A jury convicts the mayor and council on March 20; Luis Artiga is
        acquitted; Bello, Cole, Hernandez, Jacobo, and Mirabal are found
        guilty. Judge Kennedy declares a mistrial for remaining counts, and
        orders a new trial

2013   In March, the California Court of Appeals rules in favor of the
        California Attorney General in People ex rel. Harris v. Rizzo that the
        Attorney General has standing to sue former Bell officials

2013   On April 8, the five former councilmembers plead no contest and
        agree to pay restitution to the city

2013   Rizzo pleads no contest to sixty-nine charges on October 3

2013   In October 2013, California Court of Appeals rules in City of Bell v.
        Superior Court that the City of Bell does not have to pay Rizzo's
        legal fees or otherwise indemnify him for actions related to
        corruption

2014   Rizzo pleads guilty to tax charges on January 13

2014   Spaccia is sentenced to more than eleven years in prison and ordered
        to pay more than $8 million in restitution

2014   On April 11, Adams and the City of Bell settle their civil lawsuits
        concerning salary by agreeing that Adams would pay Bell $214,000

2014   Rizzo is sentenced on April 14 to thirty-three months in federal
        prison for tax evasion

2014   Rizzo is sentenced on April 16 to twelve years in state prison and
        ordered to pay $9 million in restitution; he is allowed to serve his
        federal prison sentence concurrently with state court sentence;
        which allows him to serve half his time in federal prison

2014   On July 11, Mirabal is sentenced to one year in county jail and is
        ordered to pay $242,000 in restitution to the City of Bell

2014   On July 23, Cole is sentenced to 180 days of home confinement and
        ordered to pay $77,000 in restitution

2014   On July 25, Jacobo is sentenced to two years in state prison and is ordered to pay $242,000 in restitution. She receives the harshest sentence of the former councilmembers

2014   On August 1, Hernandez is sentenced to one year in county jail and ordered to pay $241,000 in restitution

2014   On August 1, Bello, the final Bell 8 defendant, is sentenced to one year in prison and ordered to pay $177,000 in restitution to Bell. His time spent in prison was minimal because the Court credited the 340 days he spent in jail in 2010 to 2011 when he was unable to post bond

2015   In March, 74 percent of voters elect to reform the Bell City Charter to remove the "assistant chief administrative officer" position, restrict councilmember pay, strengthen rules against conflicts of interest, prohibit indefinite franchise contracts with the city, and change recall election procedures

2015   Doug Willmore resigns in March to become city manager in Ranchos Palos Verdes

Introduction

It Was All About the Money

"Government ought to be all outside and no inside. . . . Everybody knows that corruption thrives in secret places, and avoids public places, and we believe it a fair presumption that secrecy means impropriety."
—Woodrow Wilson. U.S. President. From his campaign book, *The New Freedom*[1]

The judge was furious. On April 10, 2014, Los Angeles Superior Court Judge Kathleen Kennedy sentenced Angela Spaccia, assistant city administrator of Bell, California, to more than eleven years in prison and more than $8 million in restitution. The judge levied such severe punishment because of Spaccia's central role in the empire of corruption that had ruled the small southern California city for years.

Before passing sentence on what Kennedy termed "an extraordinary case of greed and an extraordinary case of mismanagement and self-dealing," she had more to say:

> . . . I think when you go through everything and you kind of get down to the core of this case, it was all about the money. . . . In her communications with [Bell Police Chief] Randy Adams ....[Spaccia] says, ". . . *you can take your share of the pie just like us. We will all get fat together. Bob has an expression he likes to use on occasion. 'Pigs get fat, hogs get slaughtered.' So long as we are not hogs, all is well.*"

> . . . Anybody that could have done something, should have done something, looked around and examined what was happening, were burying their heads in the sand. They were reaping the benefits. It was a very small number of employees that were receiving all of the benefits. And it was the taxpayers of

1

the City of Bell that were paying the price and will continue to pay the price for years. And it is horrible. It is horrible.

And ultimately what happened is that both Rizzo and Spaccia were not content with being pigs; they were hogs . . . and so, you know, the day of reckoning is finally here.[2]

Bell is a 2.81 square-mile municipality of just over 35,000 residents, located southeast of downtown Los Angeles. It is one of the poorest cities in L.A. County, with an average annual family income of $28,000 a year. About 90 percent of the city is Latino and a sizable number of residents are not in the country legally.[3]

From the outside, this little city is decidedly indistinguishable from hundreds of others. On the inside, however, a handful of officials were about to put Bell on the road to the worst kind of fame.

In July 2010, *Los Angeles Times* reporters Jeff Gottlieb and Ruben Vives were covering the nearby City of Maywood laying off nearly all its employees when they got a tip: Some Bell city officials seemed to be enjoying some unusually high salaries. The eventual result was a Pulitzer Prize-winning series that exposed an astonishing level of corruption orchestrated by the city's chief Administrator officer, Robert (Bob) Rizzo, and Spaccia, his assistant.

At the time, Rizzo was making no less than $787,000 ($1.5 million in total compensation) annually. Spaccia was earning $376,268 ($850,000 in total compensation) and Police Chief Randy Adams was taking in $457,000 ($770,000 total compensation).[4] But the city's generosity didn't end there. Other fortunate Bell employees included Lourdes Garcia, director of administrative services ($422,707 in total compensation)[5] and Eric Eggena, a former prosecutor and director of general services ($421,402 in total compensation).[6] Four of the city's five councilmembers were earning nearly $100,000 per year, rather higher than the $400 per month compensation allowed by California law for part-time councilmembers. Meanwhile, the property tax burden for Bell's mostly low-income residents had soared to the second highest in L.A. County.

In the wake of media accounts and its own investigation, the L.A. District Attorney's Office indicted eight Bell officials, including Rizzo; Spaccia; Mayor Oscar Hernandez; Councilmembers Teresa Jacobo, Luis Artiga, and George Mirabal; and former Councilmembers George Cole and Victor Bello. This was followed by numerous investigations by—among others—the California Attorney General's office, the U.S. Securities and Exchange Commission, the State Controller, and the IRS.

September 22, 2010, was the "day of reckoning" noted by Judge Kennedy: Each of the "Bell 8" was arrested and taken away in handcuffs.

Even discounting the enormous sums involved, this was no ordinary failure of governance. The picture that emerged from years of federal, state and local investigations, trials, depositions, and media accounts is of an elaborate culture of corruption led by Rizzo. And not Rizzo alone: Multiple employees, consultants, and branches of government became complicit in years of lucrative self-dealing on a huge scale.

Rizzo maintained this massive theft—and the silence that concealed it—by removing some of those who opposed him and co-opting others. He then targeted municipal institutions, diluting or dismantling the checks and balances that were built in to Bell's council-manager form of government.

Rizzo further sought to increase his authority by converting Bell into a charter city, convincing the council to support the move via a special election in 2005. The measure passed, 336 to 54. The turnout was less than 1 percent. Most ballots, 239, were absentee.

Rizzo then introduced an ordinance that supposedly limited Councilmembers' salaries but actually increased them. Through all this, he and his staff went to great lengths to hide much of their doings from the public. They operated with virtually no written policies or procedures. Rizzo created a complex network of phantom agencies in order to conceal his and the council's salaries. He created an incomprehensible and highly opaque system for conducting city businesses. There was no way for anyone to track and understand what expenses were being incurred or, indeed, what city officials were doing. When concerned residents sought answers or clarification, he lied; when staff members and the city attorney questioned his actions, he bullied them into silence.

In order to finance the bloated salaries and benefits enjoyed by a few, Rizzo extracted revenues from poor and otherwise vulnerable parties. He raised property taxes, issued bonds for imaginary capital improvement projects, and created huge debt for city residents. He had his police force and code enforcement officers target poor and suspected unlicensed and undocumented citizens and their families to meet quotas. The city impounded cars and charged a rate to recover them that was triple that of neighboring cities, including Los Angeles.

Merely increasing the price of government services for Bell's citizens was apparently not enough. Rizzo and Spaccia extracted money from local businesses through additional taxes and arbitrarily went after other businesses for minor code violations. Businesses that balked were threatened with closure. This ultimately resulted in a large exodus of businesses from the city.

After the whole scheme crashed, Rizzo pleaded guilty to state charges and no contest to federal charges. He was sentenced to twelve years in state prison and ordered to pay $8.8 million in restitution; he also received thirty-three months in federal prison, which he is allowed to serve concurrently with the state term.

Councilmember Luis Artiga was acquitted. Teresa Jacobo was sentenced to two years in prison. Victor Bello, George Mirabal, and Oscar Hernandez were all sentenced to one year in the county jail and five years' probation. George Cole was sentenced to 180 days of home confinement.

The two leaders of the "Bell 8," Rizzo and Spaccia, are still behind bars, while the others have served their official punishment. Newly elected councilmembers and their officials—with some help from the county and state governments—are trying to put their damaged city back together. They're hoping that new elected representatives, new professional staffers, new businesses, and a new resolve by citizens to stay engaged in their local government will gradually assure outsiders—and themselves—that the conditions that unleashed such massive corruption no longer prevail in a little town that is still battling a big, bad reputation.

In 2012, more than a thousand public officials across the country were convicted of bribery, fraud, perjury, and/or theft. Over the preceding twenty years, an average of 1,013 public corruption convictions were recorded every year.[7] Given this level of routine corruption in America, why is the story of a tiny East Los Angeles city worthy of a book?

Because this corruption was far from routine. Bell witnessed the emergence of a truly astonishing level of public wrongdoing—a level succinctly described by Los Angeles District Attorney Steve Cooley as "corruption on steroids."

On July 9, 2010, after discovering Bell officials' extraordinarily inflated salaries and benefits, *Los Angeles Times* reporters Jeff Gottlieb and Ruben Vives wrote a front-page story entitled: "Is a city manager worth $800,000?" It struck a nerve, both locally and nationally. Gottlieb later commented that the two were flooded with emails and phone calls from people "wanting us to investigate their cities—in New Jersey, Connecticut and Kentucky. Editors across the country were sending their reporters to city hall to find out how much local officials were earning."[8]

The officials' misuse of municipal funds via the collection of exorbitant salaries triggered nationwide outrage and calls for more transparency in government. Meanwhile, the corruption nearly bankrupted the small, blue-collar city and burdened Bell residents with a massive debt that they still bear today.

Public corruption—broadly understood as placing private interests over the public good in public office—lay at the root of much of the distrust citizens have towards government. While the need to uncover and combat corruption has been a persistent theme throughout American history, our collective inability to stem its spread remains a genuine threat to our nation's democracy.

An avalanche of investigations by federal, state, and local authorities uncovered an outrageous mixture of dishonest, illegal, and unethical practices by Robert Rizzo, Angela Spaccia, and several councilmembers who collectively made up what became known as the "Bell 8." Rizzo orchestrated a form of collective corruption in which numerous employees, consultants, and governmental branches became complicit in the plundering of the city. Anyone that could have done something was either looking the other way or benefiting financially.

The Failure of Governance in Bell California: Big-Time Corruption in a Small Town details how Bell was vulnerable because of its disengaged public, lack of media coverage of government, and poor or non-existent governing practices. Yet, this still fails to fully explain how such large-scale corruption could have occurred. More specifically, how did such rampant corruption emerge in a system—the council-manager form of government—that was specifically designed to combat corruption and promote good governance? And how did so many officials and employees conspire to participate in or overlook the ongoing corruption?

The story of the corruption in Bell will be presented through the prism of four theoretical frameworks or contexts: political monopolies; geographic corruption contagion (regional diffusion model); the corrupting effects of fiscal systems that enable revenue extraction; and a professional public-sector ethics lens. After chronicling the story of Bell, the last chapter will use these frameworks to analyze how this corruption occurred.

Political Monopolies

The two primary forms of local governance that have emerged in the United States are best characterized as the strong-mayor (or mayor-council) and the council-manager form of government. The strong-mayor form of government dominated cities through the first half of the twentieth century. In this form, an elected mayor serves as CEO and holds overall authority to appoint and dismiss department heads. Currently, this type of government is typically found in the largest cities in the United States. However, in response to the history of widespread corruption in many large cities, progressive reformers in the early 1900s introduced new approaches to the way cities were governed by having the council appoint a non-partisan professional city manager to oversee operations. While not as popular in cities with populations over 500,000, the council-manager form remains the most common today.

These two forms of government are often thought of among public administration scholars in terms of "machine" versus "reform." However, Jessica Trounstine suggests that the council-manager form is less a barrier to corruption than simply an alternative power structure. Either side of this traditional divide, she said, could be used to form "political monopolies."[9]

She argues that elections are what keeps local government officials honest; when leaders stop worrying about reelection, they're free to pursue policies that do not reflect the desires of citizens. Under her theory, using political monopolies to remain in power and reducing concerns about reelection can lead to corruption. [10]

Geographic Contagion

A relatively new area of research explores the contagious effect of corruption. Similar to the study of a contagious disease, researchers seek to describe a cascading effect of corruption, whether vertically within an organization or geographically from one neighboring region to another. It is assumed that a minimal threshold of corruption already exists before it spreads and becomes the social norm; this process is influenced by a variety of factors such as cultural norms, a lack of transparency, weak or nonexistent check-and-balance systems, and inadequate regulations and laws. Much of the research on the geographical spread of corruption has focused on how one county's corrupt practices spread to another. This can be driven by a variety of factors such as trade, tourism and immigration. [11]

These studies have found that corruption is indeed contagious between some neighboring counties, but that it diminishes as the distance between the counties grows. [12] [13] The regional-diffusion model posits that governments are influenced primarily by other governments in their geographic region with which they share a physical border. [14] Most of the research in this area focuses on the adoption of policy innovation. [15] There is a good deal of empirical evidence of regional diffusion across jurisdictions, and scholars have used this framework to identify both intra-state and interstate influences on policy adoption. [16] [17] [18]

Revenue Extraction

The economic consequences of corruption for the growth and development of municipal economies has been explored through a number of economic theories. These include rent-seeking behavior—where rewards flow to those who have inside connections within private business and/or public officials; [19] the role of corruption in distorting policy choices; [20] and how corruption raises transaction costs. [21] The mainstream view is that corruption diverts resources from productive activities, and "that extra costs arising from paying commissions to politicians/bureaucrats for big contracts or bribing local officials for licenses/permits, utilities connections, police protection, tax assessment, etc., raise the overall costs of doing business, lower profitability of investment and breed inefficiencies" [22]

Public officials are attracted to municipal corruption, these theories posit, primarily by the opportunity to engage in revenue extraction—the appropriation of material wealth from citizens. When revenue extraction is done by illegal means, it is considered graft. However, Rebecca Mendes notes that a powerful limit to municipal corruption is the "ability of wealth to leave the city. A corrupt government can only steal if the wealth both exists and cannot escape." (p. 3)[23] She notes that many U.S. cities survived corruption during the Progressive Era (1890–1920) because city officials balanced graft with investment in the city. They could not afford to drive businesses out of their municipalities.[24]

This is reinforced by McGuire and Olson's theory of the "stationary" and "rover" bandit governments. The stationary bandit government pursues economic development so it can extract more wealth from its wealthier citizens. The officials may act purely out of self-interest, but still provide a surprisingly high level of public goods and services. The problem arises when a dishonest official operates with only a short-term horizon, becoming a roving bandit unconcerned with investing in the city and interested only in extracting public resources.[25] Generating revenues through extraction can be accomplished in a variety of ways, such as property tax increases, the shakedown of businesses, and encouraging large and unnecessary infrastructure projects that are easier to skim from.

It can also be done by raising revenue from poor and otherwise vulnerable parties through the abuse of code enforcement and police stops and citations. A recent example is Ferguson, Missouri, which gained national notoriety following the August 2014 shooting of Michael Brown by a Ferguson police officer. The U.S. Department of Justice (DOJ) investigated the city's police department and municipal court. The DOJ's 2015 report described a consistent pattern of revenue-orientated city practices, including policing, code enforcement, and court processes, mostly targeting poor and minority residents. The report concluded, "The City budgets for sizeable increases in municipal fines and fees each year, exhorts police and court staff to deliver those revenue increases, and closely monitors whether those increases are achieved."[26]

The report found that, under direction from city leadership, the finance director communicated to both the city court and police department to increase their revenue by specified percentages. This anticipated revenue was then used by the city leadership in budgeting and planning decisions.

Public Sector Ethics

Ethics refers to principles by which behavior is evaluated as right or wrong. Public sector ethics deals with the ethics of those who work in the public sector. It is not limited to elected officials, but encompasses any position included in governance and the public administration field. It includes the political level, where policies are formulated, and the administrative level that implements them.

It is useful to distinguish descriptive ethics, the empirical study of moral beliefs and practices, from normative ethics, the study of the principles, rules, and theories that guide actions. For example, descriptive ethics tries to determine what proportion of the population believe that killing is always wrong; normative ethics attempts to determine whether it is correct to hold such a belief. When examining ethical behavior, there are two prominent theories that advance different criteria for evaluating whether an act or practice is acceptable. One is teleological ethics, which examines the consequences of an act; the other is deontological ethics, which evaluates the extent to which an act would conform to certain universally accepted guiding principles.[27]

Deontological ethics looks at the adherence to principle, and disregards the consequences of an act in determining its moral worth. Each approach has both benefits and drawbacks; however, they have been used together to create guidance to public sector workers.[28] The practice of corruption and unethical behavior has been evaluated from both these perspectives, and there exists strong consensus that corruption is ethically indefensible. While there are arguably many principles in operation when referring to public-sector ethics, Niamh Kinchin suggests that there are five basic virtues: transparency, fairness, efficiency, responsibility, and no conflict-interest.[29]

Both scholars and practitioners have attempted to identify the ethical responsibilities of public leaders and to offer frameworks for use.[30] [31] [32] [33] The common method has been the promulgation of codes of ethics, guidance standards, ethics training, organizational guidelines, and enforcement mechanisms.[34] Codes of ethics vary widely in terms of content and enforceability; they also are often vague and difficult to apply to specific situations.

The International City/County Management Association (ICMA) Code of Ethics was initially adopted in 1924. It does incorporate sanctions and allow for expulsion of members.[35] The first code of ethics adopted by the American Society for Public Administration (ASPA) was in 1984. A new version was approved in 2013 that broadened the scope of values and standards and focuses on eight principles based on formal roles, relationships and societal responsibilities.[36] To be effective, however, codes need an implementation process, an educational component, and an enforcement mechanism, which until recently was lacking with ASPA.[37] A procedure for reviewing complaints was recently approved by the ASPA governing body.

Formal ethics training is typically provided by public sector organizations and primarily focuses on skill-building to deal with current laws and policies. Likewise, organizations frequently adopt an array of guidelines and policies to create an internal culture of ethical behavior.[38] Establishing standards and policies to guide ethical behavior is challenging; the existence of these within organizations, although important, will not necessarily prevent an elected or public official from debasing professional standards and undermining the ethical behaviors of others.

AUDIENCE

This book is aimed at a wide variety of individuals and groups: policymakers, activists, public managers, elected officials, university students, civic and business groups, and concerned citizens from all sectors. It was written as a resource for anyone concerned about the ability of local governments to operate in the public interest, as well as in ways to identify and combat municipal corruption. It is envisioned that colleges and universities would be the primary market for the book, using it as a supplemental text in public administration and public policy courses (graduate and undergraduate) and in human resources, ethics, governance, leadership, finance, local government, public management, organizational behavior, urban studies, and/or capstone classes.

OVERVIEW OF THE CONTENTS

In this overview, I outline the key frameworks and contexts that will be used to analyze the Bell story as well as provide an overview of the book. Given the extent and complexity of the corruption, I provide a brief introduction to each of the key players. This is followed up by a chronology of the major events connected to the Bell scandal. In chapter 1, a history of Bell is presented along with the city's current demographic, economic, civic, and municipal makeup. I cover an earlier scandal, one that involved the California Bell Poker Club in the late 1970s and early 1980s and led to the conviction of Bell's then-mayor and city administrator on corruption charges. The chapter concludes with the introduction of George Cole, who was elected to the council in 1984 as a reformer, only to become caught up in Bell's more recent and much larger web of corruption woven chiefly by Robert Rizzo.

Chapter 2 introduces Rizzo, detailing his early years in city government and chronicling his steady accumulation of enormous power during nearly two decades in Bell. I then scrutinize Rizzo's relentless, multi-faceted schemes to extract money from businesses and residents; his systematic removal or co-opting of those around him; and his dismantling of the traditional check-and-balance system built into the council-manager form of government.

Chapter 3 looks in depth at Angela Spaccia, Rizzo's assistant and accomplice. Was she duped by her boss, as she later claimed, or was she the real brains behind the plot to plunder the largely immigrant working-class community? Spaccia's detailed emails, uncovered during the subsequent investigation, appear both embarrassing and incriminating, and reveal a more sinister undercurrent to the corruption that was pushing Bell towards bankruptcy. Next, I discuss the details surrounding the hiring of Bell Police Chief Randy Adams, who was never criminally charged despite enjoying a salary of hundreds of thousands of dollars.

In chapter 4, I cover the formation of a citizens' group, Bell Association To Stop The Abuse (BASTA), and the activities of several whistleblowers who attempted—in vain—to alert officials to the underlying civic rot.

Chapter 5 describes the corruption hearings, detailing the extensive civil and criminal cases against the so-called "Bell 8" and the city itself. This includes discussions of two landmark state court appellate decisions resulting from the Bell litigation that have significant implications for other municipalities dealing with public corruption. Chapter 6 covers the legal and financial mess that Bell's residents were left with after the convictions. This includes the strategies they employed to address the recovery as well as the challenges still facing the community.

Finally, chapter 7 considers the origins of such large-scale corruption in a small town, focusing both on the council-manager form of government and the collective nature of the officials and employees involved or complicit in this remarkable municipal tragedy. Political monopolies; geographical corruption contagion (regional diffusion model); the corrupting effects of fiscal systems that generate revenue extraction; and a professional public sector ethics lens are used as frameworks to analyze the story.

As the story unfolds, the analyses of municipal operations will hopefully enable the reader to gain deeper insight into the inner workings of city governments—corrupt and otherwise.

NOTES

1. Woodrow Wilson, "The New Freedom." 1912. Retrieved from: https://www.gutenberg.org/files/14811/14811-h/14811-h.htm.

2. People v. Spaccia. BA376026, BA382701. Sentencing Minutes. April 10, 2014. pp. 61–72.

3. City of Bell, *City of Bell 2012/13 Budget*, Annual Budget Report, (Bell, CA: City of Bell, 2011). A6.

4. Center for the Advancement of Public Integrity at Columbia Law School. "The City of Bell Scandal Revisited." Retrieved from http://web.law.columbia.edu/public-integrity/city-bell-scandal-revisited.

5. People v. Hernandez, Jacobo, Mirabel, Cole, Bello, & Artiga. BA376025. Preliminary Hearing. February 14, 2011.

6. Gottlieb. J., Becerra, H., & Vives, R. "Bell Admits More Hefty City Salaries." *Los Angeles Times*. August 7, 2010. Retrieved from http://articles.latimes.com/2010/aug/07/local/la-me-bell-salaries-20100807.

7. Depangher, E. "An In-Depth Look at Public Corruption in California." *California Common Sense.* August 14, 2014. Retrieved from http://cacs.org/research/depth-look-public-corruption-california/.

8. Gottlieb, J. "Bell: A Total Breakdown." 2015. (White paper at the City of Bell Scandal Revisited Conference, Chapman University. 2015.)

9. Trounstine, J. *Political Monopolies in American Cities.* Chicago: University of Chicago Press, 2008. p. 217.

10. Ibid.

11. Quaz, R., Langley, S. & Tlii, A. "Corruption Contagion in South Asia and East Asia: An Econometric Study." *International Journal of Developing Societies*, 2(3), 2013, pp. 87–95

12. Ibid.

13. Das, J. & DiRienzo, C. "Spatial Decay of corruption in Africa and the Middle East. *Economic Papers,* 31(4), 2012, pp. 508–514.

14. Berry, F.S., & Berry, W.D. "State Lottery Adoptions as Policy Innovations: An Event History Analysis. *American Political Science Review*, 84, 1990. pp. 395–416

15. Grinstein-Weiss, M., Wagner, K. & Edwards, K. "Diffusion of Policy Innovation: The Case of Individual Development Accounts (IDAs) as an Asset-building Policy." *CSD Working Paper No. 05–08. 2005.*

16. Berry & Berry, 1990.

17. Stream, C. "Health reform in the states: A Model of State small group health insurance marker reforms," *Political Research Quarterly* 52(3) 1999, pp. 499–526.

18. Mooney, C. & Lee, M. "Legislating Morality in the American States," *American Journal of Political Science,* 39, 1995, pp. 599–627.

19. Mendes, R. "Corruption in Cities: Graft and Politics in American Cities at the Turn of the Twentieth Century." National Bureau of Economic Research Working Paper Series, 9990. http://www.nber.org/papers/w9900. 2003.

20. Cain, L. P. & E. J. Rotella. "Urbanization, sanitation, and mortality in the Progressive era, 1899–1929," working paper. 1990.

21. Husted, B. "Honor Among Thieves: A Transaction-Cost Interpretation of Corruption in Third World Countries," *Business Ethics Quarterly,* 4, 1994, pp. 17–27

22. Das & DiRienzo, p. 87.

23. Mendes, 2003.

24. Ibid, p. 14.

25. McGuire, M. & Olson, M. "The Economics of Autocracy and Majority Rule: The Invisible Hand and the Use of Force." *Journal of Economic Literature*, 34, 1996, pp. 72–96.

26. Civil Rights Division, "Investigation of the Ferguson Police Department," (report, United States Department of Justice, March 4, 2015), http://www.justice.gov/sites/default/files/opa/press-releases/attachments/2015/03/04/ferguson_police_department_report.pdf, 2.

27. Bowditch, J. Buono, A., & Stewart, M. *A Primer on Organizational Behavior*, 7th ed., John Wiley & Sons, 2008.

28. Svara, J. H. "The Ethics Primer for Public Administrators in Government and Nonprofit Organizations." Sudbury, MA: Jones and Bartlett, 2007.

29. Kinchin, N. "More Than Writing on a Wall: Evaluating the Role that Code of Ethics Play in Securing Accountability of Public Sector Decision-Makers." *The Australian Journal of Public Administration*, 66(1), 2007, pp. 112–120.

30. Johnston, M. "Accessing Vulnerabilities to Corruption. Indicators and Benchmarks of Government Performance." *Public Integrity,* 12(2), 2010, pp. 125–142.

31. Denhardt, R. & Denhardt, J. "The New Public Service: Serving Rather Than Steering." *Public Administration Review,* 60(6), 2000, pp. 549–599.

32. Cooper, T. L. *The Responsible Administrator: An Approach to Ethics for Administrative Role*, 3rd ed., San Francisco: Jossey-Bass, 2006.

33. Svara, 2007.

34. Condrey, S (ed). *Handbook of Human Resources Management in Government.* Jossey-Bass, 2005.

35. Benavides, A., Dicke, L., & Maleckaire, V. "Creating Public Value Sector Pedestals and Examining Falls from Grace: Examining ICMA Ethical Sanctions." *International Journal of Public Administration*, 35(11), 2012, pp. 749–759.

36. Svara, J. "Who Are the Keepers of the Code? Articulating and Upholding Ethical Standards in the field of Public Administration." *Public Administration Review*, (74) 3, 2014, pp. 561–569.

37. Ibid, p. 567.

38. Condrey, 2005.

Chapter One

The City, the Poker Club, and the Reformer

"Corruption is the enemy of development, and of good governance. It must be got rid of. Both government and the people at large must come together to achieve this national objective."
—Pratibha Patil, former President of India [1]

A few miles south of downtown Los Angeles, a maze of crisscrossing freeways carves up the southeast portion of L.A. County into a jigsaw known as the Gateway Cities. The area is a jumble of independent municipalities, each with its own city government. It consists, in fact, of twenty-six contiguous cities as well as the City of Avalon on Catalina Island just off the coast and the Port of Long Beach seaport. Several unincorporated areas of the county are sandwiched among the various city limits. [2]

Many of the Gateway Cities are tiny, no more than a few square miles. Yet some of them number among the most densely populated communities in California and even in the United States. [3] Still, area residents tend to identify with Los Angeles above all else. Ask any resident where they're from and they will likely answer "L.A." and proudly display allegiance to the Dodgers or the Lakers. People in these working-class communities think of themselves as Angelenos first, even though they live in cities called Maywood, Cudahy, Southgate, and Huntington Park.

One of them, Bell, is a 2.81 square-mile municipality with a population of just more than 35,000 residents. [4] Bell is bordered on its east by the I-710 Long Beach Freeway and the L.A. River, and is completely surrounded on its three other sides by other Gateway Cities of similar size and demographics. Bell thus sits within a vast swath of some of the most industrialized sections of the Los Angeles metro area, where individual city limits are largely indistinguishable. It is often difficult to tell where one city ends and another begins.

Before warehouses, factories, loading docks, freeways, and densely packed apartment buildings dominated this part of L.A. County, it was a different world. The basin that eventually became the City of Los Angeles and Los Angeles County is the ancestral homeland of the Gabrieliño Indian Tribe, today also known as the Tongva.[5] In the late 1700s, the native people were organized by the Spanish onto the Mission San Gabriel Arcangel as one of the series of twenty-one missions that lined the California coast.

As the native people were forced to live on the missions, large tracts of land fell open to Spanish occupation. The King of Spain began to issue land grants throughout California to loyal aristocrats; one went to Don Antonio Maria Lugo between 1810 and 1813 as a reward for his many years of service to the Spanish army.[6] As part of a petition for the land, Lugo's family first built a homestead in 1795 on the site, then established the 30,000-acre Rancho San Antonio.[7] Settlement of the land by farmers—first Spanish, then Mexican Californians—began immediately.

Don Antonio, as he was known, presided over land that would one day become the cities of Bell, Bell Gardens, Commerce, Cudahy, Huntington Park, Lynwood, Maywood, Southgate, Vernon, and Walnut Park. He was a prominent figure throughout the region, having served as mayor of Los Angeles and deemed one of the largest owners of land and livestock in California.[8] [9] He remained so even after the United States annexed California following the Treaty of Guadalupe Hidalgo in 1848 at the end of the Mexican-American War.[10] Remembered as "the most famous horseman of his day in California,"[11] Don Antonio presented a striking appearance; early American settlers recalled that even into his 80s he would ride "into town on horseback erect, with his sword strapped to his saddle beneath his left leg."[12]

By 1851, in the newly minted state of California, the worth of Don Antonio Maria Lugo's land had declined to an assessed value of $72,000 for 29,000 acres.[13] Don Antonio partitioned his Rancho into several estates held by his children, who began to sell off their lands to American buyers at rock-bottom prices as the family fortunes continued to decline.[14] In the following years these holdings were resold in smaller parcels to U.S. settlers from the East and Midwest. One of those buyers was James George Bell, who purchased 360 acres and established a farming community originally named Bell Station Ranch. In 1898 it was renamed Bell in honor of its founder. In 1927 it was then incorporated as the City of Bell.[15]

James George Bell's son, Alphonzo Bell Sr., went on to gain fame in his own right. After striking oil on the family ranch in the 1920s, he amassed a fortune in the oil business and founded Bell Petroleum Co.[16] He was a key player in the development of Bell and the nearby city of Bell Gardens as well as the wealthy West Los Angeles areas of Beverly Hills, Pacific Palisades,

Westwood, and Bel-Air—which was named for him.[17] Alphonzo Bell Sr.'s own children also went on to prominence: his son, Alphonzo Jr., served several terms in Congress and his daughter, Minnewa, married Elliot Roosevelt, son of FDR.[18]

During the late nineteenth and early twentieth centuries, other sections of the former Rancho San Antonio and surrounding areas were bought up by wealthy industrialists and developers, such as Michael Cudahy and Henry Huntington. They also subdivided these areas into smaller plots and sold them to the unceasing influx of settlers from other parts of the United States.

They left a lasting legacy. Cudahy, for example, sold one-acre plots that were long and narrow to allow room for a home with orchards or crop fields in the back. The idea was meant to appeal to Midwest farmers moving west, but the form of division influenced how the land would be used for decades to come. The one-acre narrow plots in Cudahy, which borders Bell on the south, still exist today, for example; but the farms have been replaced by long strips of apartments and small homes separated by narrow alleyways. Similarly, in Bell, farm plots were gradually replaced by small houses and multi-family housing that have helped solidify the area's identity as a low-wage working class community.

War proved profitable for southern California. This area first began to attract industrial ventures just before and during World War I as the United States ramped up production of war supplies. But industrial development mushroomed in the years before, during, and immediately following World War II,[19] thanks in part to geography and demographics. The Gateway Cities sat along the major railroad corridors to the nearby shipping points at the Port of Long Beach and Port of Los Angeles. The presence of a steady workforce in the L.A. suburbs added to its appeal for manufacturing—especially of motor vehicles, aircraft, and components for the American war effort. Following WWII, many of the plants kept operating by converting from military to civilian production of industrial supplies, motor vehicles, parts, and equipment for the booming population of the postwar West.

Manufacturing in southeast L.A. boomed along with the population during the first decades of the Cold War. The soaring economy fueled the growth of a middle class consumer base enriched by the plentiful work in the plants. The Cold War military buildup, as well as the wars in Korea and Vietnam, provided manufacturers with a continuous supply of work orders. Companies in southeastern L.A. supplied raw materials and parts for all types of military armaments, equipment, and vehicles—as well as for the region's booming demand for automobiles.

The prosperity spanned decades. Up until the 1970s, southeast L.A. County was home to the majority of all factories in southern California. There were GM, Ford, and Chrysler auto plants, and four tire and rubber plants run by big companies.[20] Major corporations like Bethlehem Steel and

US Steel operated iron and steel fabrication plants in cities just north of Bell. The constant source of reliable income for a large available workforce guaranteed that southeastern L.A. County communities like Bell and other Gateway Cities would continue to thrive as predominantly white and middle-class communities.[21]

Then, beginning in the 1950s, it began to unravel.

Several push and pull factors contributed to a rapid shift in the demographics of southeast L.A. County cities such as Bell during the second half of the twentieth century. The development of new and more spacious subdivisions in nearby Orange County began to attract white residents.[22] As in other Western cities, developers lured white middle-class families away from the aging industrial core and into master-planned commuter communities with wide streets, manicured lawns, and two-car garages. This new, family-friendly lifestyle was already spurring a "white flight" exodus out of the central and southeast cities of L.A. County when the Watts riots erupted in August of 1965. Bitter and outspoken racial divisions and whites' fears of minorities' arriving in their neighborhoods hastened the departure of white residents from southeastern L.A. County.[23]

In 1978 California voters administered a shock to the fiscal system by passing of Proposition 13. This rather famous—or infamous—ballot initiative limited the annual property taxes that governments could collect to no more than 1 percent of assessed property value, and prevented assessed property values from rising by more than 2 percent a year.[24] The result has been a total restructuring of local government property tax revenues. In 1978, the property taxes collected came evenly from homeowners and commercial properties; by 2015, the share of total property taxes collected from homeowners had increased to 72 percent.[25]

A further major shift in California's economy came in the late 1970s as East Asian consumer goods and industrial materials increasingly began to dominate the market. All along the Pacific coast—spurred in part by the 1970s energy crisis—Asian auto companies quickly eroded the United States. "Big Three's" hold on consumers as the latter began to favor smaller, more fuel-efficient Japanese automobiles. Clothing, electronics, and other consumer goods imported from Asia simultaneously began to supplant U.S. products. After 1978, southeastern L.A. County's auto plants and steel mills began to shut down as cheaper imported cars and structural steel replaced American-made equivalents.[26]

The decline was swift and dramatic. Between 1978 and 1982, ten out of the twelve largest non-aerospace production plants in the Los Angeles region shut down. More than 50,000 middle-class workers were thrown into unemployment.[27]

This mass abandonment of industrial sectors left behind a vast ruined landscape of vacant factories and warehouses. The combination of foreign trade pressures and the effects of Proposition 13 led to sharp drops in city revenues and overstretched services that tarnished the appeal of southeastern L.A. County cities. White laid-off workers left Bell and neighboring cities in droves. Into the void of abandoned industrial zones and empty apartment buildings came low-wage and labor-intensive consumer goods production facilities; newly arrived immigrants from Mexico, Central America, and Asia followed to provide the labor force. By the early 1990s, the heavy manufacturing base of southeastern L.A. County had been completely replaced by a system of sweatshop production facilities.[28] The steel works and auto plants that once brought plentiful jobs and steady incomes to the area were replaced by clothing production shops, furniture factories, food preparation and distribution companies, and grim clusters of warehouses in varying states of use and disrepair.[29]

The most dynamic changes in the demographics of southeastern L.A. County took place from the late 1970s through the 1990s. The *Los Angeles Times* reported that, according to U.S. Census Bureau data, "Asian and Hispanic populations have surged in Long Beach and the Southeast Los Angeles County area over the last decade, while the Anglo population in almost every community has dropped."[30] [31] By 1980, Bell had become a majority Hispanic city with a white population of 13 percent, down from 76 percent in 1970. The Hispanic share rose during the decade from 21 percent to 63 percent.[32]

Bell's population during the 1980s both grew and continued to shift in ethnic makeup. From 1980 to 1990, it rose by 35 percent, with 86 percent of the 34,365 residents reported as Hispanic.[33] The dual trends of an increasing city population and an increasing percentage of Hispanic residents persisted through the 1990s. The 2000 Census recorded 90 percent of Bell's residents as Hispanic/Latino in a population that had swelled to nearly 37,000.[34]

Latinos have come to dominate Bell's economy and culture, but they are not the only large immigrant group to settle in Bell. During the 1970s, Lebanese immigrants from a village named Yaroun began to arrive in Bell as they fled the civil war in their homeland.[35] What began as a small group of ten to twenty Lebanese Shiite Muslims in the early 1970s grew into a tightly knit community of about two thousand first-, second-, and third-generation Lebanese with origins mainly in Yaroun.[36] [37] Newly arriving immigrants would live with Lebanese already living in Bell until they could find work and move into their own apartments in the same neighborhood. Over many years, a sizeable Yaroun-linked Lebanese enclave emerged in Bell just a few blocks from City Hall.[38]

Many of Bell's Lebanese immigrants took jobs in the area's growing garment industry, but many started selling clothing items on their own—at first door-to-door and then at swap meets.[39] These efforts grew into small businesses that sold mostly specialized clothing and accessories to the ever-expanding Latino community in the region.[40] Lebanese-owned stores began to pop up, selling cowboy hats, shirts, belts and buckles, and other clothing that catered to Mexican and other Latino customers.[41]

Bell today is far from the solidly middle-class white community that it was for some fifty years. Its current population is quite diverse: As of 2013, about 48 percent of residents were foreign-born, with 34 percent being identified as noncitizens and 89 percent self-reported as speaking a language other than English at home.[42] Its 2013 per-capita income was $12,076 and its median household income was $35,985. Bell residents are far less educated than the rest of California, with only 45.3 percent holding a high-school degree and 5.9 percent having attained a bachelor's degree or higher. The city's unemployment rate stood at 16.6 percent in 2010, compared to 10.83 percent in 2000 and 12.37 percent in 1990.[43] Only 27 percent of residents own their homes, compared to the state average of 55 percent; the median value of Bell's homes hovers around $280,000. Just more than 36 percent of city residents live in multi-unit housing structures.[44] Bell is, in short, one of the poorest communities in southern California.[45]

For several decades, Bell has struggled to generate enough revenue to meet expenses. Over the years, city leaders have launched many initiatives to remedy this, from sanctioning gambling at a poker parlor to exchanging land with the local school district for commercial redevelopment.[46] [47] These and other efforts aimed at generating sales and property tax revenue by attracting new businesses fell short. By the early 1990s the mass deindustrialization of the region combined with the permanent closure of the poker parlor left a city desperate for a new direction.[48]

The stage was set.

This chronic fiscal instability joined with periodic scandal prompted frequent turnover in the city's top administrative position. Between 1980 and 1990, for example, Bell had three different city administrators.[49] [50] As Bell's economic and demographic landscape shifted, City Administrator John Bramble left the $85,200 job in May, 1993, to become head administrator of Adams County, Colorado, taking a $10,200 pay cut to run the much larger entity.[51] In that same month, the city council hired Robert Rizzo as an interim city administrator, then offered him the position permanently at a salary of $78,000, $7,000 less than Bramble was paid.[52]

At the time, Bell officials such as then-Mayor Ray Johnson acknowledged that "the city is going through a period of tight financial planning."[53] The council, facing a time crunch to fill the key administrator position and grateful for Rizzo's willingness to take the lowest possible salary, failed to do a thorough vetting of Rizzo's past, notably including his abrupt departure from his last position, in Hesperia.[54]

Under Rizzo's management, the city set about extracting larger and larger amounts of revenue from its residents. In a *Los Angeles Times* article, "How Bell hit bottom," for example, former Police Chief Michael Trevis claimed that his officers were encouraged by Rizzo to engage in revenue-oriented policing by writing more tickets and impounding more cars. [55]

Rizzo also orchestrated ever-increasing property tax rates upon residents. As the area deteriorated over the past several years, home property values in Bell dropped, yet property taxes have risen each year since at least 2006. [56] Since 2006, the municipal rate of property tax levied by Bell doubled so that by 2010, Bell had the second highest property tax rate among the 88 cities in L.A. County. [57] Property owners in the county each pay a base 1 percent general property tax rate; individual cities then tack on additional special or direct assessments that are usually in the tenths and hundredths of a percent. [58] The municipal levy portion of property tax brings up the countywide average total tax rate to 1.16 percent. Bell's rate is 1.55 percent, nearly 50 percent more than the rates of L.A. County's wealthiest cities like Beverly Hills, Malibu, and Manhattan Beach. [59]

Rizzo's administration also turned to local small businesses to collect revenue through what was essentially a shake-down operation. [60] Throughout Rizzo's tenure in the late 1990s and early 2000s, Bell officials collected countless thousands of dollars from business owners through an arranged payment scheme. The scheme required at least fifteen small businesses in Bell to pay thousands of dollars in arbitrary amounts to the city. Some payments were ostensibly for both conditional-use permits; others were in the form of specified levels of sales tax revenue, which businesses delivered to the city in exchange for their continued city permits. [61]

Nor were these consistent levies. Bell would issue permits to similar businesses yet charge wildly different fees. One tire shop was required to pay $144,000 to the city over four years (or approximately $36,000 per year); another tire shop had to pay just $13,000 a year—and a subsequent permit issued to an auto-repair shop did not require any annual fees. [62] As another part of the business shake-down scheme, some business owners were told that they were required to bring in a specific amount of annual sales tax revenue to the city. If they fell short, they would have to make up the difference themselves.

Local business owners admitted to the *Los Angeles Times* that "they felt intimidated or pressured to agree to the terms if they wanted to do business in the city." [63] In fact, several business owners, told they were behind on payments, were forced to close up their shops and leave town. In 2001, Willie Salazar, the former owner of a tire shop, was told he owed $16,250 to the city. [64] At first Salazar ignored the matter; then he was summoned to meet with Rizzo and make arrangements to pay down some of the balance. These payments further burdened Salazar's already-struggling business, and by 2004 he was forced to sell it.

Bell officials placed no liens against Salazar's business for the remaining several thousand dollars that he'd been told he owed to the city. [65] It became clear that Bell's fee program was nothing more than an illegal shake-down operation designed to bring revenue into the city.[66]

In the 1970s and 1980s, the de-industrialization of the southeast L.A. region, combined with the influx of Latino immigrants—many of them un-documented—resulted in a decline in civic participation in Bell and other Gateway Cities.[67] By the 1990s membership in various community organiza-tions, such as the Bell Chamber of Commerce, Kiwanis, Rotary Club, and Masonic and Moose lodges, which had long promoted community service and civic involvement, had almost completely dropped off.[68] [69] Voter partici-pation in Bell was almost nonexistent; in 1990, only 669 votes were needed to win a council seat in a city of 34,000.[70] Though by 1980 Latinos made up the majority of Bell residents, the council would not become majority Latino until 2003.[71] The first elected Latino councilmember was Joseph Raymond, who served from 1964 to 1976. The next Latino was not elected until 1986, when George Mirabal won a seat and served until 1990.[72] In 1992, Mirabal was appointed by the council to be city clerk. A year later he was appointed to serve out the remainder of the term of mayor and longtime councilman Jay Price, who had served on the council since the 1950s.[73] [74] [75]

The community's civic consciousness continued to wither. At some point in the 1990s, as voter turnout continued to drop, the council began to simply appoint and reappoint those councilmembers and city clerks who ran for election unopposed. This practice of appointing councilmembers instead of electing them persisted until the scandal broke in 2010. Council resolutions presented as evidence in court showed that all councilmembers serving at the time had been appointed at least once.[76] In 2003, under Rizzo's auspices, three Latinos were appointed to the council. Victor Bello, Oscar Hernandez, and George Mirabal constituted Bell's first Latino-majority council.[77]

Gambling has long been a legal fixture of California life, having existed since statehood in 1850. Indeed, instead of authorizing only certain types of gaming, State statutes prohibit only a few specific forms.[78] One long-stand-ing form has been the card club, also sometimes referred to as card casinos or California casinos. These offer several types of card games, including vari-ous forms of poker such as Texas Hold 'Em and Omaha, as well as other so called "Asian Games." These latter games offer legalized variations of other types of traditional casino games such as Blackjack, Baccarat, and Roulette. Players are not permitted to bet against the house, but instead bet against one another in "player-banked games." These operations have become quite lu-crative, as the house charges fees to players per hand or by seat time. The proceeds offer an attractive source of tax revenue that many California cities have sought to help prop up their waning tax bases.

Still, however, a relatively small number of municipal officials clung to power in the Gateway Cities. As factories closed, residents—mostly white, middle-class residents—moved away, to be replaced by largely politically uninvolved immigrant laborers. The closures also dramatically undermined union locals' influence in local elections decreased. It became commonplace for councils, mayors' offices, and city managers' departments to be controlled by a rotating set of the same people from the 1970s through the 1990s. Bell's sister cities such as Huntington Park and Bell Gardens, for example, were ruled by councils composed of the same faces for twenty years, with only an occasional reformist candidate emerging in the wake of a local corruption scandal.[79] The area's evolving demographics and abandoned industrial sectors appeared to these officials urban blight that needed to be remedied by redevelopment policies. Many of the developers, realtors, and other southeastern L.A. County businessmen who would directly benefit from these city-funded redevelopment projects were also among the elected and appointed officials who would administer them.[80] City administrators turned to modernization of their downtown retail sections and the building of new parks and recreation centers as ways of fighting blight. But these were expensive projects, and strained city coffers began to run short of the revenues needed to support them.

But there were card clubs. As these operations were not expressly permitted or banned under California state law in the 1880s era, they have been largely unregulated by the state. In the 1970s and 1980s, all a card club needed to operate legally was permits and a license from the local municipality. And in the absence of strong state regulation, it fell to city governments to adopt regulations to either permit or ban them. As a result, cities all over southeastern L.A. began legalizing card clubs or poker parlors in the hope of bringing in desperately needed revenue. This was done in the late 1970s and early 1980s by Bell, Commerce, Bell Gardens, Huntington Park, and Cudahy. Cities also began to offer special deals of discounted land to attract casino developers to build card clubs in their taxing jurisdictions.[81]

The lure of quick and easy cash was too strong for these cities to resist. In Bell's neighboring city of Bell Gardens, the Bicycle Club (now known as the Bicycle Casino) opened in the 1980s and quickly became one of the largest card casinos in the United States—bringing in gross annual profit in excess of $100 million during the decade. Bell Gardens itself received approximately $12 million of that money as tax revenue to subsidize the city's redevelopment projects. In much smaller Bell, the council authorized card clubs in the late 1970s, and attracted investors to build and operate the California Bell Club, a poker parlor that opened in 1980.[82] In its first years, California Bell Club brought in as much as $2 million in tax revenue to the city.[83]

Wagering a city's funding on a card club was in itself a gamble, as well as an approach that included plenty of potential for corruption. As it turned out, the potential was realized. Local businessmen and realtors who controlled the council established a pattern of profiting from their own administrative decisions. Two Bell administrators, Peter Werrlein Jr. and John Pitts, saw the California Bell Club as a money-making opportunity that had nothing to do with cards.

In 1977, Pitts, then chief city administrator, conceived of a plan to attract investors for a card club in Bell in exchange for secret shares of the club's profits. Pitts promised several local businessmen that, in exchange for their funding and operating what became the California Bell Club, he would have city ordinances changed to legalize a single poker parlor and ensure that these investors received the only card club gambling license available from the city. [84] Pitts recruited Bell councilman and former mayor Pete Werrlein, Jr. to introduce and advocate for the gambling ordinance in the council meetings, along with a necessary rezoning ordinance. In exchange, Werrlein would receive part of Pitts' share in the club. In total, Pitts and Werrlein received 51 percent of the California Bell Club's profits, which were held publicly by Santa Monica attorney Kevin Kirwan. [85]

The plan worked, for a while. In 1984, Pitts, Werrlein, and Kirwan were indicted on multiple charges related to corruption, included some pressed against all the club's investors involved—brothers George and Jean Dadanians, brothers Carl and Daniel Abajian, John Gasparian, and John Simonian.

Pitts, Werrlein, and Kirwan each pleaded guilty to their involvement in forming a secret partnership with the club operators. Gasparian cooperated as a witness and received immunity, while Simonian and the Dadanians went to trial and were convicted on corruption charges. Despite being indicted, Pitts refused to vacate his position as chief city administrator, instead notifying the council that he would be going on indefinite sick leave at the end of April 1984. His trial was set to begin in June. [86]

Testimony at several of the trials revealed the depth of Werrlein's involvement in the corruption. Investigators had at first believed that he had merely been approached by Pitts to introduce the gambling and card club ordinances. But the testimony of Pitts and Gasparian recounted that, at a 1977 meeting among Pitts, Simonian, and the Abajians, Werrlein drew a circle onto a piece of paper, then divided it into nearly equal segments: 51 percent for Pitts and himself and 49 percent for the partners. [87] On an FBI tape of a conversation between Werrlein and Gasparian, Werrlein voiced his true intentions. "Now, my full intent from the day I started getting involved with you . . . was to make money," Werrlein said. Gasparian agrees, "Naturally, we all had that intention." Werrlein: "It wasn't to glorify the city and, uh, bring the city $3 million per year. It was to fatten our pockets." [88]

The 1984 indictment wasn't the first time Werrlein had been under investigation; he was no stranger to unscrupulous deals and working with shady characters. Not long after the California Bell Club began operating in 1980, the L.A. County District Attorney's office revealed that, in the late 1970s, Werrlein, a city administrator and a former Huntington Park police chief, had engaged in sex parties in the neighboring city of Cudahy with teenaged prostitutes supplied by cousins Kenneth Bianchi and Angelo Buono Jr.—the latter convicted in the infamous "Hillside Strangler" serial murderers.[89] [90] The news torpedoed Werrlein's popularity; he lost his council seat after sixteen years in the 1980 election.[91]

After losing his seat, Werrlein went on to manage the California Bell Club until he resigned in 1984 when he was indicted for, pled guilty to, and was subsequently convicted of mail fraud and running an illegal gambling operation.[92] Werrlein had also served as executor of the estate of notorious Los Angeles mobster Mickey Cohen (Bugsy Siegel's former partner) after his death in 1976; shortly thereafter Werrlein helped to broker the backroom poker parlor deal in Bell.[93] Werrlein was sentenced to three years in prison for his conviction for mail fraud and conducting an illegal gambling business.[94] He was also sentenced to five years of probation, to perform one thousand hours of community service, and to contribute $50,000 to a charity that assists homeless offenders with preparation of their probation reports.[95] Werrlein had also to forfeit his share of the illegal gambling, $400,000, to the federal government.[96]

Following the scandal, Bell worked to reform the California Bell Club. But even aside from their racketeering scheme, the operation never benefited the city as much as Werrlein, Pitts, and the other club partners had promised. The card club in Bell struggled to stay afloat throughout the 1980s and into the 1990s, as revenues dropped and the city's share of those revenues (via taxes) dropped as a result. It was estimated in early 1985 that the California Bell Club was losing $4,000 a day.[97]

During the early 1980s, neighboring cities began to approve and open larger card club casinos, driving up the competition for steady shares of the gambling market. The opening of the California Commerce Club in 1983 in Commerce and the Bicycle Club in 1984 in Bell Gardens resulted in successive 18 percent drops in revenue each year for Bell's California Bell Club.[98] This plunging revenue further undermined Bell's financial stability, given that the club functioned as the city's largest source of revenue.[99] California Bell Club was not only losing out on profits, but the new club partners had also inherited some $350,000 in bad checks and loans from the period under Werrlein's management.[100]

In response, club partners pushed the Bell Council to permit new versions of Asian betting games, like *pai gow*, as a way to attract new business and lift sagging profits.[101] But card clubs in neighboring cities like Gardena and Huntington Park were quick to adopt resolutions permitting *pai gow*, which includes an element of side betting in which non-participating players can bet on another player's game. The game was under much scrutiny at the time and was feared to be illegal in some formats, depending on how betting was structured.[102]

But a Los Angeles Superior Court judge ruled in January 1985 that *pai gow* was in fact legal, and all the clubs in the county quickly began to offer the game.[103] Club operators saw *pai gow* and other Asian games such as *mah-jongg, pai gow* poker, and super-pan nine as a means of attracting a fresh set of customers, mostly newer Asian immigrants and wealthy Asian businessmen. By the early 1990s, Asian games had evolved into exclusive high-stakes forms of play that accounted for more than half the revenues of most L.A. clubs.[104]

Smaller clubs like those in Bell, Cudahy and Huntington Park continued to struggle to stay afloat against fierce competition from larger casinos like the vast Bicycle Club in neighboring Bell Gardens. By the late 1980s, Bell, which had once counted on the card club as the largest source of city revenue, began to rely more and more on general sales tax and property taxes to fund the city budget.[105] Meanwhile, successive ownership changes and a court-enforced bankruptcy, caused the California Bell Club to close and reopen several times in the late 1980s and early 1990s. After reopening as the Bell Jackpot Casino in 1995, the club closed its doors for the final time in August of 1995 after operating for only seven months.[106]

Former councilman and card club manager Pete Werrlein served only ten and a half months of his three-year sentence before he was released from federal prison.[107] And despite his criminal record, Werrlein was hired back by Bell in 1993 to work as a consultant.[108] Werrlein's company, Western Gaming Associates, was chosen to monitor the struggling poker parlor during an attempt to reopen the club following its closure after bankruptcy.[109] Under the terms of the plan adopted by the council, Werrlein would receive 15 percent of the city's revenues in the first year of operation and 10 percent of revenues in the following years.[110]

Officials with the California Department of Justice were vocally concerned with Bell's decision to hire a convicted felon as a consultant for internal monitoring. An investigator with the department, N. Whitt Murray, said, "It raises a red flag for us. I don't know why the city would take the risk."[111] When questioned about the hire, Councilman George Cole responded, "Sure, it sounds crazy, but is it any crazier than hiring a convicted burglar to teach people how to secure their houses against break-ins? He knows how to spot loan-sharking, he knows how to spot skimming, he knows how to spot rip-offs. . . . We want to put in place the toughest monitoring system in California."[112]

To outsiders, the idea of hiring Werrlein as the internal monitor of Bell card club—and paying him handsomely to do so—offered a perfect example of the fox watching the henhouse. Yet despite his ties to shady characters and illicit activities, as well as the felony convictions, Werrlein managed to move past his image as a corrupt public official and continue to maintain close relations with Bell officials.

In 2010, when another corruption scandal emerged in Bell, it was re-vealed that Werrlein's family trust had been the recipient of a $4.6 million deal for the sale of his Western Auto car parts store to Bell's Redevelopment Agency under the leadership of Robert Rizzo.[113] Werrlein appeared to have formed a close relationship with Rizzo during the latter's tenure as city administrator. In an interview with the *Los Angeles Times*, Werrlein told a story about how he once confronted a drunken Rizzo at City Hall on the night of an election and told him "you're going home," slapped him across the face, and then said, "Let's go."[114]

Following the convictions of several of the California Bell Club conspira-tors, a *Los Angeles Times* retrospective on the scandal from 1985 included the following statements from then Mayor Clarence Knechtel:

> "It's fortunate that we caught them," he said. "Maybe it's a good example for the whole industry." The council wrote a good ordinance, he said, "but you still can't keep people from deception. If they lie to you, what can you do? The best thing to do," Knechtel said, "is to have a good honest city administra-tor."[115]

Mayor Knechtel's words proved to be prophetic when the primary actor in the 2010 Bell scandal turned out to be Robert Rizzo, far from "a good honest city administrator."

In the spring of 1984, two Bell Councilmembers, Donna Caddy and Lou Ida Caster, were facing reelection.[116] The California Bell Club scandal became relevant to the race after former Councilman Peter Werrlein Jr. and then-City Manager John Pitts were indicted along with several other local businessmen in December 1983.[117] After he was indicted, Pitts refused to resign from his position, and the council refused to terminate or even permanently suspend him from his job.[118] Caddy and Caster stated publicly that Pitts should be allowed to continue in his position until his guilt or innocence was deter-mined by a jury.[119]

Initially, Pitts was put on thirty days' leave with pay, but he was allowed to return to his position "because he has not been proven guilty of anything," as Caster stated at the time.[120] Caddy and Caster's public support for Pitts' retaining his taxpayer-funded job while awaiting a verdict at trial did not play well with the public. The incumbents' challengers knew this and exploited the opportunity.

In 1984, George Cole and Ray Johnson ran against Caddy and Caster. Johnson, 62, a retired teacher and community college administrator, had been appointed to the council in 1976, but had been defeated in 1980 when he ran on a slate with disgraced Councilman Werrlein Jr.[121] Johnson had to work to regain the public trust. He played up the city's lack of action on Pitts' job, saying, "We need to restore some confidence in city government; I believe in running an open government."[122]

George Cole, who was thirty-four in 1984, entered the council race on a platform of municipal reform. He was young and popular around Bell and the greater southeastern L.A. County region. Cole had worked as a mechanic at the Bethlehem Steel plant in Vernon for nine years before he became the financial secretary of United Steelworkers Local 1845.[123] In December 1982, the plant closed and immediately rendered thousands of workers jobless.[124] With thousands of families facing hunger, Cole, who had begun working for the union-affiliated Steelworkers Oldtimers Foundation, led an effort to create a food distribution center in the area.[125]

The Oldtimers Foundation food bank provided canned goods and other staples to retired and former steel plant workers and their families.[126] The Steelworkers Oldtimers Foundation was originally founded as the charity arm of the southern California United Steel Workers local in Fontana, California, by workers at the Kaiser Steel Plant.[127] Its mission was to provide services to aging union members and their families after they had retired from plant work.[128] In 1977, the Bethlehem Steel Plant USW local members established an Oldtimers Foundation branch in Southgate to provide similar services in the southeastern area of L.A. County.[129]

The need was great. When the steel plants began to close, many workers then approaching retirement missed out on qualifying for pensions by only a few months or even weeks. The Oldtimers Foundation quickly became one of their last bastions of hope.[130] Gradually the role of the Oldtimers Foundation expanded from focusing solely on union members into a larger community-services organization providing assistance to the broader community of seniors and the needy throughout the southeastern L.A. region.[131]

"We saw the social structure disappear," Cole said in reference to the sweeping demographic, social, and economic changes that occurred across the region from the 1970s through the 1980s.[132]

Cole's work at the Oldtimers Foundation established him as a prominent figure in the community. The Southgate-based branch of the foundation quickly became the dominant division of the organization. By 2001 it had an operating budget of $5 million and served over 600,000 meals annually in Los Angeles and San Bernardino counties. Cole was its executive director.[133]

Building upon his popularity, Cole campaigned heavily as a reformer. He pledged to bring new blood into the council and shake things up. His campaign cost $6,000, more than any other candidate's,[134] and organized door-to-door canvassers handing out literature declaring that "Caddy and Caster must go—they have lost the support of the community."[135] Cole's campaign mounted a two-pronged attack, which targeted the Council for retaining Pitts while he awaited trial and for not doing enough to get Bell back on a firmer economic footing.

Cole made the unemployment rate and the city's associated problems the primary issue, stating that the council needed to "try to confront this problem head-on and find some creative solutions to it."[136] Given his experience running social-service programs for the Oldtimers Foundation, Cole believed that Bell and its sister cities could band together and work with the non-profit sector to find solutions to the region's economic hardships.

In April of 1984, Cole and Johnson were swept into office with 930 and 901 votes respectively, compared to the 742 and 607 that Caddy and Caster had won.[137] Both new councilmen saw the wide margin of victory as a referendum on the Council's actions to retain Pitts after he had been indicted. Cole immediately went to work. He called for Pitts' resignation on the day he was sworn in. He delivered a letter to Pitts and the council that said the voting results showed that voters supported a "city administrator free of criminal indictments."[138] Another incumbent councilman George Simmons stated in response that the council had a "unanimous belief in Pitts' innocence," and that it was their belief that Pitts "always had the best interests of Bell in his heart."[139]

Cole questioned Simmons on his own involvement with Pitts and why he had failed to initiate an investigation into Pitts, Werrlein, and the California Bell Club when John Gasparian, the eventual FBI informant in the case, had come to Simmons with allegations of corruption and hidden interests as early as 1982.[140] By 1984, Simmons had been on the city council for twenty-two years, and had served as mayor when Pitts was hired as city manager in 1965. In response to Cole's questions, Simmons claimed he had not had adequate information at the time to warrant further investigating the allegations of malfeasance. Cole rejected this claim. After the council meeting, Cole said Simmons "very clearly failed to carry out an obligation that he has to the people of Bell."[141] By the end of April 1984, Pitts went on an indefinite sick leave. He soon pleaded guilty to the charges against him and never returned to his position as city manager.

The Oldtimers Foundation, which Cole ran, continued to grow over several decades into one of the largest providers of social services in the entire southeastern region. Cole remained on the council and served in the rotating position of mayor several times over twenty-four years until he left his seat in October 2008.[142] During his dual tenure as Bell Councilman and director of the Oldtimers Foundation, the non-profit began securing lucrative contracts with local city governments to provide social services to their residents. By 2010, the foundation held a $38,000-a-month contract with Bell to provide for Dial-A-Ride services for senior citizens.[143] The foundation also was engaged in the sale of property to the city in 2004, and acquired a $72,000 loan from the city in 2005.[144] [145]

Then Cole, in his turn, began a steady fall from grace. The emergence of the 2010 Bell scandal spurred investigations into the doings of other current and former officials. Cole and his dealings became a target as the state's various justice departments began investigating contracts and business dealings that Bell had pursued during the tenure of Robert Rizzo—whom Cole had played a role in hiring back in 1993. The Oldtimers Foundation fell under immediate scrutiny for contracts with Bell and other cities for which no verified financial records of payments could be located.[146] Elected as a reformer, and widely trusted in the community, Cole also directed residents' tax revenues toward the non-profits for which he worked for handsome compensation. In an ironic reversal of roles, Cole would exit the Oldtimers Foundation on medical leave in September of 2010 while under investigation for the Bell corruption case—much as Pitts had left his position thirty years before.

NOTES

1. Pratibha Devisingh Patil, "Speech by her excellency the President of India Shrimati Pratibha Devisingh Patil on the eve of demitting office of the president," (speech, eve of leaving office at the end of presidential term, New Delhi, India, July 24, 2012), http://pratibhapatil.nic.in/sp240712.html.

2. Gateway Cities Council of Governments. "An Introduction to the Gateway Cities COG." July 2012. Retrieved from http://www.gatewaycog.org/wp-content/uploads/2012/07/An-Introduction-to-the-Gateway-Cities-COG-Rev-July-2012.pdf. 3.

3. "Mapping L.A.: Southeast." *Los Angeles Times.* N.D. Retrieved from http://maps.latimes.com/neighborhoods/region/southeast/.

4. City of Bell. "Annual Budget Report." City of Bell 2012/13 Budget. (Bell, CA: City of Bell, 2011). A4–A6.

5. Moodian, M. "Unity Through Crisis: How a Latino and Lebanese American Coalition Helped Save Democracy in the City of Bell." (White paper at the City of Bell Scandal Revisited Conference, Chapman University, 2015).

6. Ibid.

7. Ibid.

8. Ibid, p. 2.

9. Barrows, H. D. "Don Antonio Maria Lugo; A Picturesque Character of California." *Annual Publication of the Historical Society of Southern California.* (Los Angeles: University of California Press on behalf of the Historical Society of Southern California, Vol. 3, No. 4, 1896). pp. 28–29. Retrieved from http://www.jstor.org/stable/41167598.

10. McGroarty, S. *History of Los Angeles County* (Chicago and New York: The American Historical Society, Inc., 1923). pp. 159–160.

11. Ibid, pp. 159.

12. Barrows, Don Antonio, p. 28.

13. McGroarty, History, p. 176.

14. Moodian, Unity, pp. 2.

15. Ibid.

16. City of Bell, A4–A5.

17. Ibid.

18. Franklin D. Roosevelt Presidential Library & Museum. "Minnewa Bell Papers, circa 1942–1962." N.D. Retrieved from http://www.fdrlibrary.marist.edu/archives/collections/franklin/index.php?p=collections/findingaid&id=73.

19. Moodian, Unity, pp. 2–3.

20. Davis, M. "The Empty Quarter." *Sex, Death and God in L.A.* Ed. David Reid (New York: Pantheon Books, 1992). pp. 56–58.

21. Goffard, C. "How Bell Hit Bottom." *Los Angeles Times*. December 28, 2010. Retrieved from http://www.latimes.com/local/la-me-bell-origins-20101228-story.html#page=1.

22. Audi, T. "In One City, an Islamic Center Unifies." *Wall Street Journal*. September 20, 2010. pp. 1–2. Retrieved from http://www.wsj.com/articles/SB10001424052 748704644404575482001778588866.

23. Ibid.

24. Willon, P. "Lawmakers Push to Scrap Prop. 13 Tax Limits for Factories and Business." *Los Angeles Times*. June 10, 2015. Retrieved from http://www.latimes.com/local/political/la-me-pc-lawmakers-prop-13-tax-limits-20150610-story.html.

25. Ibid.

26. Davis, M. "Chinatown, Revisited? The 'Internationalization' of Downtown Los Angeles." *Sex, Death and God in L.A.* Ed. David Reid (New York: Pantheon Books, 1992). pp. 29-30.

27. Davis, The Empty, p. 57.

28. Ibid, p. 58.

29. Davis, Chinatown, p. 30.

30. Fuetsch, M. & Griego, T. "Census Shows Asian, Hispanic Surge." *Los Angeles Times*. February 28, 1991.

31. Moodian, Unity, pp. 6–7.

32. Hogen-Esch, T. "Predator State: Corruption in a Council-Manager System—The Case of Bell, California." (White paper at the City of Bell Scandal Revisited Conference, Chapman University, 2015). pp. 10–29.

33. Fuetsch & Griego, Census Shows.

34. Audi, In One, p. 2.

35. Ibid, p. 3.

36. Moodian, Unity, p. 8.

37. Abdulrahim, R. "Activist Raises Profile of Bell's Lebanese Community." *Los Angeles Times*. September 10, 2010. Retrieved from http://articles.latimes.com/2010/sep/08/local/la-me-bell-lebanese-20100908.

38. Ibid.

39. Moodian, Unity, p. 8.

40. Abdulrahim, Activist.

41. Ibid.

42. Hogen-Esch, Predator, p. 10.

43. Moodian, Unity, p. 10.

44. United States Census Bureau. "Bell California Census QuickFacts." Last Modified October 14, 2015. Retrieved from http://quickfacts.census.gov/qfd/states/06/0604870.html.

45. Moodian, Unity, p. 10.

46. Ibid, p. 13.

47. Biederman, P. "Schools Trade Land to Bell for $25 Million in Future Taxes." *Los Angeles Times*. October 4, 1987, SE1, SE3.

48. Moodian, Unity, p. 13.

49. Helfand, D. "BELL: Bramble to Quit Post for Colorado Job." *Los Angeles Times*. May 2, 1993.

50. "Bell: Manager Intends to Quit." *Los Angeles Times*. December 10, 1987.

51. Helfand, BELL: Bramble.

52. Berg, M. H. "Bell City Oks Rizzo as Administrative Head." *Los Angeles Times*. August 15, 1993.

53. Ibid.

54. Goffard, How Bell.

55. Ibid.

56. Christensen, K. & Esquivel, P. "Bell Property Tax Rate Second-Highest in L.A. County." *Los Angeles Times*. July 30, 2010. Retrieved from http://articles.latimes.com/2010/jul/30/local/la-me-bell-taxes-new-20100730.

57. Ibid.

58. Ibid.

59. Ibid.
60. Esquivel, P. & Lopez, R. "Bell Demanded Extra Fees From Some Businesses." *Los Angeles Times.* November 2, 2010. Retrieved from http://www.latimes.com/local/la-me-1102-bell-fees-20101102-m-story.html#page=1.
61. Ibid.
62. Ibid.
63. Ibid.
64. Ibid.
65. Ibid.
66. Ibid.
67. Hogen-Esch, p. 13.
68. Ibid.
69. Goffard, How Bell.
70. Ibid.
71. Hogen-Esch, Predator, p. 13.
72. "BELL: Mirabal to Rejoin City Council." *Los Angeles Times.* April 4, 1993.
73. Ibid.
74. Hogen-Esch, Predator, p. 13.
75. Goffard, How Bell.
76. Knoll, C. "Bell's City Clerk is First to Testify in Corruption Case." *Los Angeles Times.* January 25, 2013. Retrieved from http://articles.latimes.com/2013/jan/25/local/la-me-bell-trial-20130126.
77. Hogen-Esch, Predator, p. 13.
78. Dunstan, R. "Section V. Gambling in California." *Gambling in California.* (California State Library: California Research Bureau, 1997).
79. Davis, The Empty Quarter, pp. 67–68.
80. Ibid, p. 68.
81. Ibid, p. 69.
82. Ibid, p. 69.
83. Burns, M. "Bell Reforms Aimed at Poker Club Corruption." *Los Angeles Times.* January 3, 1985. p. 1.
84. Ibid.
85. Ibid, p. 1, 4.
86. Burns, M. "Indicted City Official Placed on Sick Leave in Bell." *Los Angeles Times.* April 26, 1984.
87. Burns, Bell Reforms, p. 4.
88. Farr, B. "Ex-Mayor of Bell Gets 3 Years in Prison for Secret Casino Interest." *Los Angeles Times.* May 14, 1985.
89. Davis, The Empty, pp. 69–70.
90. Burns, M. "Indicted City Manager Becomes Central Issue in Bell Campaign." *Los Angeles Times.* March 18, 1984.
91. Gottesman, J. "Bell's Hiring of Felon Threatens Reopening of Card Club, State Says." *Los Angeles Times.* December 15, 1993.
92. Ibid.
93. Becerra, H. & Pringle, P. "Bell's Business Ties to Officials Probed." *Los Angeles Times.* July 31, 2010. Retrieved from http://articles.latimes.com/2010/jul/31/local/la-me-07-31-bell-properties-20100731.
94. Farr, Ex-Mayor.
95. Ibid.
96. Ibid.
97. Burns, M. "Council Wary It May Be Illegal: Bell Casino Requests Adding Asian Games." *Los Angeles Times.* January 10, 1985.
98. Ibid.
99. Ibid.
100. Ibid.
101. Ibid.

102. Ibid.

103. Churm, S. R. "Asian Game: Good Deal or Fast Shuffle for Card Clubs?" *Los Angeles Times*. February 3, 1985.

104. Davis, The Empty, p. 71.

105. Valencia, C. "Bell Club's Fiscal Health Called Better Yet Delicate." *Los Angeles Times*. January 19, 1986.

106. "Central Los Angeles: Bell Jackpot Casino Closes After 7 Months." *Los Angeles Times*. August 18, 1985.

107. Gottesman, Bell's Hiring.

108. Ibid.

109. Ibid.

110. Ibid.

111. Ibid.

112. Ibid.

113. Wilson, S. "Weapons Dealer from City of Bell Ranks 10th for Most Guns Found in Mexico." *LA Weekly*. December 13, 2010. Retrieved from http://www.laweekly.com/news/weapons-dealer-from-city-of-bell-ranks-10th-for-most-guns-found-in-mexico-2397797.

114. Goffard, How Bell

115. Burns, Bell Reforms, p. 5.

116. Burns, Indicted City Manager.

117. Ibid.

118. Ibid.

119. Ibid.

120. Ibid.

121. Ibid.

122. Ibid.

123. Einstein, D. & Burns, M. "Poker Scandal Key to Bell Upset." *Los Angeles Times*. April 12, 1984.

124. Boyer, E. J. "Steelworkers' Lament: Odes for a Lost Love: In Memory of 'Lady Beth'." *Los Angeles Times*. May 6, 1985.

125. Einstein & Burns, Poker Scandal.

126. Burns, M. "Springsteen Strikes Chord With Steelworkers." *Los Angeles Times*. October 28, 1984.

127. Marosi, R. "Clients Have Changed, but Needs Haven't." *Los Angeles Times*. September 9, 2001. Retrieved from http://articles.latimes.com/2001/sep/09/local/me-43904.

128. Ibid.

129. Ibid.

130. Boyer, Steelworkers' Lament.

131. Marosi, Clients Have Changed.

132. Ibid.

133. Ibid.

134. Einstein & Burns, Poker Scandal.

135. Ibid.

136. Burns, Indicted City Manager.

137. Einstein & Burns, Poker Scandal.

138. Burns, M. "New Bell Councilman Calls for Administrator's Ouster." *Los Angeles Times*. April 19, 1984.

139. Ibid.

140. Ibid.

141. Ibid.

142. McGreevy, P. "Former Bell Mayor Steps Down from Charity that Does Work for the City." *Los Angeles Times*. September 8, 2010. Retrieved from http://articles.latimes.com/2010/sep/08/local/la-me-oldtimers-20100908.

143. Becerra & Pringle, Bell's Business.

144. Ibid.

145. McGreevy, Former Bell Mayor.

146. Ibid.

Chapter Two

The Puppet Master

"It will be of little avail to the people, that the laws are made by men of their own choice, if the laws be so voluminous that they cannot be read, or so incoherent that they cannot be understood;"
—Alexander Hamilton, *The Federalist Papers No. 62*[1]

By all accounts, Robert Rizzo was an introvert. He rarely sought the limelight during his seventeen years as the chief administrative officer in Bell, nor during his previous employment in the cities of Rancho Cucamonga and Hesperia. This was especially true during the period from 2005 to 2010, after which he pleaded no contest to a host of illegal activities, such as falsifying public records, perjury, conspiracy, misappropriating public funds, and conflict of interest. Rizzo, along with his assistant, Angela Spaccia, and five elected Bell officials, was convicted of looting millions from one of the poorest cities in the United States.

At the time of his arrest, Rizzo's salary and benefits totaled more than $1.5 million. His assistant, Angela Spaccia, drew total compensation close to $850,000. Randy Adams, the town's police chief, earned $770,000 in total compensation. The mayor and council were paying themselves annual salaries of up to $100,000 to work part-time for a city of less than 37,000 residents, a quarter of whom lived below the poverty line.

A man of seeming contradictions, Rizzo often quoted tough-guy lines from *The Sopranos* and tolerated no challenges to his authority as chief administrative officer.[2] He owned several thoroughbreds—one named *Depenserdel'argent*, French for "spend money,"[3] and was known to have a fierce temper.[4] But Rizzo was also known to be thrifty, refusing to spend public funds to repair City Hall and keeping an office bare of any furnishings or pictures besides a plain desk.[5] In his early days, he came across as a humble public servant making flapjacks at community breakfasts.[6]

A Bay Area native, Rizzo received formal training as a public administrator by making his way through classes on human resource management and ethics in public service, as well as public finance and public budgeting, earning a bachelor's degree in political science from the University of California, Berkeley and graduating from Cal State Hayward with a master's in public administration. During his early employment he was known for being good with numbers, although during his deposition, he seemed to struggle to grasp basic accounting principles.[7] He later indulged in other questionable behaviors,[8] some of which brought accusations of sexual harassment,[9] rumored affairs with city officials,[10] intimidation,[11] [12] and alcoholism.[13]

After interning at the City of San Leandro and with the Housing Authority of Alameda County, Rizzo began his political career in the southern California city of Rancho Cucamonga as an administrative aide. There, he reportedly worked diligently and quietly, avoiding calling attention to himself while building respect and influence among city officials. Those who worked with him at the time described him as "intimidating and standoffish."[14] He maintained a flawless track record by using his aptitude for money management to link his work to quantifiable improvements, thereby associating himself with success. He would ride this success to a position of power. Within five years in Rancho Cucamonga, he had risen from an entry-level administrative position to assistant city manager. He would repeat this silent and seemingly effortless rise to power several times over the course of his career.

After eight years in Rancho Cucamonga, Rizzo was hired as city manager of Hesperia in 1988 at a pay of $78,000—about one-tenth of his salary at the peak of the Bell scandal. For the newly incorporated city of Hesperia, his reputation for aggressive and effective economic policies and his willingness to accept a modest pay scale made him an ideal candidate. City Councilmember Roth said Rizzo was "very impressive . . . and he seemed to know what he was talking about."[15]

In just the first year, Rizzo saw the city's budget more than double, from $6.9 million to $17.5 million. This time, his rising power was not tied to an escalation in position or title, but to influence over the checks and balances meant to limit that power. In four years, he gained the respect and confidence of the city council, and acquired a 25 percent pay increase for himself. However, questionable monetary exchanges with other officials began to surface.[16]

Even early in his tenure in Hesperia, Rizzo was described as legendary. He was said to have handled the building of the city of Hesperia with "down-to-earth practicality and a penchant for pomp." Described as a "short, stout man with a quick wit and friendly smile," Rizzo was said to have boundless energy—energy that was reminiscent of his two pre-school age daughters at the time. After a year in the job, Councilman Roth proclaimed Rizzo was the "best" city manager, calling him both innovative and aggressive while remarking on how much he cared about the people of Hesperia. Another councilman and resident of Hesperia for forty years, Val Shearer, echoed Roth's assertions that Rizzo was aggressive and also knowledgeable. "Bob Rizzo's mind is so far ahead of everyone else's it's amazing," he said.[17] His foresight earned Rizzo a write-up in the trade magazine *Public Manager* in 1989.[18] After the scandal, many would realize how Rizzo's calculations were, indeed, very far ahead of others.

In his first year in Hesperia, Rizzo praised the city council as cohesive and solid, but changed his story when suspicions of misconduct arose. He then characterized the council as "vindictive, very, very vindictive." Hesperia's Planning Director, Rob Zuel, said Rizzo's style and demeanor was very authoritative,[19] a trait that would continue to show up repeatedly during his seventeen years in Bell.

In April 1992, Hesperia's city council pressured Rizzo to resign. At that time, he was making $95,000 a year, a 25 percent pay increase in less than four years.[20] The council acted following an accusation that he was funneling city improvement funds to pay salaries; it was also suspected that Rizzo and other city officials were abusing their city-issued credit cards.[21] After his departure, officials found more than $7 million in poorly documented or unspecified transactions as well as more revelations that restricted funds were used for general operations.[22]

Despite being pushed out for wrongdoing in Hesperia, Rizzo managed to cut ties so stealthily that his next employer, Bell, was oblivious to his previous economic mismanagement. Did Hesperia serve as a trial run where he learned how to manipulate and deceive both subordinates and the elected officials to whom he reported? In any case, his approach in Bell would be much the same as before: Earn recognition for positive change while quietly gaining control over those who could rein in his influence.

In May 1993, Rizzo, then thirty-nine, was hired as interim chief administrative officer in Bell with an annual salary of $72,000, less than what he was making in Hesperia and less than the previous city administrator of Bell. He was offered the permanent position in August. In his cover letter applying for the position, Rizzo had written, "As you are aware, I am an experienced municipal administrator having professional experience that spans the past fifteen years. . . . The City of Bell is of particular interest to me because I have the experience to work with the City Council and community to continue the city moving positively towards the next century."[23]

Initially, Rizzo was credited with saving the cash-starved city by instituting sound fiscal measures and restructuring bonds. There were comparable commendations made regarding his other improvements: Residents said the parks were attractive and clean, trash was removed quickly, and graffiti was painted over with efficient urgency.[24] Under Rizzo's tenure, Bell also enjoyed quicker police response, cleaner streets, and more programming for youth. Rizzo helped create the conditions for a big skateboard park, playing fields, a miniature golf course, and an insistence that not just the stars of games got trophies, but every child. A former councilman said Rizzo both stabilized the finances of the city while taking an interest in its image. [25]

Even a year after Rizzo's conviction, some residents at a public hearing on a recycling collection facility told the newly installed council that when Rizzo was in charge, streets were cleaner and police response time quicker. [26] Indeed, many believed the city had looked better than it had in years.

It was also noted that, while salaries of top administrators were a bit high, they were approved in a manner consistent both with best practices and in accordance to the rules governing general law cities. The city attorney, Ed Lee, prepared employment contracts, including ones for Rizzo, which were placed on the Council's agenda for approval and made available to the public. [27]

It was a prosperous time for Rizzo and associates. In eleven years, Rizzo's compensation increased to $300,000 until 2005, when he received a 47 percent raise to $442,000. His base salary continued to increase at a rate of about $52,000, or over 11 percent, a year. [28] He and Angela Spaccia began working supplemental retirement plans to benefit a small group of city officers and employees. In 2008, even after Rizzo laid off city employees to address a budget shortfall, he approved new contracts for himself and Spaccia and automatic 11 percent raises to their base salaries. [29]

By this time, employment contracts previously prepared by the city attorney and submitted to the council for approval had ceased seeing the light of day. Prosecuting Assistant District Attorney Sean Hassert suggested it was sometime in 2004, after bringing Angela Spaccia on, that Rizzo "began becoming less of a benevolent dictator . . . and they just kept taking that money for themselves . . . and what they did wasn't just criminal; it–it is so outrageous . . . it is so offensive, it is hurtful and destructive to the city." Harlan Brown, Spaccia's attorney, said Rizzo "went nuts" at this time. [30]

In some ways, the Bell scandal officially started with the little-noticed special election on November 29, 2005, that turned Bell into a charter city. Rizzo convinced the council that becoming a charter city would give them more control over municipal business and enable them to increase salaries for the mayor and council. The vote passed 336 to 54 votes with less than 1 percent of the population voting, many by questionable absentee ballots. The majority of the ballots, 239, were absentee. [31] A Bell police sergeant who later sued Bell for being demoted after contacting federal authorities, said city officials and police officers walked door-to-door encouraging residents to vote absentee. He identified nineteen people he claimed voted in the special election despite either living outside of the country at the time, or being dead. [32]

The California Constitution gives cities the power to become charter cities. Becoming a charter city provides officials with more control and authority over municipal affairs and enables them to trump a state law governing the same issue. This is also known as "home rule." Home rule is a delegation of power from the state to its sub-units of governments. This includes counties, municipalities, and towns or townships or villages. Cities in California that have not adopted a charter are general law cities. These cities are bound to the state's general law with respect to municipal affairs.

The issue of home rule is generally governed by what is commonly known as "Dillon's Rule." The U.S. Constitution is silent on the inherent powers of local government. When the Constitution or statue is silent, the courts must intervene and interpret the silence. This is what happened in Iowa in 1868, when Judge John Forrest Dillon held that local governments only have those powers expressly granted them by the state. If specific authority is not granted to a local government, it does not exist and the local government is required to go to the state to seek legislation allowing it. Dillon concluded "municipal corporations owe their origin to, and derive their powers and rights wholly from, the legislature. It breathes into them the breath of life, without which they cannot exist. As it creates, so may it destroy. If it may destroy, it may abridge and control."[33] A common feature of a home-rule local government is its ability to raise taxes.

Dillon did not trust local governments. His beliefs were shaped during probably the lowest point in the history of America cities, a period in the late nineteenth and early twentieth centuries that was filled with corruption and inefficiency. He is quoted as saying that "those best fitted by their intelligence, business experience, capacity and moral character" usually did not hold local office, and that the conduct of municipal affairs was generally "unwise and extravagant."[34] The inflexibility of this system is the reason that many states began to adopt home rule provisions in the early 1900s. State preeminence, based on Dillon's Rule, is now accepted legal theory in all fifty states, although not all states follow it. Approximately forty states are considered "Dillon Rule" states, but the application differs widely in many states.[35]

The status of becoming a charter city also freed city officials from state salary caps. A California state law enacted in 2005 limited the pay of councilmembers in "general law" cities, a category that includes most cities in Southern California. Rizzo and the Bell Council turned the city into a charter city so they could increase their own salaries. Councilmembers received $96,000 in base salary, while state limited councilmembers of general law cities to $4,800 per year (in cites with similar population). Bell passed an ordinance titled "An Ordinance of the City Council of the City of Bell Limiting Compensation" that actually doubled the salaries of the council from $673 per month to $1,332 per month (not including the salaries they begin to receive for serving on phantom agencies Rizzo created).[36] The deceptive intent was evident in that only the title appeared in the agenda and not actual text, the backup and minutes of the meeting.[37] But Rizzo hadn't waited for the official action. He had already been signing employment contracts (including his own) and not placing them on the council agenda since early 2005, and went into high gear when he signed his and Spaccia's contract on July, 1, 2005, granting them both nearly 50 percent raises as well as a tripling of sick leave and vacation accruals. In 2008, Rizzo was awarded 856 hours (107 days) of vacation and 288 hours (36 days) of sick leave per year. This totaled 143 days of combined leave in a year containing about 250 working days. In 2009, Rizzo converted these hours into a pay rate of $304 per hour and cashed out over 1,100 hours of vacation and sick leave for more than $360,000.[38]

Not everything that Rizzo and the council did to increase their salaries was done in the dark. One of their most lucrative techniques of extracting money from the city was setting up public agencies, appointing themselves to the board, and paying themselves a salary for doing so. The council created multiple subordinate agencies for the city, including the Bell Surplus Property Authority, the Bell Community Housing Authority, the Bell Solid Waste and Recycling Authority, and the Bell Public Finance Authority.[39] In the name of efficiency, Rizzo scheduled the boards to meet concurrently with council meetings.[40] It was through these sham agencies that Rizzo and the council were eventually able to dramatically inflate their salaries.

The boards of these agencies seldom if ever actually met. The most egregious example is the Bell Solid Waste and Recycling Authority, which met one time in February 2006, one time two years later in June 2008, and then never met again under Rizzo's tenure.[41] Likewise, the Bell Surplus Property Authority did not meet at all in 2009 or the first half of 2010.

When the council did hold meetings for these agencies, little substantive work was discussed. For example, at the February 6, 2006 council meeting, the Bell Surplus Property Authority, the Bell Community Housing Authority, the Bell Solid Waste and Recycling Authority, and the Bell Public Finance Authority held meetings for the sole purpose of granting board members of the agencies—the Council—salaries of $1,100 per month for sitting on each board.[42] After the councilmembers passed their own pay raises, each of the agency meetings were adjourned without further business being conducted.[43] The infrequent board meetings were often absurdly short, usually lasting less than a few minutes, reinforcing the notion that very little of substance was discussed. The July 31, 2006 city council meeting was typical of how the agency meetings took place. The Bell Surplus Property Authority, Bell Public Finance Authority, and the Bell Community Housing Authority meetings each lasted for one minute.[44]

Despite their official titles, it remained unclear to most why these agencies existed and what if any public purpose they served. Rebecca Valdez, the city clerk, was responsible for keeping the minutes of all of the meetings held by the boards of the city agencies.[45] Still, she did not know what any of the agencies actually did, or even what their purpose was.[46] According to Lorenzo Velez, who replaced Victor Bello on the city council in 2009, none of these agencies ever met outside of the council meetings and none of the board members did any work for them.[47] In fact, he didn't know that many of the agencies even existed until he spoke with the District Attorney's Office investigating Bell after the corruption became public.[48]

The agencies proved lucrative for Rizzo and the councilmembers. By 2006 only a small fraction of the Council's earnings came from their actual salaries. In 2010, councilmembers were paid $150 per month as a base salary.[49] Due to their "service" on these agency boards, however, they were receiving more than ten times that amount, at $1,574.65 per agency per month.[50] In September, 2008 Rizzo begin breaking his salary into five separate employee contracts to hide the total from the public. As chief administrative officer, he had one primary contract for $52,325.04 per month and four additional contracts at a monthly rate of $8,467.51 for each of the four phantom agencies he created. When the corruption scandal broke, each of the councilmembers except Velez was making almost $95,000 per year to handle agency board meetings that almost never happened and to run agencies that did no work.

Rizzo's payout from the agencies was even more generous than that of the councilmembers, in part because he was appointed head of each agency and was paid accordingly. By 2010, he was receiving almost $9,300 per month for each of the agencies that he headed, which together exceeded the salary he gave himself for the chief administrative officer.[51] The phantom agencies enabled Rizzo and the council to hide their escalating salaries in plain sight.

These increases were embedded within five-year program-of-service budget that no one, including the council, understood. There was no public discussion held about a budget document that was virtually incomprehensible. In total, twelve employment contracts giving approximately 25 percent to 50 percent pay raises to twelve high-level employees were approved in this manner.[52][53][54][55] A deputy district attorney later remarked, "The budget they passed [was one] that none of them understood, because you can't understand it; it was meant not to be understood. Everything. Every resolution. Every agenda that you picked up, you cannot understand what's going on in Bell by looking at it. And it was constant disinformation given to the people month after month after month. And someone should have stopped it, and no one did."[56]

Rizzo had also been hiring law firms and other consultants, signing engagement letters, and almost never putting them on an agenda for council approval. Once Rizzo started getting cash from the 2004 General Obligation Bonds, he proceeded to disburse the money as he chose, regardless if his choices actually involved improvements to the city, as the bonds were intended. He put documents in place that enabled him to control the contracts, outside contractors and disbursement of the bond funds, which started flowing in a big way in 2006 and 2007.

One of the ways that Bell financed its ever-increasing spending was through debt. The most direct way a municipality can finance debt is to issue bonds to investors that it must pay back with interest over a set amount of time. Between 2003 and 2007, Bell and its various agencies issued six rounds of municipal bonds totaling almost $143 million in debt that would mature between 2010 and 2037.[57] At the time, bond issuances provided short-term cash for Rizzo and the council to hide their salaries and other spending. But they have left Bell and its residents with high debt load and continuing high taxes to pay off the bonds' principal and interest.

The highest amount of bonds issued during this period was connected to questionable municipal capital improvement projects, including a new sports complex. A bond levy for various projects was first publicly proposed during a council meeting in June 2003. But there was little discussion at the time, or indeed afterward, of final plans, specific budgets, timeframes, or assessments of the capital improvement projects that would be funded by the bond issuance. Despite the lack of public discussion and deliberation of the merits of these phantom projects, the council approved bonds of up to $70 million to pay for them.[58]

Since the bonds were general obligation bonds that were to be paid for by levying higher property tax on Bell property owners, the bonds were required to be approved by voters by a two-thirds supermajority.[59]

The measure was placed on the November 2003 election ballot even though no more details were provided to the council or publicly discussed. Measure A, as it was titled, painted an ambitious picture of how the funds were to be used by the city. According to Measure A, the $70 million in bonds would be used to

> develop the Bell Sports Complex to include a gymnasium for indoor soccer, basketball, cheerleading and the baseball facility; expand the Bell Community center and other parks, recreational and cultural facilities; construct a new full service Bell Community Library, Performing Arts Theatre, public safety and civic facilities.[60]

Rizzo promised voters a sports complex with mission-style architecture, sculptures, large playing fields, and beautiful landscaping. The Bell Sports

Complex was to be a place for families and children's activities for after-school activities. According to the ballot argument in favor of Measure A, "[n]ow is the time to continue Bell's transformation into the southeast's finest community."[61]

Given such promises, it is not surprising that the measure was passed by an overwhelming majority. With only 10 percent of registered voters voting in an election limited to the bond issue, Measure A received 731 "yes" votes compared to 202 "no" votes.[62]

Of the $70 million approved through Measure A, only $50 million of bonds were issued by Bell. The first issuance occurred the next year, in 2004, when $15 million in bonds were sold to investors. Unlike the later issuance, the 2004 bonds were subject to at least some outside review. The 2004 bond proceeds were deposited into an account maintained with Citigroup, which provided a cursory review of the expenditures before they were disbursed by the city.[63]

The plurality of the funds raised through the 2004 bond issuance, $6.2 million, did not go to the Bell Sports Complex, but instead went to construct Little Bear Park.[64] The park sits on 1.4 acres right behind one of the convenience stores owned by then-mayor Hernandez. The funds were used to turn the space into a children's park with a playground, soccer field, and an indoor-activities space.[65] A little over $3 million was spent on the sports complex with the 2004 bond funds,[66] mostly to purchase land for the sports complex. However, the city still lacked concrete plans on how to design and build the facility.[67]

In 2007, Bell issued a second set of bonds pursuant to Measure A, for $35 million. Unlike the 2004 bond issuance, there was no outside financial entity like Citigroup to provide even an elementary level of oversight. Instead, Rizzo acted as fiscal agent for the bonds and exercised complete discretion over how the proceeds were used.[68]

Indeed, the $35 million was not used for much. Few of the promised capital improvement projects promised by Measure A came to fruition under Rizzo's tenure. Another $2.5 million was spent on Little Bear Park; $3 million was allegedly spent working on the Bell Sports Complex, though there was little to show for it.[69] Rizzo collected over $35,000 for oversight of construction of the sports complex. During his oversight, the designs and plans changed repeatedly, and the city never settled on a final concept for the complex. Even in the absence of a final concept, the planning firm owned by Dennis Tarango, who was Bell's planning director, charged Bell almost $500,000 for its planning work on the facility.[70]

There was, in fact, almost nothing to show for the $6.1 million. The State Controller's 2010 Audit of Bell found seven years' of work on the sports complex to have accomplished nothing except for "acquiring a site that consists of a dirt lot with a masonry wall around it and a water pumping station in the middle."[71]

After Measure A was passed, amid repeated vague promises by Rizzo about the sports complex and other projects, Bell citizens began to express frustration at the lack of progress. This frustration went public as early as a 2008 council meeting. A resident, Roger Ramirez, publicly questioned Rizzo about what was happening with the sports complex and why it was taking so long. Even after this, however, Rizzo refused to provide any concrete answers.[72]

It is unclear why Bell issued the 2007 bonds in the first place. The city provided no clear rationale as to why it needed the funds, particularly since the council continued to defer any deliberation on budgetary and spending decisions related to the proposed projects.[73]

Consequently, most of the $35 million bond proceeds went unspent. Only $11.5 million was disbursed at all, with almost $5 million spent on interest payments.[74] Only $6.5 million was allegedly used for projects, less than half the $15 million spent from the 2004 bond issuance. The $23.5 million in unspent bond funds sat in a non-interest-bearing checking account owned by the city. The reason Rizzo placed this substantial sum of money into a checking account is unclear, particularly considering the 5 percent interest that the city owed bondholders for the 2007 issuance. By not putting the unspent money into an interest-bearing account, Rizzo cost the city an estimated $1.7 million in potential arbitrage earnings alone.[75]

This lost revenue adds to the financial damage the 2004 and 2007 bond issuances have done to the city. Despite having very little to show for the $50 million in bonds, Bell still has to make payments to its bondholders. In addition to the principal, the city will have to pay an estimated $38 million in interest.[76]

In 2007, Bell conducted another bond issuance that compounded its financial mess. One of the city agencies, the Bell Public Financing Authority, entered into a deal with Dexia Credit Local in October 2007. Dexia purchased $35 million in taxable lease revenue bonds issued by the Public Financing Authority. The agency was to use the money to purchase a 23.4-acre plot that it would lease to BNSF, a railroad company. Dexia would be paid out of the revenue generated from the BNSF lease.[77]

It was supposed to be a sure thing. It turned out not to be. Five days prior to the bond deal's closing, BNSF and Bell were sued under the California Environmental Quality Act to enjoin BNSF from using the property as it intended to under the lease. It was unclear if Ed Lee, the city attorney, was aware of the lawsuit, but he allowed the bond deal to go forward.[78]

After the bonds were issued, a court found that BNSF's intended use of the property would violate the California Environmental Quality Act and enjoined the company from improving the land. With BNSF unable to act under the lease, the Public Financing Authority could not collect the intended rent.[79] For Bell, this meant that, without the rent, the city could not make its bond payment obligations.

Bell was required to make biannual interest payments, with the principal, $35 million, due on November 1, 2010.[80] Because of the judgment against BNSF, Bell was unable to make its final interest payment on May 1, 2010, or to the repay the principal on November 1, 2010.[81] This default ruined Bell's credit rating. In August 2010, after the missed interest payment and the *LA Times* story exposing the city's corruption, Bell's bond rating fell from A+ to junk status.[82] [83]

Meanwhile, the money to pay the inflated salaries and benefits for Rizzo and other city officials had to come from somewhere. Over the years that Rizzo was chief administrative officer, officials found ways to shift the burden of their raises onto residents. This was mainly accomplished through higher property tax rates and increased assessments and fees. By 2010, Bell had one of the highest property tax rates in Los Angeles County, as well as substantially higher fees that made living and working in Bell much more expensive.

Like other California municipalities, Bell was affected by the "tax revolt" of the late 1970s that limited the amount of taxes that could be assessed. Specifically, Proposition 13, passed in 1978, limited property taxes to a maximum 1 percent of the assessed value of the property, plus "the rate necessary to fund local voter-approved bonded indebtedness."[84] Pursuant to this law, Bell was subject to a 1 percent property tax assessed by Los Angeles County; approximately 5 percent of the revenue generated from this tax is given the city to spend as part of its general fund.[85]

In addition to the county's 1 percent tax, Bell property owners were also subject to a city property tax to help fund pension obligations. This property tax override was first approved by Bell voters in 1944 to pay for city employee pension contributions and for medical insurance premiums for former employees. This type of pension override property tax was not uncommon in Los Angeles County, and more than 10 percent its cities had a similar provision.[86] Bell's pension override tax rate was relatively stable, and from the 1980s remained unchanged for more than twenty years at 0.187554 percent.[87] Starting in 2007, however, this stability began to wobble.

In order to fund the increasingly lavish pension benefits of Bell officials and employees, the council passed Resolution No. 2007-42. This set out a series of increases in the pension override tax rate over the next three years. The rate would top out at 0.277554 percent for the fiscal year 2009-2010. This final rate represented an almost 50 percent rise from the pre-2007 rate.[88] This enabled the city to collect an additional $2.9 million from property owners than under the old tax rate.[89]

It is doubtful that the city council had the legal authority to increase the pension override tax rate. Specifically, California Revenue and Taxation Code Section 96.3(a) set a maximum allowable property tax rate to pay for pension benefits to equal the higher of the rates assessed in the 1982–1983 or in the 1983–1984 fiscal years.[90] California law does not permit a council to increase the pension override tax rate above 0.187554 percent, which was the tax rate assessed in the 1983–1984 fiscal year. After the corruption was exposed, the State Controller ordered Bell to refund the excessive property tax collected by reallocating the money to the city's public school district.[91]

Bell property owners were hit by yet another property tax increase during this time. By 2010, interest payments on the $15 million bond issuance in 2004 started coming due. This bond, as well as the 2007 bond issuance, were paid for through a property tax increase. In 2010, the city property tax rate increased by 0.9 percent to accommodate the bond payments.[92]

These increases added up to a substantial tax hike in a few short years. By 2010, Bell's total property tax rate was 1.55 percent, the second-highest rate in Los Angeles County.[93] [94] Bell residents, despite having substantially below-average household income, paid a much higher rate than the county average of 1.16 percent. The city with the highest property tax rate, Industry, had only twenty-one residential properties subject to its property tax. Bell taxed more than 2,000 homes and 1,500 rental units.[95]

High property taxes were not the only means by which Bell residents were made to foot the bill for the salary and pension increases. Around the time the council started increasing the property tax rate, they brought in even more money by increasing assessments charged for basic services. Specifically, in 2007, the council passed a series of resolutions that dramatically raised the assessments charged by the Sanitation and Sewerage System District, the Refuse Collection District, the Recycling and Integrated Waste Management District, and the Landscaping and Lighting District. Starting in fiscal year 2007–2008, the rates almost doubled.[96] For example, after the council passed the increases, the average cost to a single-family home for refuse collection rose from $14.71 per month to $26.48.[97] But the city coffers swelled with new revenue. The assessment rate increases for those four districts resulted in an increased revenue of over $4.7 million, which overlapped the dramatic salary increases for Rizzo and Spaccia.[98]

Like the property tax rate increase, the assessment rate increases were probably not legal. In particular, Article XIIID of the California Constitution governs how municipalities like Bell can add or change assessments and other fees charged to residents. In order to increase assessment rates, the municipality must mail notices to the affected property owners, as well as win a majority vote of those property owners.[99] The city council did not follow these procedures and increased the assessment rates by a simple council vote without regard to the constitutional requirements.

Increasing the price of basic government services was not the only way Bell increased residents' cost of living. The city also increased the business license tax charged to the approximately one thousand businesses that operated in Bell. The increases started in 2000, when the city raised the business license tax by 20 percent. This was followed in 2005 by a 19 percent tax increase. The official justification for the increases was that the city was applying retroactive cost-of-living tax rates for the years that it did not raise the tax rate, even though the Bell Municipal Code did not provide for such cost-of-living increases. The State Controller General in its 2010 audit of Bell found that the ten years of increased business license taxes were lucrative for the city coffers, and estimated that $2.1 million more was collected from businesses than had the tax rate had not been raised.[100]

Like the other tax and fee increases enacted while Rizzo was in control, the additional business license taxes were not approved by voters. They were not even approved by the city council.[101] They were, however, quite similar to other tactics the city used to shake down and otherwise extract money from businesses.

Rizzo originally contended that the new charter gave him the authority to sign employment contracts. In fact, he began signing employment contracts and not taking them to the council in early 2005, well before the November charter vote. In reality, the charter never gave Rizzo this authority; it merely said the council could, if it so chose, delegate certain authorities to Rizzo. At some point, one of the legal consultants he hired, Clifton Albright, told Rizzo the council may need clarification that the charter allowed Rizzo to sign for employment contracts. Albright drafted Resolution Number 2006-42, which passed on July 31, 2006. Albright did testify that the charter and resolution never gave Rizzo the authority to sign his own contract.[102] However, Ed Lee, Bell's city attorney, testified that even after the passage of this resolution, the council retained the right to sign off on employment contacts.

Another significant problem with Rizzo's assertion regarding the Council's approval was that the document execution provision of the resolution was not actually part of the resolution the council passed. In court, Deputy District Attorney Sean Hassett shared the following provision with jurors: "The Bell City Council authorizes the Chief Administrative Office to execute all business documents on behalf of the City."[103] However, the original agenda packet containing the 2006 resolution did not have this provision included. Spaccia confirmed this, although she maintained that she was not aware of the provision's absence when the resolution was passed in 2006.

The resolution delegating to the chief administrative officer the ability to bind the city in labor and services contracts passed unanimously after Albright appeared before the council in a closed door meeting. Rizzo cited this resolution as the basis for his authority to approve employment contracts (including his own) without taking them to the council. This was crucial to the corruption charges against Rizzo and subsequently to the decision by the California Public Employee Retirement System (CALPERS), California's largest pension administrator, not to count any salaries of Rizzo, Spaccia, Randy Adams (Bell's police chief), and others after 2005 for calculation purposes towards their retirement. CALPERS's reasoning was that the contracts were not legally executed and approved by the council in an open meeting where the public was noticed. A central argument of the prosecution—upheld by the judge and jury—was that the resolution did not give Rizzo the authority to sign contracts by himself.

The resolution delegating labor and service contracts to Rizzo also was seriously flawed. When such delegation powers are given to city managers and chief administrative officers, they always include a dollar limit. Typically, there is a $25,000 or $50,000 cap on this delegation with larger amounts requiring council approval. This limit ensures there is a check and balance system in place that can serve to protect the city managers and administrators if issues arise. Resolution Number 2006-42 contained no dollar limit.

The consent calendar was designed in local governments to handle routine, non-controversial items. Issues placed on the consent calendar are supposed to have titles that clearly identify what action is to take place and to have backup materials attached to each item. The materials are required to be made publically available. The calendar can be taken and approved in one motion by local government officials. Best practice dictates that the public, staff, or elected officials should be allowed, after reviewing the title and the backup materials, to identify items and request one or more to be taken separately and publically discussed.

Under the Open Meeting Laws of California and the Brown Act of 1953, meetings of public bodies must be "open and public." Local government business may not be secret, and any action taken in violation of open meetings laws are required to be voided.

The Brown Act basically guarantees the public's right to attend and participate in meetings of local legislative bodies. Under the Brown Act, all local governments must post notice and an agenda for any regular meeting and mail notices at least three days before regular meetings to those who request it; post notice of continued meetings; deliver notice of special meetings at least one day in advance to those who request it; deliver notice of emergency meetings at least one hour in advance to those who request it; notify the media of special or emergency meetings if requested; hold meetings that are places accessible to all, with no fee; and not require a "sign in" for anyone.

There is also a requirement that the local government provide backup staff reports or the data that would support the position of staff in asking the local government to take action to approve or disapprove matters appearing before them. The Brown Act requires that all this information be available to the council and well as the public. Closed sessions are permissible; however, the body must report on final action taken in closed session. If action is taken as it pertains to contracts or settlement agreements, the public may receive copies of such records upon request. Both civil and criminal sanctions can be imposed on individuals or local governmental bodies that violate the act.[104]

However, the practice of mislabeling agenda items was quite common under Rizzo's tenure. Rizzo controlled the agenda, including what items went on the consent agenda. These latter items often went onto the consent calendar under extraordinarily misleading titles, some of which were incomprehensible. At times, backup materials on items differed from agenda packages, and the council and the public received different versions. Other times, backup materials were added after the council voted. City Clerk Rebecca Valdez testified about "switching pages" of City Attorney Ed Lee's and other key signatures and using them for multiple purposes.

When Rizzo and Spaccia had Bell purchase five years of Additional Retirement Service Credit (ARSC) from CALPERS for themselves and the council, the consent item agenda read "Section 5.03, Approval of Budget Amendments." There was no mention anywhere that the city was buying five years of retirement benefits.[106] No ordinance or resolution was passed to purchase these credits, nor was there any agenda item to be voted on or any approved increases in salary.

Before the practice was prohibited on January 1, 2013, California government workers were allowed to purchase additional years of service that could be counted toward their pension when they retire. Most workers in the public sector have employer-sponsored pension benefits known as defined benefits. In a defined benefit plan, the employer guarantees a certain level of retirement benefit to the employee based on several factors, such as the employee's age, years of employment (or a combination of years and age), and final average salary.

The practice of buying additional years to be used toward final retirement calculations is also known as "air time." Buying the years allows employees to retire earlier. However, when these years are purchased, they are almost always purchased by the employee, not the employer. Only in rare circumstances would a city agree to purchase these years of service; if it were to occur, it would be required to be voted on by the elected officials in a public meeting. Not in Bell. Rizzo, Spaccia, other city executives and the council used taxpayers' money to purchase these years.

Valdez, initially hired by Rizzo at the age of seventeen, ended up testifying with the promise of immunity. She never received any training for the job of city clerk, which she took in December 2007.[107] And it showed. Gottlieb said Valdez took the "worst minutes ever." Consent agendas never had backup documentation, and Valdez falsified records at Rizzo's request. The importance of the lack of backup documentation cannot be underestimated, as it supposedly freed up time for debate of any controversial items. The fact that virtually no backup documentation was kept by Valdez, under Rizzo's instruction, made it difficult to determine what the council was actually voting on.

Valdez's testimony also revealed that she signed minutes for meetings she didn't attend and sometimes made mistakes in her records. Also brought to light was the fact that she was clerk in name only for three years, when she was asked to perform almost none of the required duties. [108] Valdez also did a poor job of keeping backup documentation for meetings, a common practice by Rizzo. She only began recording meetings in 2010; before, she just summarized meetings and placed the notes in a vault. [109] [110] [111] [112] Her signature, she said, was often forged. Asked why she followed along with information she knew to be false, Valdez said she feared losing her job. As it turned out, she did not. Valdez continued to work for Bell until she secured another city job in October 2015.

City Attorney Ed Lee testified that he had no recollection of signing various documents that bore his signature. In fact, there existed a signature page containing Lee's signature that was paper-clipped; Rizzo would periodically ask Rebecca Valdez to slip it into documents. After being presented in court with ten employment contracts bearing his signature, Lee testified that he asked the L.A. District Attorney's Office to have them forensically examined to see if there were an explanation other than that he had actually signed them. [113]

Even though Lee served as the legal authority for Bell from 1993 to 2010, Rizzo increasingly began to rely less on him and instead to seek legal advice from others, notably Tom Brown and Clifton Albright. In addition to representing Bell, Lee also represented the Los Angeles cities of Maywood, Downey, and Covina. Typically, the city attorney and legal teams are hired by and report directly to elected local government officials to ensure a check-and-balance system. In Bell, the city attorney and legal advisors were hired by and reported directly to Rizzo. Further, Lee was associated with a large legal firm, Best Best & Krieger, LLP that possessed expertise in most of the municipal matters that Rizzo began obtaining counsel on elsewhere. It seems clear that Rizzo was not getting the advice he wanted from Lee. [114] [115]

Albright was with Albright, Yee and Schmit. He started working for Bell in late 2004, first on a Workman's Comp audit, and next on issues concerning the Independent Cities Risk Management Authority (ICRMA). Then, suddenly, he became involved in an unusual matter involving Bell and the city of Vernon. [116] Albright explained that his engagement with Bell was "to give legal advice regarding municipal law, contracts, and legal problems which might arise in the City." [117] As noted before, Albright and his firm drafted Resolution 2006-42, which attempted to clarify that Rizzo had authority to sign employment agreements as well as other official matters and contracts on behalf of the city.

Rizzo also employed Tom Brown, a former assistant U.S. Attorney in the major frauds section of the criminal division from 1991 to 1995. Brown, whose firm was initially called Brown & White, started working for Rizzo in 2006 on medical and other council reimbursements, and changed the firm's name to Brown White & Newhouse in 2008. Brown was also engaged by Bell to look at ethics, risk-management issues, and litigation matters. The 2006 retainer agreement with Brown & White stated that the firm was "to represent the City of Bell in connection with its investigation of the reimbursement of city council members of business and medical expenses" (hereafter the matter).[118]

Ultimately, Brown became Rizzo's key advisor, and quickly became involved in a number of issues surrounding the Bell scandal. He accompanied Rizzo to the initial meeting with *L.A. Times* reporters Gottlieb and Vives at Bear Park on July 9, 2010. The meeting was set up in response to the public records request concerning the salaries of top Bell appointed and elected officials and was how the reporters first confirmed what everyone in Bell was making. The meeting led to the widely quoted front-page headline: "Is a City Manager worth $800,000?" After the meeting concluded and the room emptied out, Brown stayed behind and told the reporters that he was the one that told Rizzo he had to give them the documents they requested. "I told them they'd take a hit, but things would blow over," Brown added.[119]

Brown was at most of the meetings between Police Chief Randy Adams and Bell officials during Adams's contract negotiations. Adams was hired at a salary of $457,000, double what he was making as chief at his former post in Glendale, and considerably higher than the chief of the LAPD. Emails flowing between him and Spaccia during their employment negotiations suggest there was a conscious effort to conceal his compensation from the public.

During his later deposition, Adams testified that he specifically asked Brown "if there was clarifying information, support information as to Mr. Rizzo's authority in reference to my contract. And he said, yes, it is in the charter." Adams said "[Brown] just had always represented to me that Rizzo had the authority to do what he was doing. . . . From the very beginning, when I first met Tom Brown and found out about his background, that he was a former U.S. attorney and that he'd been working in the City of Bell for about five years, I asked him—I took him aside.

"And I asked him," Adams testified, "you've been working here for five years. You're legal counsel, so forth. You've got an inside look at the city, that kind of thing. I said, 'Is there anything I need to worry about in coming to this city?'"[120]

In an email exchange between Rizzo and Lee regarding Adams' employment agreement, Lee asked Rizzo if the Adams' hiring needed to be added to the next Council meeting agenda and whether he should work on a contract. Rizzo responded that he had

> "never been asked by the city council to show, review, discuss or, anything else with any other Department head contract since the Charter became effective." Rizzo then listed 11 instances in which he executed contracts. Then in boldface type, he asks, '*What makes this one so special*! Ed—With our 15 years of working together and the City of Bell's continuing with you at BBK just because of our relationship. . . .'"

Then, in capital letters, Rizzo told Lee to be part of the "solution" and not the "problem." And signed it "your pal, Bob."[121] Lee also testified that, after several email exchanges with Rizzo and Tom Brown, he met with them in Rizzo's office. Lee said they handed him Resolution 2006-42 and asserted again that Rizzo had the authority to sign Adams' contract. Lee said he made it clear that, in his legal opinion, Rizzo did not have the authority to sign Adams' contract.[122] Yet Lee then seemed to go silent on the issue and did not challenge Rizzo further.

Brown was also heavily involved with the employment contract that had Victor Bello leaving the council but keeping his $100,000 salary while becoming coordinator of the food bank. Brown was also involved when Rizzo was arrested for DUI in Huntington Beach in 2010 after crashing through a neighbor's mailbox. Rizzo pleaded not guilty and hired Brown's firm to represent him, but ended up being sentenced to eighty hours of community service, treatment for alcohol abuse, and three years' probation.

Brown later testified to the grand jury that Rizzo paid him $2,900 in cash for his firm's work on the DUI during a trip to Rizzo's horse ranch. Brown testified that he passed the money to a staff member who was responsible for the firm's banking, but the cash wasn't actually deposited into the firm's account for four months. The judge overseeing the Bell trial, Kathleen Kennedy, was skeptical of Brown's story, questioning the timing and method of payment and saying they were "suspect at best." Rizzo pleaded guilty to conflict of interest for his dealings with Brown.[123] [124]

Brown also knew of Bell's illegal loan program. Rizzo oversaw the practice in which he, Spaccia, Mayor Hernandez, Councilman Artiga, and the majority of city employees—nearly fifty—received loans, mostly collateralized with unused vacation and sick leave. The council never approved the program. Brown and his firm actually received a wire payment from Bell from a loan given to a councilman. Rizzo oversaw the program in which forty-four employees and two councilmen received nearly $1.5 million in loans, including $160,000 to Rizzo himself. Rizzo also authorized $400,000 in loans to two businesses without collateral. None of these loans received any public discussion or council approval. [125] [126] [127]

Lourdes Garcia, Bell's director of administrative services, testified that she received phone calls and emails from Brown about wiring $20,000 directly to the bank account of Brown, White & Newhouse, LLP from a loan given to Councilman Artiga. Confused, she testified that she spoke with Rizzo directly, who assured her that Brown was handling certain matters for Artiga and it was okay to wire the funds to his office. [128]

The additional legal counsel Rizzo sought from Albright and Brown did not come cheap. Between January 1, 2005 and September 30, 2010, Albright billed and received payment for $1,376,160.32. [129] Brown's firms received payments between January 1, 2007 through December 31, 2010 in the amount of $1,380,545.70. [130]

Both men and their firms were involved separately in the infamous South Gate corruption case of former Mayor Albert Robles (Big Al). Robles served as an elected official in South Gate for a dozen years and became the city's youngest mayor at twenty-six. It was later alleged that Robles exerted power over city managers, firing those who refused to follow his orders and rewarding those who did. As mayor and city councilman, he had no authority to do so. He was convicted of corruption and sentenced to ten years in federal prison in 2005. In April 2013, the US 9th Circuit Court of Appeals threw out some of the convictions but let stand five counts of bribery. He was sentenced to time served (seven years). [131]

South Gate sued both firms for overbilling the city for defending Robles. In 2005, Brown's firm, Sheppard, Mullin, Richter and Hampton, agreed to pay South Gate $2 million to settle the suit. This occurred after a Los Angeles Superior Court judge ruled that the firm overcharged the city when defending Robles in a criminal trial. In his decision, Judge John P. Shook said the city should not have been charged more than $150,000 for the defense of Robles. Shook wrote in his opinion that

> Sheppard Mullin's redactions and block-billing entries make it impossible for the court to determine how much time was spent on nearly all specific activities, such as media relations, unfiled motions, unnecessary research and motions, and the like. The Court must therefore weigh all of the evidence to ascertain a reasonable fee, and has done so in accordance with the preceding discussion. The court finds that the fees charged the city by Sheppard Mullin were more than excessive and unreasonable, transcending beyond the stratosphere into deep outer space. The Court finds that a reasonable fee in this case should not have exceeded $150,000. The court finds that the City is the prevailing party and is entitled to judgment on its first cause of action for Restitution, because the evidence shows that Sheppard Mullin billed fees and costs that are unreasonable and unnecessary. [132]

Albright and his firm, Albright, Yee & Schmit, filed suit against South Gate in 2003. [133] South Gate countersued, seeking $1.8 million in damages for the firm's role in assisting Robles to assert control over the city's administration. [134] South Gate and Albright's firm agreed to a settlement in 2007 in which the firm paid $350,000 into a trust account. [135] The total amount was then split equally and paid to both South Gate and Albright, Yee. Each side received $175,000 in exchange for the dismissal of all claims by both sides. [136] In effect, Albright, Yee & Schmit paid a net of $175,000 to South Gate, far from the $1.8 million the city had sought.

Best Best & Krieger, LLP, the firm where Lee worked, ended up paying $2.5 million in 2013 to settle a suit with Bell for faulty legal advice and failing to properly advise Bell on a $35 million bond offering in 2007. A mutual release form was signed on August 26, 2014, between Bell and Brown, White & Newhouse, LLP releasing the city from unpaid legal fees and costs in the amount of $304,439.42 in exchange for the city's agreeing not to pursue potential claims against the firm. [137] [138]

While Lee and Albright were each deposed and required to testify during the Bell trials, neither was required of Brown, although he was a witness during the Grand Jury investigation. The prosecution did use the fact that Brown provided comprehensive ethics training to the council as evidence that they knew that what they were doing was wrong.

Ironically, *L.A. Times* reporters Gottlieb and Vives launched their investigations into Bell while looking into a sound idea of Rizzo's—combining police forces in Bell and neighboring Maywood with other small cities to form a regional force. Maywood was experiencing financial woes, and turned to Bell for help. Despite Rizzo's many years of keeping Bell out of the spotlight, even going so far as to ban employees from attending conferences, suddenly the small town came into focus. In fact, Rizzo assigned Spaccia to serve as Maywood's interim city manager under a mutual-aid agreement. She had held the position for seven months when the scandal broke. [139]

When the story did burst into public view, Rizzo was notably unapologetic about his salary, which had a $787,637 base pay and a total compensation package of $1.5 million. "If that's a number people choke on, maybe I'm in the wrong business," he said. "I could go into private business and make that money. This council has compensated me for the job I've done." [140]

However one characterizes Rizzo's performance, he kept Bell and its employees under tight rein. It may have been alcohol-fueled paranoia, but numerous former employees reported Rizzo tried to micromanage even the private lives of his subordinates, demanding to be the first to know about major life events that could affect their work. Rizzo also did not socialize and piloted Bell under the radar, barring employees participating in training outside his purview where they might have interacted with colleagues from other municipalities.

Descriptions of Rizzo tended toward a "diminutive and rotund"[141] figure with the "egg-shaped body of the Penguin in the movie *Batman Returns.*"[142] Along with the physical appearance, some added, Rizzo took on the characteristics of Danny Devito's character from the 1992 film.[143] His actions and manner increasingly painted him as a money-hungry, cigar-chomping, godfather-like figure,[144] surrounded by those who remained loyal in pursuit of power and influence.

In her testimony, Rebecca Valdez echoed others' descriptions of how Rizzo exerted control over people. "It was pretty well-known to the employees that important events that happened in your life, like going to school, having a baby, or buying a house—he had to be the first one to find out," Valdez said. When she got married, she said, Rizzo was the first to know.[145] Like many others, Valdez was loyal to Rizzo because she started at Bell as an intern at fourteen.

This systematic practice of cultivating loyalty was further described by Doug Willmore, Bell city manager after Rizzo, who helped clean up some of the challenges plaguing the city after Rizzo's and other councilmembers' departure. Willmore called it a "program" whereby Rizzo would hire highschool students, with a particular eye toward Latinas, and promise them that, "I'll keep you employed part-time all the way through college if you get a degree, and then I'll give you a job."[146] This meant, for example, that when Rizzo would ask for money to be wired, his subordinates would not question it.

Willmore said he spoke with four or five young Latinas about Rizzo's management style. They all described him with words like "benefactor," "father figure," or "favorite uncle." He had a temper, they agreed, but their image of him remained father-like. Former staff members also told Willmore that if they did speak about Bell in any public forum, they would either have to call Rizzo for regular check-ins and/or get remarks approved beforehand. Rizzo would tell them what they could or could not say.

From his own observations of the aftermath, Willmore described Bell's official environment as a "fear-based kind of dictatorial sort of thing, and he filled it with people who were sort of beholden to him."[147] Nor were the mayor and councilmembers spared Rizzo's micromanagement. It was reported that Rizzo required them to call him before coming to City Hall. If they showed up unannounced, Rizzo told staffers to let him know.

Rizzo's management style also included keeping no written records of anything, which made it difficult to audit and find out what actually happened in numerous circumstances and how to recover money. He also was careful to minimize what city business was available to the public. When the council wanted to take video of city meetings and put them on the Internet, for example, Rizzo promptly vetoed the idea.[148]

Rizzo was deposed on December 15, 2011, and ended up invoking his 5th Amendment rights over 115 times; however, Bell's lead civil litigator, Anthony Taylor, was able to gain some insight into Rizzo's management style.[149] Asked during his deposition whether his style as city manager was more "hands-on" or if he tended to delegate tasks, Rizzo responded, "I was management by wandering around."[150] He said he learned this style of management while studying for his master's in public administration. He said he relied on department heads and staff to do their work while he would "wander" and occasionally check in to make sure people were on task or if they needed assistance. He did not manage day-to-day affairs, he said, because he was busy working in the council. Asked if he held staff meetings, Rizzo said, "I didn't—no, I actually never really believed in staff meetings."[151] He called them a waste of time and said he would rather deal with department heads directly when issues arose.

Similarly, Rizzo acknowledged that he did not respond directly to emails, but instead would forward them to the appropriate department head with the instruction "please handle."[152] In other words, Rizzo's own descriptions of his management style did not seem to mirror micromanaging approach noted by others. In fact, testimony indicated that Rizzo used a myriad of different tactics to control and manage the city. Some of these tactics were evident to the reporters who first started talking to him about his salary.

One tactic was intimidation, such as in the infamous Little Bear Park meeting, which was the first time Rizzo met with Gottlieb and Vives. The *Los Angeles Times* reporters requested a meeting with Rizzo but were denied. They were told it would take ten days to provide the documents they requested from Valdez, the city clerk. However, on the ninth day they were told Rizzo wanted to meet with them. Thinking they would meet at City Hall, Gottlieb and Vives were surprised to learn that Rizzo wanted to meet them in a park. When they arrived, they found Rizzo with nine other people, including attorneys Lee and Brown, Spaccia, Mayor Hernandez, Councilman Luis Artiga, Valdez, Police Chief Randy Adams, Councilman George Cole, and Pedro Carrillo, a contractor from the city.

Gottlieb described it this way:

> "When I walked into the room, which had a fireplace surrounded by American and Cub Scout flags, I saw Rizzo had brought nine people with him, obviously trying to intimidate us. There were two attorneys, a couple city councilmen, the police chief, the assistant city manager, the city clerk and a councilman from Maywood," he said. "Rizzo, who has the egg-shaped body of the Penguin in the movie *Batman Returns*, sat at the back in an open collared shirt."[153]

This meeting, along with the stack of documents they took with them, provided the basis for the story Gottlieb and Vives broke.

Gilbert Miranda, a senior investigator for the L.A. District Attorney, similarly described how Rizzo cultivated fear, and put people in place to carry out his plans as a way to continually expand his influence. Miranda acknowledged that the councilmembers were "negligent," but said Rizzo's had them fearful of losing their jobs if they did not comply with his requests. It a type of loyalty fostered through fear.[154]

Rizzo's propensity for creating a chilly environment could also be seen in his office, which was virtually bare—devoid of family photos or personal touches that might humanize him. Asked about this, Rizzo said he preferred to not get too comfortable, and valued the ability to leave at a moment's notice should an opportunity arise. Yet Rizzo spent nearly twenty years in Bell, and throughout had little more in his office than a television for religiously following stock market updates.[155] When it came to the city's offices in general, Rizzo pinched pennies and refused upgrades, such as changing the carpets. Curiously, the makeup of the offices included a one-way mirror where staff could be watched without knowing it. The only elected official with an office was the Mayor.

James Corcoran, the Bell police sergeant who exposed the questionable tactics the city used in illegally impounding vehicles, described Rizzo as "autocratic." Corcoran admitted that Rizzo was an effective manager who was very good at "dollars and cents" even if this aptitude for money management was predicated on false pretenses. Corcoran also attested to Rizzo's growing reputation as a "drunk." Corcoran had also been privy to the sexual assault accusation, shared with him by Lourdes Garcia, director of administrative services. Corcoran said Rizzo's overextension of power meant that he didn't believe in checks and balances, and completely disregarded this philosophy. "He was the monarch, he was the king," Corcoran said. "He was like the little guy in the *Wizard of Oz*; when the curtain fell . . . that was Rizzo."[156]

Rizzo also raised money by targeting property owners and businesses through a covert and mostly undocumented process that amounted to little more than a business shakedown. The main actor in this effort was Eric Eggena, who was originally hired as the city prosecutor and later became director of general services. In the latter position, Eggna supervised code enforcement.[157] In Bell, this division "enforces the Bell Municipal Code and City Ordinances created to maintain the welfare of residents and business owners."[158] This is supposed to be achieved by "work[ing] proactively and respond[ing] to neighbor and business-owner complaints" and issuing violations to the offending property owner or business if necessary. Only if the violation is not corrected can the city issue a fine and refer the case for court supervision.[159]

This is not what happened under Eggena. The city aggressively targeted residents and businesses for the most minor of code violations. This enforcement often involved the police. For example, police would stop people collecting aluminum cans to redeem the refund value and issue a fine for unauthorized trash collection or other trumped-up code infraction.[160] In one case, police stopped a woman who was getting back in her car after delivering an Avon bag to a residence. The police issued her a citation when she admitted that she did not have a business license. They then impounded her car as "evidence" after finding more Avon products in the back seat.[161] By impounding the car, the city could not only gain leverage over the woman to pay the fine, or "settlement," but also charge a $400 release fee, despite the fact that police would seldom actually collect evidence from the impounded vehicles.[162]

In another case, a business owner was threatened with closure if he failed to comply. The payments affected at least fifteen small businesses, including a tire shop, restaurants, a market, and auto detailers. In addition, the fees seemed to be arbitrarily required and collected. City records indicated that a tire shop owner paid at least $144,000 over a four-year period while another tire shop owner paid $13,000 a year. Yet another permit with city approval for an auto repair shop did not require annual fees. One auto dealer had to generate $80,000 a year in sales taxes or had to pay the difference back to the city. Gerardo Quiroz, a car-wash owner, was so upset about his $300 monthly fee that he often would write "bribe" in Spanish on the memo line of his checks.[163]

And instead of allowing a person or business to correct the violation, Eggena and others would pressure them to settle the case and pay an arbitrary fine. Even though Eggena almost never filed a code enforcement case in which the court became involved, he would present targeted residents with papers made to look like court documents to persuade them to pay the fine.[164]

It is impossible to know how much money the city extracted from its citizens in this manner. Even though Eggena and other officials operated under the color of law, the lack of actual court involvement means this activity was poorly documented. Much of the code enforcement activity was unreported. Furthermore, it is unclear what actually happened to much of the property that was seized. While many people did pay release fees get their property back, a substantial amount of property simply disappeared.[165] Many allege that Eggena and other officials would sell the seized property for the city or for themselves.[166] [167]

As noted above, Rizzo claimed credit for lowering crime and shortening police response times. To the degree this was true, it may have been due to Rizzo's cozy relationship with the police union. Rizzo encouraged police to target undocumented workers and their families—which whistleblower Corcoran called "racial profiling." Corcoran said one officer told him, "If you see ladders or paint cans in a truck, pull it over."

Corcoran said, "They talked about generating revenue by impounding motor vehicles of unlicensed drivers. It started and we did it for years and we would tally up—I remember we'd take 50 cars a night and the sergeant would sit there and tally up what—'cause each car was $300."[168] The fee was triple what Los Angeles County and nearby cities charged. At the height of this scheme, the police force was said to be impounding up to eight vehicles a day. Since many of the targeted community members were undocumented, they were unlikely to challenge the grounds by which their vehicles were impounded. The practice ended up spurring a federal investigation into civil-rights violations. One Bell officer admitted, "We'd look for younger guys in their 20s and 30s, guys with junkier cars, broken lights, loud music or tinted windows."[169]

Other Bell officers said there was a daily quota for towing cars and that their jobs would be at risk for not meeting them. Records showed the city made $800,000 from the vehicle impound scheme in 2009.[170] Controller John Chiang's office found that Bell overcharged businesses with fees and taxes to the tune of $5.6 million.[171]

Among all these dubious practices, the one scheme that led to most of the charges against Rizzo was the loan program he established for himself, the council, and city employees. Outside experts called this practice unprecedented. Under the program, Spaccia received three loans totaling more than $300,000; Lourdes Garcia, the administrative services manager, obtained two loans for $177,500; and Annette Peretz, Bell's director of community services, got a $95,000 loan. Rizzo approved all of the loans, and the audit showed that vacation and sick pay were often used as collateral.[172] Councilman Artiga and Mayor Hernandez also received loans of $20,000.

Some businesses received loans as well. It is notable that these loans were made without any public notice or approval from the council. In addition, Rizzo borrowed money from his retirement accounts in two $50,000 increments in 2004. He also received two $80,000 loans from the program.[173] Willmore said other rank-and-file employees had also taken out loans, many of which were repaid before he got to the city. For those that had not been, it was Willmore's job to collect the repayments: "We finished up the process of making sure that everybody paid those loans back."[174]

The audit by Chiang's office also found that more than $93,000 in city funds was used to repay personal loans taken out by Rizzo, which did not appear to have authorization or justification for any public benefit.[175] In total, $1.5 million in loans were made to the council, other public officials, and city employees at Rizzo's discretion.[176] Council and administrative oversight and internal controls were virtually non-existent, the audit found, allowing for waste, fraud abuse, and misappropriation to be unusually widespread.[177]

During Rizzo's sentencing hearing, Judge Kathleen Kennedy commented on the loan program:

> Almost every employee I ever heard about with Bell had a loan with the city. There was no authority for that, but it sort of made Rizzo kind of a godfather like character where people would come to him when they were in need and get loans, and so it gave him power, respect and authority by the employees that were able to take advantage of that.[178]

However, James Spertus, Rizzo's attorney, said

> The criminal case involved the loan accounts which were really, basically, Mr. Rizzo administering a program that had been in place since the early 80's. . . . In fact, the city attorney at the time had the opinion that it was lawful to administer the loan program. Is that a crime? The law was unclear. . . . they (the prosecutors) believed the law was strict liability. That is Mr. Rizzo authorized the loan, and he was not authorized to make those loans, that's a misappropriation of funds. . . . He clearly wasn't personally profiting from the loan counts. In fact, five chiefs of police have taken loans."[179]

Rizzo found a mentor in another corrupt politician, Bruce Malkenhorst, city administrator in the small city of Vernon for twenty-nine years who earned a salary upwards of $900,000. Vernon, a town four miles south of downtown L.A. that shares a border with Bell, had the smallest population of any incorporated city in California, with 112 residents. Malkenhorst left office in 2005 after being indicted for corruption. He was convicted in 2011 for misappropriation of funds after accepting a plea deal.

Malkenhorst was sentenced to three years' probation and ordered to repay Vernon $60,000 and $10,000 in fines. Upon his retirement, Malkenhorst became the highest-paid retiree under CALPERS, collecting $509,664 a year. However, in 2012 CALPERS reduced his pension to $115,000, concluding that his salary was improperly obtained and in November 2015, and CALPERS moved to collect $3.4 million.[180] Some believe that Rizzo may have taken Malkenhorst as a model. Rizzo's plan, of course, was to retire along with Spaccia before the corruption the two had fostered was discovered.

In 2005, Rizzo bought a luxurious ranch in the state of Washington and started breeding thoroughbreds. The ten-acre farm in Auburn was assessed at $875,000—perhaps because in 2004 Rizzo's horses earned him $678,000.[181] The property is a 2,600 square-foot parcel on the Green River, complete with a pool and barn. Rizzo's horse-breeding ultimately lead to his conviction for federal tax fraud. On the other hand, this federal conviction may have enabled his attorney to work out a deal to have Rizzo's federal sentence run concurrently with his state term, enabling him to serve about half of his time in federal prison instead of harder time in state prison.

Other questionable business exchanges followed, such as in 2006 when Bell spent over $1 million on a law firm for only three months of work that year. The firm happened to employee Eugenia Chiang, who would become Rizzo's second wife. Rizzo divorced his first wife in 2001, blaming the breakup on the stress of his job. But people who knew Rizzo from Auburn said he loved his horses and would dote on them almost as much as his wife and three daughters,[182] two from his previous marriage and one with Chiang.

Rizzo also formed a horse-owning partnership with Dennis Tarango, who served as Bell planning director while also being a private contractor who secured multiple contracts with the city.[183] This seemed to be a theme for Rizzo, since under his leadership, the city also bought property owned by Mayor Oscar Hernandez, the circumstances of which are unclear. In addition, the city purchased a social services organization headed by former Councilman George Cole.[184] These transactions and affiliations further cemented the loyalty Rizzo was fostering among officials across all levels of the municipality.

Rizzo did not call attention to himself. He regularly dressed in clothing that did not suggest that he was making nearly $1.5 million in total compensation. And track officials and trainers at Emerald Downs said he bought relatively inexpensive horses. He also listed the owners of most of the horses as three California companies he formed—Rizzo Racing Stable Inc., R.A. Rizzo Inc., and Golden Aggie Ranch Inc.[185] This way he spread his assets and sought not to be linked to the massive amounts of money he was collecting, or the tax fraud he ended up committing through this scheme.

Rizzo ended up pleading guilty to federal tax charges. According to court documents from 2006 through 2009, he claimed illegal losses of $571,530 on his Washington ranch, which he falsely claimed was rental property. In total, he was charged with over $770,000 in counterfeit losses, most of which came from the ranch. Rizzo was paid over $200,000 by one of his corporations for personal expenses in 2009 and 2010, according to the plea agreement. This included $120,000 he was paid for work on his Huntington Beach home, work that is speculated to have been carried out by Tarango's firm.[186]

For his role in the Bell scandal, Rizzo pleaded no contest to sixty-nine corruption counts and was sentenced to thirty-three months in federal prison and twelve years in state prison. Chief United States District Judge George H. King recommended the federal sentence run consecutive—one after the other—to the state term;[187] however Judge Kennedy allowed the federal and state terms to run concurrently—at the same time. With time off for good behavior, he would serve 80 percent of his federal sentence which would give him a release date of October 19, 2016, when he would be transferred to state prison. As with his federal sentence, with time off for good behavior he would end up serving an additional five or six years of his state sentence. Rizzo was also ordered to pay $8.8 million in restitution to Bell. One district attorney's investigator concluded that Rizzo should receive the maximum sentence because "the craftiness with which [Rizzo] committed the crime [was] amazing." Senior investigator Gilbert Miranda said, "the financial losses incurred by the city of Bell will cause a ripple effect which will be felt by all California taxpayers."[188] Willmore further noted the corruption's impact by noting that, for eighteen years, Rizzo ignored much-needed economic development in Bell, which was known as "the commercial center of the southeast."

Rizzo asserted his Fifth Amendment rights throughout all legal processes. During his sentencing hearing on April 16, 2014, Anthony Taylor, attorney for Bell, said "What you have never heard him say is that he is willing to tell the people of Bell everything that happened so that the truth can come out in every single matter."[189] Rizzo was not even interviewed for his own probation report, which ended up containing incomplete and inaccurate information.[190] Rizzo was never asked to testify in any of the cases, which caused Harland Braun, Spaccia's attorney, to get into a heated debate with Judge Kennedy.

Braun later called Kennedy the "Rizzo of the judicial system" during a panel discussion at Chapman University and insisted that she just didn't want to sit through another trial. He also suggested that the Judge had an issue with the two women standing trial, Spaccia and Teresa Jacobs. "I think it's a women thing," Braun said. "I just can't figure it out. She didn't like my client as a woman, because the only one that really went to prison of the city council people was a female who testified. She didn't like her testimony. She said that."[191]

Braun said the plea deal should have forced Rizzo to cooperate with the prosecution and be interviewed extensively. Of the interview that was conducted, Braun lamented, "[The interview] doesn't talk about the agreements they had, who said what to whom about the authority they had or—versus what authority he did not have." In Braun's opinion, the probation interview was "useless."[192]

In addition, Braun remarked on how Rizzo had insisted there be no press present when he made his plea bargain, and insisted that the district attorney couldn't tape record his interview. To Braun, this meant that Rizzo was "leading everyone by the nose" and further ignited his argument that Spaccia did not receive a fair trial.

Rizzo's silence continues today. In multiple requests for an interview for this book, Rizzo kept insisting that he could not be interviewed because the district attorney's office and the U.S. Securities and Exchange Commission still had open investigations. However, he was willing to take a look at a list of topics and potential questions to be presented. All previous correspondence had been in handwritten notes, but the letter he sent after receiving a list of questions was typed and claimed that the questions indicated a "strong negative bias" with respect to his seventeen years of service in Bell.

Rizzo claimed that any response he made would be misconstrued.[193] As of this writing, Rizzo has not spoken out about the events in Bell. Some speculate that his silence indicates that there were others involved who he has to protect. For example, Mayor Nestor Valencia suggested that former Councilman George Cole was the real mastermind behind the corruption.[194]

The one time Rizzo did speak, in his sentencing hearing, he had the following to say:

> Your Honor, I started in Bell in 1992. For the first 12 years, we ran a very good, tight ship, because we didn't have any issues. And beginning in the 13th year, I breached the public's confidence by starting to look at the position more towards myself than towards the community. I'm very, very sorry for that. I apologize for that. If I could go back and make changes, I would. I've done it a million times in my mind. All I can do today is ask you to please understand that I'm sorry. I will never do anything like this again. I will never have an opportunity, but I did breach the public's confidence and I do apologize.[195]

But Taylor challenged Rizzo's apology, saying he did not think he showed any remorse throughout the process, as from the beginning Rizzo had been seeking legal fees from the city.[196] And Bell residents were also angry at Rizzo's silence. During the public comment section of the sentencing hearing, one said:

> As a manager, he did a great job. That's not why we are here. He stole the money. He hurt a lot of people in Maywood and in Bell. People are still hurting. And that's going to go on for a while. So he did what was easier for him because even today, he is still trying to figure out, through his attorney, what he can get for himself.[197]

Perhaps Rizzo is simply biding his time before writing his own bestseller, telling the world what really happened in the tiny town of Bell. For now, it remains largely a mystery.

NOTES

1. Alexander Hamilton, Federalist No. 62. The Senate. February 27, 1788. Retrieved from http://www.constitution.org/fed/federa62.htm.

2. Pringle, P., Knoll, C., & Murphy, K. "Rizzo's Horse Had Come In." *Los Angeles Times*. August 22, 2010. http://articles.latimes.com/2010/aug/22/local/la-me-rizzo-20100822.

3. Grad, S. & Yoshino, K. "Bell's Robert Rizzo Pleads No Contest, To Get 10 to 12 Years in Prison." *Los Angeles Times*. October 3, 2013. Retrieved from http://articles.latimes.com/2013/oct/03/local/la-me-ln-bell-robert-rizzo-pleads-no-contest-prison-20131003.

4. Doug Willmore, interview with author, February 12, 2015.

5. Ibid.

6. Pringle, Knoll, & Murphy, Rizzo's Horse.

7. People v. Rizzo. BC445497. Videotaped deposition of Robert Rizzo. December 15, 2011.

8. Ibid.

9. Ibid.

10. Knoll, C. & Gottlieb, J. "Bell Trial – 'Were You Robert Rizzo's Girlfriend?' DA Asks." *Los Angeles Times.* February 13, 2013. http://latimesblogs.latimes.com/lanow/2013/02/bell-trial-were-you-robert-rizzos-girlfriend-da-asks.html.

11. Nestor Valencia, interview with author, February 12, 2015.

12. Willmore, interview.

13. Lopez, S. "Robert Rizzo is Service Time Behind Cars." *Los Angeles Times.* January 13, 2011. http://articles.latimes.com/2011/jan/13/local/la-me-0113-lopez-20110113.

14. Ibid.

15. Ibid.

16. Ibid.

17. Nordyke, P. "Hesperia's City Manager Uses Pomp, Practicality to Set Pace for New Town." *Public Management*, 71(12), pp. 28. 1989. http://search.proquest.com/docview/204162893?accountid=13758.

18. Ibid.

19. Pringle, Knoll, & Murphy, Rizzo's Horse.

20. Edwards, B. "Hesperia on the Hook for $80,000 of Rizzo's Pension." *Hesperia Star.* August 10, 2010. Retrieved from http://www.hesperiastar.com/article/20071103/SPORTS/311039986/0/SEARCH.

21. Pringle, Knoll, & Murphy, Rizzo's Horse.

22. Ibid.

23. B013634. Robert Rizzo's Cover Letter. June 24, 1993.

24. Goffard, C. "How Bell Hit Bottom." *Los Angeles Times.* December 28, 2010. Retrieved from http://www.latimes.com/local/la-me-bell-origins-20101228-story.html#page=1.

25. Ibid.

26. City of Bell. "Regular Meeting of the Bell City Council/Bell Community Housing Authority/Successor Agency to the Bell Community Redevelopment Agency/Bell Public Finance Authority/Planning Commission." February 11, 2015.

27. People v. Spaccia. BA 376026, 382701. Sentencing Minutes. April 10, 2014.

28. California Public Employees' Retirement System Office of Audit Services. "City of Bell Public Agency Review." November 2010.

29. People ex rel Brown v. Rizzo, Spaccia, Adams, Hernandez, Jacobo, Cole, Bello, and Mirabel. BC445497. First Amended Complaint. November 15, 2010.

30. People v. Spaccia. BA 376026, 382701. Sentencing Minutes. April 10, 2014.

31. Gottlieb, J. "Bell Council Used Little-Noticed Ballot Measure to Skirt State Salary Limits." *Los Angeles Times.* July 23, 2010. Retrieved from http://www.latimes.com/local/la-me-bell-council-used-ballot-measure-state-salary-limits-20130117-m-story.html.

32. James Corcoran, Interview with author, February 12, 2015.

33. Beale, J.H. *A Selection of Cases on Municipal Corporations.* Cambridge: Harvard University Press, 1911. pp. 132–133.

34. Dillon, J. F. *Treatise on the Law of Municipal Corporations.* Chicago: James Cockroft & Company, 1872. pp. 21–22.

35. Ibid

36. People ex rel Brown, BC445497, First Amended, November 15, 2010.

37. People ex rel Brown v. Rizzo, Spaccia, Adams, Hernandez, Jacobo, Cole, Bello, and Mirabal. BC445497. Attorney General's Motion for Appointment of a Monitor for the City of Bell and Supporting Filings. November 17, 2010.

38. People ex rel Brown, BC445497, First Amended, November 15, 2010.

39. Gottlieb, J., Winston, R., & Vives, R. "Bell Council Was Paid For Board That Seldom Met." *Los Angeles Times.* August 25, 2010. Retrieved from http://articles.latimes.com/2010/aug/25/local/la-me-bell-meetings-20100825.

40. Ibid.

41. People v. Hernandez, Jacobo, Mirabel, Cole, Bello, & Artiga. BA376025. Preliminary Hearing. February 7, 2011. pp. 17–18.

42. Ibid, p. 17.

43. Ibid, p. 18.

44. Gottlieb, Winton, & Vives, Bell Council Was Paid.

45. People v. Hernandez, Jacobo, Mirabel, Cole, Bello, & Artiga. BA376025. Preliminary Hearing Transcript. February 7, 2011.

46. Ibid, pp. 94–95.

47. Ibid, pp. 12–13.

48. Ibid, p. 63.

49. People v. Hernandez, Jacobo, Mirabel, Cole, Bello, & Artiga. BA376025. Preliminary Hearing. February 14, 2011. pp. 111-112.

50. Gottlieb, Winton, & Vives, Bell Council Was Paid.

51. People v. Hernandez, Jacobo, Mirabel, Cole, Bello, & Artiga. BA376025. Preliminary Hearing Transcript. February 14, 2011.

52. Lee, E. Testimony. October 28, 2013.

53. People ex rel Brown, BC445497, Attorney General's, November 17, 2010.

54. People v. Bello. BA376025. People's Sentencing Memorandum. July 25, 2014.

55. People v. Cole. BA376025. People's Sentencing Memorandum. July 23, 2014.

56. People v. Cole. BA376025-04. Sentencing Minutes. July 23, 2014. p. 27.

57. City of Bell. "Investments (Bonds)." ND. Retrieved from http://cityofbell.org/?NavID=177.

58. California State Controller. "Audit Report: Administrative and Internal Accounting Controls July 1, 2008 through June 30, 2010." September 22, 2010. p. 10.

59. City of Bell, Investments.

60. California State Controller, Audit Report, pp. 10.

61. Esquivel, P. "Bell Voters OKd Bonds for Sports Complex that Remains Unbuilt." *Los Angeles Times.* April 29, 2011. Retrieved from http://articles.latimes.com/2011/apr/29/local/la-me-bell-park-20110429.

62. "Los Angeles County Election Results." *Los Angeles Times.* November 6, 2003. Retrieved from http://articles.latimes.com/2003/nov/06/local/me-la1final6.

63. California State Controller, Audit Report, p. 10.

64. Ibid, p. 27.

65. Esquivel, Bell Voters.

66. California State Controller, Audit Report, p. 27.

67. Esquivel, Bell Voters.

68. California State Controller, Audit Report, p. 10.

69. Ibid, pp. 10–11, 27.

70. Esquivel, Bell Voters.

71. California State Controller, Audit Report, p. 11.

72. People v. Rizzo, Spaccia, Artiga, and Hernandez. BA376026. Preliminary Hearing. February 22, 2011. pp. 28–29.

73. Ibid.

74. Ibid, p. 27.

75. Ibid, p. 11.

76. City of Bell. "Annual Financial Report for the Fiscal Year Ended June 30, 2011." June 28, 2013. pp. 38–39.

77. Willmore, D. "City of Bell Agenda Report RE: November 13, 2013. Consideration of Stipulation for Settlement with Dexia Credit Local Including Limited Settlement Terms with BB&K." April 3, 2013.

78. Ibid.

79. Ibid.

80. Aleshire, D. & Taylor, A. "Corruption on Steroids: The Bell Scandal from the Legal Perspective." (white paper at the City of Bell Scandal Revisited Conference, Chapman University, 2015).

81. Ibid.

82. Christensen, K. & Gold, S. "Bell's Bonds Downgraded to Junk Status." *Los Angeles Times.* August 11, 2010. Retrieved from http://articles.latimes.com/2010/aug/11/local/la-me-bell-ratings-20100811.

83. Marois, M. "California City With $800,000 Manager Gets Rating Cut by Fitch." *Bloomberg.com.* August 17, 2010. Retrieved from http://www.bloomberg.com/news/articles/2010-08-17/california-city-with-800-000-manager-has-ratings-lowered-to-junk-by-fitch.

84. California State Board of Equalization. "California Property Tax: An Overview." July 2015. Retrieved from http://www.boe.ca.gov/proptaxes/pdf/pub29.pdf.

85. City of Bell. "A Summary of the City of Bell's Property Taxes." N.D. Retrieved from http://www.cityofbell.org/home/showdocument?id=4525.

86. Ibid.

87. Chiang, J. Letter to County of Los Angeles Auditor – Controller Wendy Watanabe. August 13, 2010.

88. California State Controller, Audit Report, p. 13.

89. Ibid.

90. CA. RTC § 96.3(b). *See also, Ibid.* at p. 14.

91. Chiang, Letter.

92. Christiansen, K. & Esquivel, P. "Bell Property Tax Rate Second-Highest in L.A. County." *Los Angeles Times.* July 30, 2010. Retrieved from http://articles.latimes.com/2010/jul/30/local/la-me-bell-taxes-new-20100730.

93. Ibid.

94. "Paying Too Much? Comparing Property Tax Rates for L.A. County Cities. [2010]." *Los Angeles Times.* N.D. Retrieved from http://www.latimes.com/local/la-me-city-property-tax-table-htmlstory.html.

95. Christiansen & Esquivel, Bell Property Tax.

96. State Controller's Office Bell Audit. September 2010. p. 12.

97. Christiansen, K. & Esquivel, P. "Bell Property Tax Rate Second-Highest in L.A. County." *Los Angeles Times.* July 30, 2010. Retrieved from http://articles.latimes.com/2010/jul/30/local/la-me-bell-taxes-new-20100730.

98. California State Controller, Audit Report, p. 12.

99. California Constitution Art. XIIID § 4. *See* Ibid.

100. California State Controller, Audit Report, pp. 14–15.

101. Ibid.

102. Albright, C. Testimony. November 4, 2013.

103. Gottlieb, J. & Vives, R. "Several Documents Point to Questionable Action in Bell." *Los Angeles Times.* November 15, 2013. Retrieved from http://www.latimes.com/local/la-me-angela-spaccia-20131116,0,2375241.story.

104. Ibid.

105. Brown Act. "A Pocket Guide to Open Meeting Laws in California: The Brown Act." December 3, 2003. Retrieved from http://www.thefirstamendment.org/Brown-Act-Brochure-DEC-03.pdf.

106. People v. Spaccia. BA 382701, BA376026. Spaccia's Testimony. November 15, 2013. pp. 6119.

107. People v. Hernandez, Jacobo, Mirabel, Cole, Bello, & Artiga. BA376025. Preliminary Hearing. February 9, 2011.

108. Gottlieb, J. & Knoll, C. "Bell City Clerk Says: 'I Couldn't Ask Any Questions.'" *Los Angeles Times.* January 29, 2013. Retrieved from http://articles.latimes.com/2013/jan/29/local/la-me-0130-bell-trial-20130130.

109. People v. Rizzo, Spaccia, Artiga, and Hernandez. BA376026. Preliminary Hearing. March 4, 2011.

110. People v. Rizzo, Spaccia, Artiga, and Hernandez. BA376026. Preliminary Hearing. March 7, 2011.

111. People v. Rizzo, Spaccia, Artiga, and Hernandez. BA376026. Preliminary Hearing. March 10, 2011.

112. Lee, E. Testimony. October 28, 2013.

113. Ibid.

114. Ibid.

115. People v. Bello. BA376025-05. Sentencing Minutes. August 1, 2014.

116. Michael Kratzer, personal correspondence with Thom Reilly, Augsut 17, 2015.

117. Albright, C. "Declaration of Clifton Wade Albright." December 14, 2012.

118. Brown & White LLP. "RE: Retainer Agreement for Representation by Brown & White LLP." August 10, 2006.

119. Gottlieb, J. "Bell: A Total Breakdown." (white paper at the City of Bell Scandal Revisited Conference, Chapman University, 2015).

120. Adams v. Bell. BC489331. Deposition of Randy Adams. May 1 2013. pp. 12–13

121. People v. Spaccia. BA376026. People's Exhibits 1 to 71. Exhibits 1 of 4.

122. Lee, Testimony.

123. People. v. Rizzo. BA276026, BA377197, BA382701, Plea Minutes. October 2, 2013.

124. People v. Rizzo, Spaccia. BA3760626, BA377197, BA382701. Consolidated Criminal Complaint. Count 29. September 12, 2013

125. Gottlieb, J., Winston, R., & Vives, R. "Bell's Rizzo Gave $400,000 in City Loans to Two Businesses Without Council Approval." *Los Angeles Times.* September 1, 2010. Retrieved from http://articles.latimes.com/2010/sep/01/local/la-me-bell-loans-20100901-26.

126. People v. Rizzo, Spaccia, Artiga, and Hernandez. BA376026. Preliminary Hearing. February 28, 2011.

127. People v. Rizzo, Spaccia, Artiga, and Hernandez. BA376026. Preliminary Hearing. March 1, 2011.

128. BA376026, Preliminary Hearing Transcript, February 28, 2011.

129. Albright, C. "Paid Invoice History By Vendor January 1, 2005-September 30, 2010." October 4, 2010.

130. Brown, T. "Paid Invoice History By Vendor January 1, 2007-December 31, 2010." August 17, 2011.

131. Dolan, M. "Corruption Convictions Reduced for Former South Gate Official." *Los Angeles Times.* April 15, 2013. Retrieved from http://articles.latimes.com/2013/apr/15/local/la-me-ln-corruption-south-gate-20130415.

132. Guillermo Salazar, et al v. City of South Gate, et al. BC280158. Statement of Decision. January 19, 2005.

133. Albright, Yee & Schmit, LLP. v. Henry Gonzales, et al. BC297983. Case Summary of Court Case, Superior Court of California, County of Los Angeles. 2007.

134. Becerra, H. "South Gate Chases Legal Firms." *Los Angeles Times.* January 23, 2005. Retrieved from http://articles.latimes.com/2005/jan/23/local/me-southgate23.

135. Albright, Yee & Schmit, LLP. v. City of South Gate. BC297983, BC311748, BS090172. Case No. 1220031340. Settlement Agreement and Mutual Release. February 22, 2007. pp. 1–8.

136. Ibid.

137. City of Bell. "Agenda Report." 2014.

138. Brown White & Newhouse LLP and City of Bell. "Mutual General Release Agreement." August 26, 2014.

139. California Public Employees' Retirement System Board of Administration. "Pier'Angela Spaccia Compensation Review. OAH No. 2012020198. Proposed Decision, Attachment A." February 26, 2013.

140. Gottlieb, J. & Vives, R. "Is a City Manager Worth $800,000?" *Los Angeles Times.* July 15, 2010. Retrieved from http://www.latimes.com/local/la-me-bell-salary-20100715-story.html#axzz30rdlU3Zb.

141. Goffard, C. "How Bell Hit Bottom." *Los Angeles Times.* December 28, 2010. Retrieved from http://www.latimes.com/local/la-me-bell-origins-20101228-story.html#page=1.

142. Gottlieb, Bell: A Total.

143. Goffard, How Bell.

144. Gottlieb, J., Vives, R., & Leonard, J. "Bell Leaders Hauled Off in Cuffs: Eight Are Held in Scandal the D.A. Calls 'Corruption on Steroids.'" *Los Angeles Times.* September 22, 2010. Retrieved from http://articles.latimes.com/2010/sep/22/local/la-me-bell-arrest-20100922.

145. Knoll C. & Vives, R. "Bell City Clerk Testifies Signatures on Documents Were Forged." *Los Angeles Times.* January 30, 2013. Retrieved from http://articles.latimes.com/2013/jan/30/local/la-me-0131-bell-trial-20130131.

146. Willmore, interview.

147. Ibid.

148. People v. Hernandez, Jacobo, Mirabel, Cole, Bello, & Artiga. BA376025. Preliminary Hearing. February 15, 2011.

149. People v. Rizzo. BC445497. Videotaped deposition of Robert Rizzo. December 15, 2011.

150. Ibid.

151. Ibid.

152. Ibid.

153. Gottlieb, Bell: A Total.

154. Gottlieb, J. "After Vowing to Cooperate, Robert Rizzo Skips His Sentencing Interview." *Los Angeles Times.* April 17, 2014. Retrieved from http://www.latimes.com/local/lanow/la-me-ln-rizzo-probation-report-20140417-story.html.

155. Goffard, How Bell.

156. James Corcoran, interview with author, February 12, 2015.

157. Gottlieb, J. "Ex-Bell Official Seeks $837,000 Payout." *Los Angeles Times.* August 28, 2012. Retrieved from http://articles.latimes.com/2012/aug/28/local/la-me-bell-20120829.

158. City of Bell. "Code Enforcement." N.D. Retrieved from http://cityofbell.org/?NavID=59.

159. Ibid.

160. Corcoran, interview, p. 17.

161. Ibid.

162. Lopez, R. & Esquivel, P. "Bell Collected Hefty Fines in Numerous Code-Enforcement Cases." *Los Angeles Times.* December 16, 2010. Retrieved from http://www.latimes.com/local/la-me-bell-code-enforcement-20101216-story.html.

163. Esquivel, P. & Lopez, R. "Bell Demanded Extra Fees From Some Businesses." *Los Angeles Times.* November 2, 2010. Retrieved from http://www.latimes.com/local/la-me-1102-bell-fees-20101102-m-story.html#page=1.

164. Ibid.

165. Ibid.

166. Corcoran, interview.

167. Valencia, interview, p. 9–10.

168. Corcoran, interview.

169. Winton, R., Esquivel, P. & Vives, R. "Federal Probe Targets Possible Civil Rights Violations in Bell." *Los Angeles Times. September* 10, 2010. Retrieved from http://articles.latimes.com/2010/sep/10/local/la-me-bell-feds-20100910.

170. Ibid.

171. Gottlieb, J., Yoshino, K., & Vives, R. "Bell Doubled Public Service Taxes and Funneled $1 Million to Rizzo, Audit Finds." *Los Angeles Times.* September 23, 2010. http://articles.latimes.com/print/2010/sep/23/local/la-me-bell-audit-20100923.

172. Ibid.

173. Ibid.

174. Willmore, interview.

175. California State Controller, Audit Report.

176. Ibid.

177. Barnes, W. "Audit findings in the City of Bell by the Office of State Controller." N.D.

178. People v. Rizzo. BA376026, BA377197, BA382701. Sentencing hearing. April 16, 2014.

179. Spertus, J. "Drawing the Line Between Crime and Mistake." (white paper at the City of Bell Scandal Revisited Conference, Chapman University, 2015).

180. Vives, R. & Becerra, H. "Top Public Pension Earner Sues Vernon After CALPERS Cuts His Benefit." *Los Angeles Times*. July 22, 2013. Retrieved from http://articles.latimes.com/2013/jul/22/local/la-me-highest-pension-20130723.

181. Seattle Times Staff. "Ex-Official in Bell, Calif., Scandal Has Auburn Farm." *Seattle Times*. September 22, 2010. Retrieved from http://www.seattletimes.com/seattle-news/ex-official-in-bell-calif-scandal-has-auburn-farm/.

182. Ibid.

183. Gottlieb & Vives, Is a City Manager.

184. Pringle, Knoll, & Murphy, Rizzo's Horse.

185. Ibid.

186. Gottlieb, J. "Former Bell Administrator Robert Rizzo Pleads Guilty to Tax Charges." *Los Angeles Times*. January 14, 2014. Retrieved from http://www.latimes.com/local/la-me-0114-rizzo-20140114-story.html.

187. U.S. District Court Central District of California criminal minutes and sentencing judgement, CR 13-878 GHK, April 14, 2014.

188. Gottlieb, After Vowing.

189. BA376026, BA377197, BA382701, Sentencing, April 16, 2014.

190. Gottlieb, After Vowing.

191. Bell Legal Panel. Chapman University. February 19, 2005.

192. People v. Spaccia. BA376026, BA382701. Sentencing Minutes. April 10, 2014.

193. Rizzo, R. In discussion with the author. March 27, 2015.

194. Valencia, interview.

195. BA376026, BA377197, BA382701, Sentencing, April 16, 2014.

196. Ibid.

197. Ibid.

The Accomplice and th

"Secrecy, being an instrument of conspiracy, ought never to be the system of regular government." —Jeremy Bentham [1]

Angela Spaccia was fifty-five at the time of her sentencing. It was obvious that the trial and publicity had taken its toll. She had become despondent and contemplated suicide after the Bell scandal surfaced, and was hospitalized for a time. [2] She had a lot to lose. When she resigned her position as assistant chief administrative officer, she was making $376,268 ($850,000 in total compensation) annually with the same twenty-six weeks of paid annual vacation and sick leave (143 days combined) that Rizzo received.

But unlike Rizzo, who rarely spoke to anyone, never testified, took the Fifth during most of his deposition, and skipped out on his probation interview, Spaccia seemed to want to talk with everyone. She refused to plead and instead sought a jury trial, during which she talked and talked and talked.

But the content of her words was suspect. Deputy District Attorney Sean Hassett, who lead the prosecution, said that Spaccia would lie about everything. And indeed during the trial she fabricated facts, revised history, argued with the prosecutors, and make nonsensical statements that clearly exasperated Los Angeles County Superior Court Judge Kathleen Kennedy.

Spaccia attempted to portray herself as merely a dupe of her boss, Robert Rizzo, who made a plea deal with prosecutors. Her lawyer's defense centered on the premise that she was not in a position of authority and she was just following Rizzo's orders. Others suggested, however, that she was the real brain behind the operation and that the governance of Bell seem to enter a downward spiral shortly after her arrival. [3] Prosecutors portrayed her as an enthusiastic partner with Rizzo in a plot to plunder the low-income working class city that they ran.

Spaccia received her Bachelor of Science, Business Management
from the University of La Verne, California.[4] She began her career in
service at the age of twenty as an accounting clerk in Ventura. At first
temporary position, her job turned into full-time employment and afforded
her opportunities for professional development. She received several promo-
tions, ultimately serving as director of management services.[5] The city's
finance director, Terry Adelman, oversaw Spaccia's work when she became
an accounting manager, and lauded her management abilities. Of particular
note, he said, were the "outstanding audits" she conducted each year. When
the Bell scandal broke, Adelman confidently remarked, "I don't believe for a
minute she was any part of it. My perception is she became a political
pawn."[6]

Spaccia's time in Ventura had its challenges, particularly in 1989 when
Spaccia accused a colleague of sexually and physically harassing her.[7] She
went on full disability from her job for some time, and tried to get the council
to vote down a pay raise for then-City Manager John Baker; she felt that
Baker did not handle the incident properly, since the accused colleague only
received a twenty-day suspension without pay.

When she ended her employment in Ventura, she began working for the
Los Angeles County Transportation Commission (LACTC) in 1990. The
LACTC merged with the Southern California Rapid Transit District. Spaccia
was promoted to director of management services and remained employed
there until 1994. She married in 1994 and moved to Idaho, where she worked
as an associate director at the YMCA and as a finance director for Kootenai
County. In 2000, Spaccia returned to California with her son and was employed briefly by the Old Globe Theater in San Diego and then by the North
County Transit District.[8]

Spaccia became chief financial officer of Ventura County in 2001, a post
she held for only five months. She left when the administration of the county
changed, but her former employer declined to disclose the conditions under
which she left. Spaccia then got a job with Moreland and Associates; it was
through her employment there that she became associated with Bell.[9]

In 2003, Spaccia was hired as a fulltime Bell employee with a starting
salary of $102,310. A year later, after receiving a 27 percent increase, she
was making $130,000. This was followed by a 42.3 percent increase in 2005
and an average 11 percent yearly increase thereafter.[10] In all, Bell employed
her from July 1, 2003 until October 1, 2010, when she resigned along with
Rizzo and Police Chief Randy Adams.

The original Agreement for Employment stated that Bell desired to employ
Spaccia as assistant to Rizzo, the chief administrative officer. Initially, Spaccia organized an annual car show, planned a skateboard park, and attended to

other duties assigned by Rizzo. She reported directly to him and did not have a formal job description, supervisory duties or budgetary responsibilities.[11]

Spaccia was also assigned oversight and mentoring of Lourdes Garcia, the director of administrative services. Garcia began working for the city in 1991, and became director in 2003. During her employment, she earned an undergraduate degree in Business Administration from California State University, Los Angeles, and a master's degree in Public Administration (MPA) from Cal State Northridge. For her testimony at trial, she was granted immunity by the prosecution.[12]

When the scandal surfaced, Garcia was earning $422,000 in total compensation and had benefited from some of the same perks as Rizzo and Spaccia. She was receiving forty hours of vacation and two days of sick leave per month, and was able to cash these out every paycheck. Garcia also was one of the Bell employees for whom the city purchased five years of service pension credits from CALPERS.[13] Neither Garcia nor Spaccia included the pension service credits on their W-2 form. Both said they just overlooked doing this.[14]

Garcia testified that, even when she thought some activities might be illegal, she didn't think to question them because Rizzo would assure her that everything was fine. She said Rizzo purposely tried to make documents complicated so councilmembers wouldn't understand them.[15] Her position was eliminated in 2011 when the interim city manager concluded that she was underqualified for a position in Bell's reorganized government.

During her years at Bell, Spaccia spent a great deal of time crafting pension and retirement plans that would benefit her, Rizzo, and a small group of officials and employees. As soon as she was hired in 2003, she began working on a supplemental retirement plan for the city. She and Rizzo retained Bryan, Pendleton, Swats & McAllister, LLC, and a Wells Fargo Company to draft the plan. Between April and June of that year, Spaccia was exchanging emails with Alan Pennington, a consulting actuary with Wells Fargo in Tennessee, about how to craft the Bell Supplemental Retirement Plan to avoid laws capping pension amounts, how to conceal it from the public, and how to structure it so that it could not be repealed by any council in the future.[16]

During the period that Rizzo and Spaccia worked at Bell, employees were covered by a pension or defined benefit plan with the California Public Employees Retirement System (CALPERS), known as "2 percent at 55." Under this plan, Bell guaranteed a certain level of retirement benefits based on several factors. These would include an employee's age, years of employment and final average salary. Benefits for Bell employee retiring at 55 would be calculated by taking 2 percent (also known as a "multiplier") of the worker's highest 12-month salary and multiplying it by the number of years in CALPERS. An employee who worked for Bell for twenty-five years could retire at age fifty-five and would receive 90 percent of their final pay.[17] Bell covered the entire cost of its employee pensions, unlike the State of California and most other local governments, where public employees contribute a portion of the pension costs.

After the Bell scandal, several changes were made to state laws governing public-sector pensions. In 2012, California raised the retirement age for maximum benefits to sixty-two, from sixty, and included measures designed to avoid pension spiking—the increasing of compensation in the last years of a worker's career that often included adding unused sick and vacation leave. The new law also included a provision for new workers that caps the amount of annual salary that can be applied to their defined benefit plan at $110,000 (if they are eligible to collect social security; $132,000 for those ineligible for social security). The law also ensures that all state and local employees' contribute half of their pension costs.

As if their retirement benefit plan under CALPERS wasn't generous enough, Rizzo and Spaccia created the Bell Supplemental Retirement Plan in 2003. This was also paid entirely by Bell taxpayers. The plan was made available to forty-one employees, including all elected officials. The supplemental plan increased the 2 percent multiplier to 3.7 percent at age 55; as the CALPERS limit was 2.7 percent, the city picked up the remainder.[18]

Spaccia and Rizzo didn't stop there, but sought to increase their plans even further by trying to raise the multiplier to 5.175 percent at age fifty-five.[19] Such increases would have cost millions and benefitted only the two.

At trial, Deputy D.A. Hassett pointed out to the jury that Spaccia started working on this plan almost immediately after her work began at Bell, to what he called "the utter ruin of the city."[20] Spaccia continually gave Pennington directions to recalculate benefits for herself and Rizzo to increase their take. Hassett continued: "that pension plan is so outrageous and so exorbitant; her cost alone to the city was going to be $8 million. $8 million of the public's money just to fund her special portion of the plan. $7 and a half million to fund Mr. Rizzo's, which is ironic given that his was the larger salary."[21]

Rizzo and Spaccia continued their quest for enhanced retirement benefits even after laying off park employees on Christmas Eve.[22] In fact, Spaccia's determination to lock in her retirement money was evidenced by her contacting Pennington to obtain her retirement forms shortly after the scandal broke. In one email exchange, Spaccia acknowledged that she no longer had access to her email at Bell. Spaccia said, "The whole situation is absolutely horrendous. . . . and I pray that nothing was done illegally."[23]

She told Pennington she hoped the request for her forms wouldn't pose any difficulties for him, and that she just wanted to "end this misery."[24] Pennington responded that at that time it was more than ever prudent to avoid any appearance of impropriety.[25] He said he could prepare the paperwork, but that the request would need to come from someone at the city. Pennington also expressed concern at the city's agreeing to start payments and processing with the investigation still underway. In keeping with her demeanor throughout the investigation, Spaccia responded that she had "read something" about the investigation.

In 2005, Spaccia became focused on special projects and claimed to have told Rizzo there were improprieties with the Housing Authority. After that, she said she was "removed" from finance completely, even though her initial employment agreement did not enumerate a specific financial role. Throughout her trial, Spaccia emphasized this new role in special projects, claiming that it removed her far from any of the decisions regarding how the city was appropriating funds.

In 2010, Spaccia claimed to have brought additional discrepancies to Rizzo's attention, and was then sent to Maywood, a neighboring city experiencing financial woes, to act as its interim city manager. This, however, conflicts with the accounts of numerous others, who claimed that Spaccia pushed to get the Maywood position, and that Rizzo did not want her to go, preferring to keep Bell's affairs under wraps and loyal confederates close by.

This time, perhaps, Rizzo's paranoia was on target. Doug Willmore, the subsequent city administrator, said the relationship with Maywood is what ultimately "blew this wide open." He cited emails between Spaccia and Rizzo in which he asked her not to go, noting that they had a "good thing" going on. In fact, Willmore believed that Spaccia was the "brains" of the operation, calling Rizzo a "smalltime crook" and saying that Spaccia turned their efforts into a "big-time operation."[26]

Spaccia didn't seem to earn the best reputation in Maywood in her short time there. At her sentencing, a resident of Maywood took advantage of the public comment portion and said:

> Angela Spaccia was running the city of Maywood for a couple of months, and there was no Bob Rizzo. She did all the decisions in our city. And she destroyed it. She fired all our employees. We—we always—that's why I am up here because all I keep hearing is Bell. But she destroyed Maywood. We are still trying to recover from Maywood. After she fired all our employees, there was no public works. There was no nothing you could do at city hall. And I have never heard her once say she is sorry.[27]

Spaccia's tenure at Maywood was turbulent enough that, whether justified or not, she employed a bodyguard and bought a device that enabled her to start up her car from a distance, in case it was rigged to explode.[28]

Also during her seven months at Maywood, Spaccia claimed to have learned that Rizzo and Police Chief Randy Adams encouraged City Clerk Rebecca Valdez and Chief Financial Officer Lourdes Garcia to alter documents to show that they were making less money. It was odd that Spaccia still maintained ignorance about Bell's inflated salaries since emails between her and Adams—with whom she had worked previously in Ventura—revealed an implied intention to steal from Bell's citizens.

For example, here's a line from an email Spaccia wrote to Adams: "LOL…well you can take your share of the pie..just like us!!! We all will get fat together…Bob has an expression he likes to use on occasion…Pigs get Fat … Hogs get slaughtered!!! So long as we're not Hogs … all is well!! Have a nice night….see you tomorrow."[29]

During her trial, Spaccia testified that she was merely trying to be "clever" and "humorous" since she and Adams were old friends. Adams also testified that he was joking when he told Spaccia in an email that he was looking forward to taking all of Bell's money.[30]

Other inappropriate email exchanges with Adams included a strange request from Spaccia while recruiting Adams for Bell—she asked him for a $350,000 loan. This happened while she was the negotiator for his contract, prompting Kennedy to ask aloud: "Who does that?"[31] Given her generous salary in Bell, it is surprising Spaccia would even need a loan; but the context of the email indicates she was trying to buy property in Idaho. However, court documents later revealed Spaccia had a $6,000 mortgage on a multimillion dollar home. Another curious deal made by Spaccia occurred in 2010 when she took out a loan from Rizzo's mother-in-law for a property in Idaho for which she was paying $1.6 million. The amount of the loan was $200,000.[32]

The tone of some emails between Spaccia and others were also "sexually charged," with Spaccia sending suggestive texts and even photos to Adams. At least one photo showed Spaccia in a robe, smoking a cigar. The subject line read: "A photo for my ID on ur phone!!LOL."[33] Willmore learned that many in the city were aware of Spaccia's "multiple affairs" and described her as a "bombshell" when she first arrived in Bell.[34] It was Willmore's understanding that Angela used sex appeal to her advantage, flirting with several of the men in the city to get what she wanted. Corcoran had similar feelings, calling Spaccia "a very personable, beautiful lady," however, with an air of arrogance and hubris. He was aware that she had known Adams since the 1980s during her time in Ventura.[35]

Kennedy concluded that Spaccia had a different weapon in addition to her reputation as an attractive and intelligent woman in an occupation typically dominated by men. While admitting that Spaccia was "charming, attractive and well-educated," Kennedy added: "Her weapon is not the weapon that I usually see in cases that come before me. It's not a gun, it's not a knife. It's the trust that people had in her."[36] Kennedy said that, due to her other attributes, Spaccia would not have been seen as someone who would have been "stealing [people] blind."[37]

Kennedy said the case was "extraordinary" in terms of mismanagement and self-dealing. She dismissed a letter Spaccia wrote to the court detailing some challenges she had been facing during the period. In her letter, Spaccia pointed out that, although she worked in Bell from 2003 through 2010, there was about a year and a half total when she never showed up to work. This was also a significant part of Braun's defense. During that time, Spaccia said, she went to Idaho to take care of her dying grandfather, nursed her son after he nearly died in a motorcycle accident, and had several surgeries herself.

However, since Spaccia admitted to being paid her full salary while away, did not deduct any sick or vacation days, and continued to accrue days off, the strategy ended up working against her.[38]

At Spaccia's sentencing, Braun tried everything in his power to get his client a new trial. He acknowledged that Spaccia wasn't in Bell for large periods of time, and claimed specifically that her absences coincided with many of the allegedly illegal actions that were taking place. In an attempt to win Kennedy's sympathy, Braun reiterated the personal tragedies Spaccia had experienced. For example, he noted an email to consultant Alan Pennington in which Spaccia shared some details about her son's accident:

> My son was in a horrific motorcycle accident a month and a half ago. He was in a coma and on life support for 8 days, but is doing well now. He came home about 10 days ago for some bone healing and will return to the hospital for in-patient acute rehab in about a month. Fortunately, he has no brain damage, and his spine and neck are fine.....just injured everywhere else.[39]

Spaccia's son, Sean Sheffield, was an aspiring hockey star. Shortly after his accident, he was assaulted and beaten, adding yet another layer of challenges to Spaccia's personal life. Kennedy was not sympathetic about these circumstances, nor about Spaccia's own health issues, which included asthma and a genetic form of chronic obstructive pulmonary disease. When anyone else faces family tragedy or illness, the judges said, they use vacation time or take unpaid leave to do what they have to do:

> I am sure that there were citizens of the City of Bell during the course of time that Miss Spaccia was working for them that had tragedies that happened in their own family, illnesses that happened in their own family that they were not in a situation to be able to easily pay for, and certainly the city of Bell didn't pay them. But they did, in Miss Spaccia's case.[40]

Spaccia's denial of responsibility for any of the corruption in Bell seemed to represent a claim of "willful blindness," which legal scholars say carries little weight in courtrooms. "It's sort of ironic," Spaccia said, "that I'm now being accused of heinous crimes on a community when my whole career I've spent uncovering any sort of improprieties in government agencies and was really trained by the city of Ventura to be an honest and fair leader."[41]

Taylor called the twenty-four months Spaccia had off with full pay "staggering." He also noted that she did not dock herself a single vacation or sick day during seven years of employment, which he claimed was "completely unheard of."[42] Kennedy continued, "to be absent basically for twenty-four months and receive your full pay, and not only that, accrue vacation benefits on that pay, and not only that, for that pay and the vacation benefits, to then pay back loans that you were getting, huge loans that you were getting from the City, I mean, it is really appalling."[43]

During her trial, Spaccia was asked by Assistant District Attorney Hassett whether she thought the people of Bell should have to pay the approximately six months of time off when she did no work for the city. Spaccia responded, "That's an interesting question. I have never even looked at it that way. So I . . . yeah, I don't even know how to answer that. I guess I look at it as my employer made a decision as to how to handle my pay and my accruals. And I went along with that. Is that fair or unfair? I don't really know."[44]

Still portraying herself as Rizzo's victim, Spaccia blamed the unethical act on her employer, arguing that, because she was permitted to do so, that made it acceptable. But an email to Rizzo from Spaccia dated February 21, 2010, shows that Spaccia knew that taking leave with pay was unusual and, therefore, that the director of administrative services, Lourdes Garcia, required specific instructions:

> Hi Bob,
> Just wan [sic] to make sure that we are protected .... can you please make sure that Lourdes puts me on 90 clays [sic] Administrative Leave effective as of the date of Maywood's Council action to hire me ...... meaning two Fridays ago. But.. .. please make sure it is Amin Leave WITH Pay LOL ....[45]

It was clear that Kennedy was not going to go easy on Spaccia. One reason was that she and Deputy District Attorney Hassett repeatedly caught Spaccia lying, even about seemingly small issues. Hassett said she was a chronic liar. During her trial, Angela kept denying that she attended council meetings, even though minutes and others' testimony contradicted this. City Attorney Ed Lee said she was at certain meetings which she denied attending. Roger Ramirez, the Bell resident who first inquired about Rizzo's and the council's salaries, said he saw Spaccia at another meeting she denied attending.[46] Spaccia also consistently denied that she ever had authority to sign any official city documents, despite being presented with numerous documents bearing her signature: ". . . approved for payment, City of Bell, office of the Chief Administrative Officer, by A. Spaccia."[47] Her response: "Well, I don't even know that I said I had authority to sign on my own. But I know that these bills would have been handed to me by Mr. Rizzo. And I think it is kind of strange that I didn't put 'A. Spaccia for R. Rizzo, actually.'"[48]

At the pivotal Little Bear Park meeting, *Los Angeles Times* reporter Gottlieb thought Spaccia was lying when he asked her how much she made and she answered "I don't know."[49] However, this time Spaccia may have in fact been telling the truth, given how complex the city's employment contracts got, not to mention the retirement schemes and the abuse of sick pay and vacation pay.

Another important issue was whether or not Spaccia was a "public official." In an Agreement for Employment dated June 30, 2008, Spaccia's title changed from assistant to the chief administrative officer to assistant chief administrative officer, which came with a 20 percent increase followed by the 11 percent annual increases, similar to Rizzo's contract. Given the title change, there was some disagreement as to which title made her a public official. Kennedy instructed the jury that the assistant chief cdministrative officer title did make her a public official. Braun disagreed, saying Spaccia's authority depended on what the charter said. He maintained that the authorization given Spaccia's job title in the charter did not make her a public official and, therefore, she should not be held to the same standard.[50] Braun claimed that City Attorney Ed Lee, who wrote the charter and wrote many of the resolutions, also said Spaccia did not have authority.

Hassett said this was untrue, and that the jury found Spaccia stole Bell's money and that she was "laughing out loud while she did it repeatedly for years."[51] Kennedy also pointed out an email from Spaccia to incoming police chief Randy Adams, in which Spaccia noted that, "we have crafted our agreements carefully so we do not draw attention to our pay."[52] This did not bode well for Braun's argument that Spaccia did not have authority and, further, that she did not understand that she was doing wrong. Braun insisted that this issue should have gone to the jury, adding "that will be another issue for the appellate courts to decide."[53]

Spaccia's propensity for self-dealing was further demonstrated by a strange 2008 contract between Bell and Pacific Alliance Group. She said the firm provided a "pass-through" for payments to another company that was conducting a phone survey regarding city services.[54] In an email exchange with Todd Remington, owner of the firm tapped to conduct the survey, Spaccia notified him that Pacific Alliance Group would be the subcontractor through which his company would bill the city for the survey, which was intended to function as risk-management analysis. Spaccia, using her personal email, wrote that the reason for using Pacific Alliance was to "minimize opportunity for data to be subjected to public access."[55] She said the signature authority was Sean Sheffield, president of the firm. What Spaccia neglected to mention to anyone, including the council who approved the contract, or outside counsel Todd Remington, was that Sheffield was her son.

Pacific Alliance Group then entered into an agreement with Bell to provide the survey, with Remington as the subcontractor, for a fee of up to
$30,000. However, the scope of work did not reflect any of the work per-
formed. The project was purportedly "Research and analysis to determine
risk management options at the city of Bell." However, the actual work
concerned a telephone survey about the city's parks.[56]

After continued questioning on what qualifications her son had to perform any of these duties, Spaccia said it was a pass-through and "I thought I
was helping. My son didn't get any huge benefit out of this and now I am
being badgered by you as if there was something nefarious and not that my
son actually took $30,000 and that did not occur."[57] After presenting two
canceled checks for $14,000, Hastert pointed out that this would leave
$2,000 in her son's pocket.[58]

Pacific Alliance Group had already been under contract with Bell to
handle Health Insurance Portability and Accountability Act (HIPAA) compliance for medical reimbursements for various councilmembers and employees. This third-party administration took place from 2006 to 2010 and
generated nearly $75,000 in fees, as indicated on vendor invoices. Upon
further investigation, however, it did not appear that Sheffield had any qualifications or previous knowledge of HIPAA compliance. Further, the firm did
not appear to have any other clients.

Spaccia was found guilty on 11 felony counts. The counts included
"drafting illegal contracts, receiving more than $200,000 in illegal loans from
the city and helping create a pension plan for Rizzo and herself that would
have cost the city $15.5 million had it been funded." She was sentenced to
more than eleven years in prison and more than $8 million in restitution.[59]

While many thought justice had been served, Spaccia's attorney certainly
did not. Braun claimed that the judge had played up the story for the media.
He further defended Spaccia by saying she was probably delusional, in the
sense that she thought everyone was getting the compensation they deserved
for turning the city around—which indeed seemed to be the sentiment of the
"Bell 8" and other complicit officials. He desperately wanted to get Rizzo on
the stand to show the mutual culpability the two shared in orchestrating the
corruption, thinking it might help Spaccia at sentencing.

Braun heavily criticized Kennedy, claiming she "played to the cameras,
made the comments, rolled her eyes, interrupted her testimony with snide
remarks. The most serious thing she did was she illegally plea-bargained. . . .
She plea-bargained for 12 years maximum (for Rizzo) and an amount of
restitution concurrent with the federal case. . . . Now to me," Braun said,
"that's a violation of basic rules. A violation of the basic standard that is set
by the Supreme Court. A violation of your judiciary duty."[60]

Hassett wrote in his sentencing memo that it was clear from Spaccia's
conduct and actions that she believed she would never be caught, and, if

caught, she could lie her way out of any consequences. He claimed Spaccia was an active participant in the crimes, and had aided and conspired with Rizzo for years. He added:

> She created their illegal pension plan; she created their illegal contracts; she created Adams illegal contract; and secreted his illegal disability letter. The crimes at issue are not part of a single isolated event, but instead comprise a very sophisticated pattern of corruption. Defendant Spaccia's criminal conduct occurred over a seven year period and required great secrecy. Defendant Spaccia's crimes were carefully planned and executed, and she took great care to conceal them. This was not a one-time lapse of judgment on defendant Spaccia's part; it was a criminally sophisticated conspiracy that drove the City of Bell to the edge of bankruptcy.[61]

During the sentencing, Hassett used words like "outrageous," "hurtful," and "destructive," saying Spaccia "laughed out loud the entire time she was stealing Bell's money."[62] When Kennedy handed down the sentencing, she claimed that greed overtook Spaccia, transforming her into a hog, not a pig. Nor did Kennedy believe Spaccia felt sorry for her actions: "She has never expressed any remorse other than sorrow that she finds herself in this position."[63] To this day, however, Braun maintains Spaccia's innocence, maintaining she did not know she was doing anything illegal.[64]

Many observers were surprised that Adams was not included in the September 2010 indictments of the Bell 8. Adams was among the highest paid of the former city officials, and as the details surrounding his hiring became better known, it seemed increasingly likely that he would face prosecution. When he was named as a defendant in the civil suit brought by then-Attorney General Jerry Brown in September 2010, it was widely expected that criminal charges would also be brought against him.

But this didn't happen. The next week, when the Los Angeles District Attorney's Office brought criminal charges against the Bell 8, Adams was not among them. When then-Los Angeles District Attorney Steve Cooley was asked about why Adams was not arrested along with the others, he said, "Being paid excessive salaries is not a crime. . . . [T]o illegally obtain those salaries is a crime."[65]

Adams' avoidance of criminal charges caused a public backlash, with many people publicly calling for him to be criminally investigated and indicted as a veritable ninth member of the Bell 8.[66]

It is unclear what happened in the initial investigation concerning Adams' potential role in the scandal. Many believed that the ultimate reason he was spared was his relationship with Cooley. Critics charged that Adams and Cooley had been close friends for years.[67] [68] They noted that, as recently as 2008, Cooley had presented Adams with the President's Award on behalf of the Peace Officers Association of Los Angeles. [69] Those calling for Adams to be prosecuted included officers from the Bell police officers union who had repeatedly clashed with Adams during his short tenure as chief. Sgt. James Corcoran, who was forced by Adams to resign after reporting Bell's corruption to the District Attorney and Attorney General's Offices, agreed that Adams and Cooley were "buddies." [70]

Cooley downplayed the significance of their relationship and its impact on the investigation. He and Adams were "not friends," Cooley said; theirs was purely a professional working relationship. In any case, Cooley denied that the relationship had any bearing on the investigation. [71] However, by October 2010, more than two weeks after the Bell 8 were arrested, Cooley announced that his office would investigate Adams's employment agreement with Bell, which allowed him to collect a tax-free disability pension. And in order to avoid any appearance of impropriety, Cooley said he had removed himself from the investigation. As it happened, the subsequent investigation of Adams proved fruitless. He has never been charged with a crime associated with his employment in Bell.

The fact that Adams was not criminally prosecuted was questioned by Judge Kennedy. In December 2011, more than a year after Cooley announced the investigation into Adams, the topic of Adams' hiring came up at a court hearing. James Spertus, Rizzo's attorney, told Kennedy that Adams was selected by Rizzo as police chief "because of his reputation for integrity." Judge Kennedy replied, "[Adams] is not a man of integrity. This is not the man who is going to clean up the Police Department." She added: "I don't know why he is not a defendant in this case," and that "I don't make decisions on who is charged, but it does seem rather curious to me." Deputy District Attorney Max Huntsman responded that "it was our assessment and still is our assessment that there isn't enough evidence to make a conviction beyond a reasonable doubt likely as to Adams." [72]

The District Attorney's Office decided not to prosecute Adams because, unlike the Bell 8, his questionable employment contract was not signed while he was a Bell employee, and he did not have control over Bell's finances. As such, it would be difficult to prove that Adams committed a crime against Bell. [73] While the Attorney General's suit was dismissed, Adams settled with the Bell for $214,715, an amount described as a "rollback of compensation." The settlement included a provision allowing Adams to revoke the agreement if he were again named in a revised complaint by the state Attorney General's Office.

Even though Adams was not among the Bell 8, he remained embroiled in the scandal because of his $457,000 salary and the emails with Spaccia in which they tried to hide his full salary from the public, and in which he claimed a disability before he began work and joked about taking Bell for all its money.

The well-educated, thirty-eight-year law enforcement veteran, formerly chief in Simi Valley and Glendale, had enjoyed a stellar record in policing before his employment with Bell. He obtained a Bachelors of Science degree from Cal State University of Los Angeles in police science administration as well as two master's, one in administration of justice from Cal Lutheran University and one in management from Cal Poly Pomona. He earned numerous law enforcement certifications and served on several local, national and international police organizations, including a stint as president of the Los Angeles County Police Chiefs Association. [74] [75]

Adams served as police chief for Bell for little more than a year before his resignation. Prior to that, he served six years as chief in Glendale and seven and a half years as chief in Simi Valley. Before that he worked in Ventura for twenty-three years as officer, assistant police chief, and chief. It was in Ventura that he became acquainted with Spaccia.

Spaccia called Adams in early 2009 after she and Rizzo had watched his online interview as a finalist for the sheriff's job in Orange County. Spaccia told Adams they were impressed with him and wanted him to be chief in Bell. Adams at first demurred, telling Spaccia it was "Because you couldn't afford me. It would take all Bell's money to hire me. And I've been working basically for free here at Glendale and I'm not going to do that anymore." [76]

It turned out that he wouldn't have to. The Orange County job paid approximately $250,000. Adams ended up negotiating with Bell for $457,000.

Over six meetings, Adams met with various Bell elected officials, department heads such as Eric Eggena and Lourdes Garcia, the president and vice president of the police association, as well as Spaccia, Rizzo, and outside city council Tom Brown, who were present at all of the meetings. His compensation was never discussed. When Adams concluded that they were serious about offering him a job, he checked in with Ron Ingels, the liaison from the L.A. District Attorney's office to police officers. Ingels told him that the DA's office was not aware of any issues or corruption at Bell, and that there was a longtime city manager there. Ingels said the only problem was with the police department, and that Bell could really use someone like Adams to fix it. [77]

At a face-to-face meeting, Rizzo, Spaccia, Mayor Hernandez, and Brown implored Adams to fix their police department. They felt that the officers did not work full days, had low morale, were having sex on duty and that their "police department was an embarrassment and they wanted to bring in best practices to it." [78] Spaccia assured Adams that they had the necessary funds, stating that "Bell has done really well as a city. The city manager has taken it from a nearly bankrupt city during his tenure to $15 to $20 million in reserves. And for a small city, that's a large amount of money. And we believe that we have to pay what we have to pay to get the talent we need to address the issue of the city."[79] What Spaccia failed to disclose was that, earlier in 2009, they were exploring layoffs at City Hall.

Financially, Adams had done well in his career. He'd gained his maximum allowable retirement formula amount in each of the cities he'd served, had worked under CALPERS and was at the "3 percent of 55" that would allow him to retire making approximately $270K annually. In his April 14, 2009 letter to Rizzo outlining his salary and compensation request, he outlined what it would take to get him to come to Bell:

> My law enforcement tenure and reputation make me highly marketable for interim police chief opportunities. In those positions, I could reasonably expect to make anywhere from 150 to 250K annualized, per assignment. I believe the Police Chief has been paid from 160 to 190K per year. Therefore if my starting salary per year, plus the deferred compensation package we have discussed, I will be able to make a similar amount to what I could expect to make doing my interim police chief jobs.

Adams requested a $69,000 deferred-compensation plan per year; 10 percent annual raises with consideration for a greater increase for outstanding performance; a police car for his personal use, including his wife's ability to use the car; the same 3 percent at 55 CALPERS Plan with a 5 percent cost of living provision; lifetime medical fully paid for; the maximum accrual for vacation and sick leave allowable under Bell current policies with an initial seeding of a vacation bank of 80 hours and sick leave with 160 hours; and 100 hours of management leave.[80]

While Bell didn't grant all of these requests, Adams was able to secure a $457,000 salary, along with a controversial side agreement that seemed to grant him a disability before he ever started. Adams negotiated directly with Rizzo and they "came to an agreement of . . . $457,000 a year which encompassed the $270,000 or the 260-70 I was going to lose, and the normal chief's salary added onto that."[81] His original contract was for $200,000. But that was padded by another $257,000 for his role as "special police counsel." Thus the documentation made it appear that he was only making $200,000 as chief.

Prior to his employment, Adams discussed with Rizzo and Spaccia the possibility of creating a joint police force between Bell and Maywood. This would require a Joint Power Agreement between the two cities. Adams testified that he was later given two contracts; Rizzo said "we will divide your salary into two contacts for that J. P. A. (Joint Powers Authority). One will be for the police chief's salary of the new police department. The other contract will be for consulting for our department." Adams said he was given two envelopes and told that adding them together would equal his current salary.[82] Adams signed them, but when he later asked for copies he was told by Rebecca Valdez that the City had decided not to use them and they were destroyed. Prosecutors said Adams' contract was deliberately drawn up so that citizens would be unable to learn the real size of his paycheck.

About a month after his compensation agreement, Adams also drafted a "Medical Retirement side agreement," or MOU, that many felt was designed to allow him to retire with a preapproved disability pension even before he began employment at Bell. Adams said he merely wanted to memorialize the various concerns that he had in terms of his medical injuries after thirty-eight years in law enforcement.

Rizzo signed the pension disability agreement, which read in part: "The job-related back injury is currently being litigated by the cities of Simi Valley, Ventura and Glendale. . . . It's fully understood and accepted the City of Bell recognizes that Mr. Adams qualified for and will be filing for a medical disability retirement in conjunction with his service retirement when he retires from the City of Bell. The City of Bell agrees to support this retirement and agrees that a service/medical retirement is justified and appropriate."[83] [84]

Pension experts have questioned the legality of Adams contract, partially because it meant that the city had determined him unfit for the position's full-time duties yet employed him anyway. This came to light because Adams' lawsuit alleged that he was trying to get pension payments under disability, meaning they would not have been taxed. However, Glendale officials maintained that Adams was not disabled when he retired from Glendale in 2009.[85]

A series of embarrassing emails surfaced providing some insight into how Spaccia ended up negotiating Adams' employment contract. When Adams asked why a "pay period" was not defined, Spaccia explained: "We have crafted our agreements carefully so we do not draw attention to our pay. The word Pay Period is used and not defined in order to protect you from someone taking the time to add up your salary."[86] The final contract made no mention to pay period and just stated "Employee shall be paid (hereinafter the "Basic Salary) $17,577.00 per pay period."[87] It was after concluding the negotiations that Adams made the remark about "taking all of Bell's money," in the same email exchange in which Spaccia's infamous "pigs vs. hogs" quote occurred. Adams claimed the two were only joking and that the emails were taken out of context.

In his deposition, Adams discussed how he wanted to make sure everything in his contract was going to be legal. He said he was repeatedly assured by Rizzo, Spaccia, and Brown that his contract did not need to be placed on the council agenda for approval because Rizzo had the authority to sign his contract. In one exchange, Spaccia told Adams:

> Re: your attorneys suggestion that you should receive something in writing indicating what Bob's authority is to issue the contract. It is a shame that he is so unwilling to recognize that you (I think) already have. We have painstak-

ingly and carefully, and with attorney assistance made sure of what authority Bob has vs., what the City has. So, for your attorney's information Bob has the proper authority to enter into a Contract with you, and we are not interested in educating him on how we did that . . . [88]

Adams also said that Brown was present each time he met with Bell officials, and that, in response to Adams' inquiries, Brown assured him that everything in Bell was fine.[89] Adams said Brown also told him that the city's salaries and other activities were " in the charter."[90]

In April, 2009, Adams wrote to Rizzo, noting "unusual" recruitment process and expressing his interest in becoming part of the "moral compass" of the community by accepting the position, and calling the job with Bell the "opportunity of a lifetime."[91] This was a fair characterization: Adams would take over Bell's much smaller police force at a salary twice that of the Los Angeles Police Chief and Los Angeles County Sheriff. The Bell force contained 36 sworn officers, while Simi Valley had 122 and Glendale had 245.[92]

If Adams' $400,000 pension had been later deemed appropriate, he would have been the third highest-paid pensioner in California. But when his contract was ruled invalid, the amount was cut to $268,175. Adams sued the city for additional retirement. The CALPERS Board had previously decided that, because Adams and the city had effectively hidden his true salary from the public, his pension would be based on his previous salary as chief in Glendale ($235,000 per year) rather than his $457,000 salary in Bell. The decision read, in part: "To be the basis for a pension, a public official's salary must be readily available to the public. In Mr. Adams' case, the administrative law judge who decided the case in the first instance held that Bell and Mr. Adams had affirmatively hidden Mr. Adams' compensation from the public."[93]

Even though Adams was only chief for little over a year, police sergeant and whistleblower James Corcoran spoke extensively about Adams' role in the department's illegal vehicle impounds. He said Adams supported the illegal seizures fully and was even in negotiations with a contractor to install cameras at red lights, which would help them further identify "problem" vehicles. He said Adams justified this practice by saying the drivers were dangerous because they were unlicensed—which many were—but Corcoran was most concerned with how the fines were determined. He said that a neighboring city, Downey, charged $69 for vehicle impounds while Bell was charging $300 on average.[94]

Shortly after the *Los Angeles Times* broke the corruption story, Adams filed a cumulative trauma claim on his back and left Bell. Soon after the high salaries were reported, several Bell officials ended up at Rizzo's horse ranch in Washington. During his testimony at Spaccia's trial, Adams was asked about the meeting: "Did the 'Oh, my gosh you were making $1 million' issue come up?" Adams said that it did not.[95]

NOTES

1. Bentham, Jeremy. "On Publicity." The Works of Jeremy Bentham, Vol. 2, part 2. 1839. Retrieved from: http://oll.libertyfund.org/titles/1921.

2. Deutsch, L. "Bell Assistant City Manager Angela Spaccia Convicted in Corruption Case." *Los Angeles Daily News.* December 9, 2013. Retrieved from http://www.dailynews.com/general-news/20131209/bell-assistant-city-manager-angela-spaccia-convicted-in-corruption-case.

3. Doug Willmore, interview with author, February 12, 2015.

4. People v. Spaccia. BA376026. People's Exhibits 1 to 71. Exhibit 53. N.D.

5. California Public Employees' Retirement System Board of Administration. "Pier'Angela Spaccia Compensation Review. OAH No. 2012020198. Proposed Decision, Attachment A." February 26, 2013.

6. Martinez, A. "Angela Spaccia, Former Ventura Employee Embroiled in Bell Pay Scandal, Maintains Innocence." *Ventura County Star.* February 6, 2013. Retrieved from http://www.vcstar.com/news/former-ventura-employee-embroiled-in-bell-pay.

7. Overend, W. "Official Says Colleague Sexually Harassed Her." *Los Angeles Times.* June 8, 1989. ProQuest Historical Newspapers.

8. Ibid.

9. Ibid.

10. California Public Employees' Retirement System Office of Audit Services. "City of Bell Public Agency Review." November 2010.

11. California Public Employee, OAH No. 2012020198, February 26, 2013.

12. People v. Hernandez, Jacobo, Mirabel, Cole, Bello, & Artiga. BA376025. Preliminary Hearing. February 14, 2011.

13. Ibid, pp. 201–209.

14. People v. Spaccia. BA 382701, BA376026. Spaccia's Trial. November 15, 2013. p. 6371.

15. People v. Hernandez, Jacobo, Mirabel, Cole, Bello, & Artiga. BA376025, Preliminary Hearing, February 14, 2011.

16. People v. Rizzo, Spaccia. BA382701. Criminal Indictment. March 29, 2011.

17. Gottlieb, J. "Pensions for Rizzo, 40 Other Bell Employees Will be Larger than First Estimated." *Los Angeles Times.* September 30, 2010. Retrieved from http://articles.latimes.com/2010/sep/30/local/la-me-rizzo-pensions-20100930.

18. Ibid.

19. People v. Rizzo, Spaccia. BA382701. Criminal Indictment. March 29, 2011.

20. People v. Spaccia. BA376026, BA382701. Sentencing Minutes. April 10, 2014.

21. Ibid.

22. Ibid.

23. People v. Spaccia. BA376026. People's Exhibits 1 to 71. Exhibit 57. July 29, 2010.

24. Ibid.

25. Ibid.

26. Willmore, interview.

27. People v. Spaccia. BA376026, BA382701. Sentencing Minutes. April 10, 2014.

28. Lee, E. Testimony. October 28, 2013. pp. 2456/58.

29. People v. Spaccia. BA376026. Defense's Exhibits EE to ZZ. Exhibit GG.

30. Adams, R. Testimony. November 6, 2013. pp. 4323

31. Ibid.

32. People v. Spaccia. BA376026. People's Exhibits 201 to 209. Exhibit 204. March 6, 2010.

33. People v. Spaccia. BA376026. People's Exhibits 72 to 100. Exhibit 80. N.D.

34. Ibid.

35. James Corcoran, Interview with author, February 12, 2015.

36. Knoll, C. & Mather, K. "Former Bell Second-in-Command Gets 11 Years in Prison for Corruption." *Los Angeles Times*. April 2014. Retrieved from http://www.latimes.com/local/la-me-spaccia-sentencing-20140411-story.html.

37. BA376026, BA382701, Sentencing Minutes, April 10, 2014.

38. People v. Spaccia. BA 382701, BA376026. Spaccia's Trial. November 15, 2013. p. 6839.

39. Spaccia, Angela. Email Exchange to Alan Pennington. November 5–18, 2007.

40. BA376026, BA382701, Sentencing Minutes, April 10, 2014.

41. Martinez, A. "Angela Spaccia, Former Ventura Employee Embroiled in Bell Pay Scandal, Maintains Innocence." *Ventura County Star*. February 6, 2013. Retrieved from http://www.vcstar.com/news/former-ventura-employee-embroiled-in-bell-pay.

42. BA376026, BA382701, Sentencing Minutes, April 10, 2014.

43. Ibid.

44. BA 382701, BA376026, Spaccia's Trial, November 15, 2013, p. 6379.

45. People v. Spaccia. BA376026. People's Exhibits 72 to 100. Exhibit 74. February 21, 2010.

46. People v. Spaccia. BA 382701, BA376026. Spaccia's Trial. November 14, 2013. p. 5737.

47. Ibid, p. 5809.

48. Ibid, p. 5810.

49. Gottlieb, J. Bell: A Total Breakdown. (white paper at the City of Bell Scandal Revisited Conference, Chapman University, 2015).

50. BA376026, BA382701, Sentencing Minutes, April 10, 2014.

51. Ibid.

52. Ibid.

53. Bell Legal Panel. Chapman University. February 19, 2015.

54. Gottlieb, J. & Vives, R. "Several Documents Point to Questionable Action in Bell." *Los Angeles Times*. November 15, 2013. Retrieved from latimes.com/local/la-me-angela-spaccia-20131116,0,2375241.story.

55. BA376026, People's Exhibits 71 to 100, Exhibit 97, August 15, 2008.

56. BA 382701, BA376026, Spaccia's Trial, November 15, 2013, p. 6146.

57. Ibid, p. 6147.

58. Ibid, p. 6148.

59. Ibid.

60. Bell Legal Panel, February 19, 2015.

61. People v. Spaccia. BA376026, BA382701. Sentencing Memorandum. January 22, 2014.

62. BA376026, BA382701, Sentencing Minutes, April 10, 2014.

63. Ibid.

64. Bell Legal Panel, February 19, 2015.

65. Gottlieb, J., Vives, R., & Leonard, J. "Bell Leaders Hauled Off in Cuffs: Eight Are Held in Scandal the D.A. Calls 'Corruption on Steroids.'" *Los Angeles Times*. September 22, 2010. Retrieved from http://articles.latimes.com/2010/sep/22/local/la-me-bell-arrest-20100922.

66. Maddus, G. "D.A. Steve Cooley Under Pressure from City of Bell Police Union to Fully Investigate Ex-Chief Randy Adams." *LA Weekly*. September 27, 2010. Retrieved from http://www.laweekly.com/news/da-steve-cooley-under-pressure-from-city-of-bell-police-union-to-fully-investigate-ex-chief-randy-adams-2390716.

67. Corcoran, interview.

68. Nestor Valencia, interview with author, February 12, 2015.

69. Maddus, D.A. Steve Cooley.

70. Corcoran, interview, p. 22.

71. Pringle, P. "Injury Cited By Ex-Bell Police Chief In Disability Pension Claim Didn't Prevent Him from Exercising." *Los Angeles Times*. October 5, 2010. Retrieved from http://articles.latimes.com/2010/oct/05/local/la-me-randy-adams-20101005.

72. Ibid.

73. Gottlieb, J. "Judge Questions Why Bell's Former Police Chief Isn't Facing Corruption Charges." *Los Angeles Times*. December 19, 2011. Retrieved from http://articles.latimes.com/print/2011/dec/19/local/la-me-bell-adams-20111220.

74. People v. Spaccia. BA 382701, BA376026. Spaccia's Trial. November 6, 2013.

75. Adams v. Bell. BC489331. Deposition of Randy Adams. May 1, 2013.

76. Ibid, p. 61.

77. BA 382701, BA376026, Spaccia's Trial, November 6, 2013. p. 4220.

78. BC489331, Deposition of Adams, May 1, 2013, p. 68.

79. Ibid.

80. BA376026, Defense's Exhibits, Exhibit FF, April 14, 2009.

81. BA 382701, BA376026, Spaccia's Trial, November 6, 2013.

82. Ibid, pp. 4283.

83. BC489331, Deposition of Adams, May 1, 2013, p. 148.

84. BA376026, People's Exhibits, Exhibit 63.

85. Leonard, J., Blankstein, A. & Gottlieb, J. "In E-mails, Bell Official Discussed Fat Salaries." *Los Angeles Times*. February 14, 2011. Retrieved from http://articles.latimes.com/print/2011/feb/14/local/la-me-bell-emails-20110215.

86. BC489331, Deposition of Adams, May 1, 2013.

87. BA376026, People's Exhibits, Exhibit 28.

88. BA376026, People's Exhibits, Exhibit 82.

89. BC489331, Deposition of Adams, May 1, 2013.

90. Ibid.

91. BA376026, Defense's Exhibits, Exhibit FF, April 14, 2009.

92. BC489331, Deposition of Adams, May 1, 2013.

93. California Public Employees' Retirement System Board of Administration. "Randy G. Adams Final Compensation Calculation. Case No. 2011-0788. Precedential Decision." March 18, 2015.

94. Corcoran, interview.

95. BA 382701, BA376026, Spaccia's Trial, November 6, 2013, p. 4350.

Exterior of the California Bell Club poker club in Bell, California in 1985, once one of the largest card club casinos in the state. Rick Corrales, Copyright © 1985, *Los Angeles Times*, Reprinted with Permission.

The vast room of poker tables inside the California Bell Club poker club in Bell, California during its heyday in the early 1980's. Rick Corrales, Copyright © 1985, *Los Angeles Times*, Reprinted with Permission.

Poker players at one of the California Bell Club's gaming tables. The poker club catered to a clientele of mostly older and lower income Los Angeles area residents. Rick Corrales, Copyright © 1985, *Los Angeles Times*, Reprinted with Permission.

Former Bell City Administrator John Pitts admitted to masterminding the plan to profit from the California Bell Club poker club in 1977. In 1984, just before going to trial on corruption charges, Pitts pleaded guilty on two counts of mail fraud and in 1985 he was sentenced to six months in federal prison. Rick Corrales, Copyright © 1985, *Los Angeles Times*, Reprinted with Permission.

Former Bell Councilman Peter Werrlein Jr. working with John Pitts introduced measures to the city council that paved the way for the building of the California Bell Club poker club. Werrlein lost his seat on the council in 1980 after it was revealed he was under investigation for involvement in a prostitution ring run by the "Hillside Strangler" serial murderers. Werrlein then worked as the manager of the Bell poker club until he was indicted in 1984. Subsequently, in a plea deal with federal prosecutors, Werrlein pleaded guilty on one count of mail fraud and one count of conducting an illegal gambling business. Werrlein was sentenced to three years in federal prison, but served only ten and a half months. Rick Corrales, Copyright © 1985, *Los Angeles Times*, Reprinted with Permission.

George Cole (left) and Ray Johnson (right) celebrate their election to the Bell City Council along with Cole's wife Judy (center) in April 1984. Cole and Johnson were elected to the council after making reform and ousting corrupt city officials a major campaign platform. The two successfully unseated two incumbent councilmembers that had decided not to suspend City Administrator John Pitts without pay after he was indicted by a federal grand jury on corruption charges. Rick Corrales, Copyright © 1984, *Los Angeles Times*, Reprinted with Permission.

Robert Rizzo is led away in handcuffs from his Huntington Beach home on September 21, 2010, after he was arrested on sixty-nine counts related to his role in the corruption in Bell. Robert Lachman, Copyright © 2010, *Los Angeles Times*, Reprinted with Permission.

Bell community members conduct a demonstration out front of the Bell City Hall following the arrests of eight current and former Bell officials. The photo of Rizzo's arrest held by demonstrators from BASTA became an iconic symbol used by the residents that had organized community groups in support of reforming the Bell city government. Jay L. Clendenin, Copyright © 2010, *Los Angeles Times*, Reprinted with Permission.

The Bell Eight sit during their arraignment in court following their arrests in September 2010. From left to right are Robert Rizzo, Angela Spaccia, Victor Bello, and Oscar Hernandez. Al Seib, Copyright © 2010, *Los Angeles Times*, Reprinted with Permission.

Several former Bell city officials in court during their trial in 2013. From left to right are former Councilmembers Luis Artiga, George Cole, George Mirabel, Teresa Jacobo, and former Mayor Oscar Hernandez. Artiga was the only former official out of the eight indicted to be acquitted of all charges. Irfan Khan, Copyright © 2013, *Los Angeles Times*, Reprinted with Permission

Former Bell Police Chief Randy Adams attends the Bell City Council meeting in July 2010, just after the corruption scandal began to gain public attention. Adams was hired as Bell's chief of police in 2009 and served until he resigned in 2010. Adams was investigated in September 2010 by the Los Angeles County District Attorney's office, but he has never been formally charged for any crimes. Liz O. Baylen, Copyright © 2010, *Los Angeles Times*, Reprinted with Permission.

Former Bell City Attorney Ed Lee testifies on the witness stand during the trial of Angela Spaccia in October 2013. Lee's signature appeared upon multiple contracts granting Spaccia and Rizzo exorbitant salary increases, but Lee said he did not recall ever drafting or signing the documents, though he confirmed that the signatures appeared to be his own, suspecting they were either forged or unknowingly signed by him. Irfan Khan, Copyright © 2013, *Los Angeles Times*, Reprinted with Permission.

Judge Kathleen Kennedy presided over the trials of the Bell Eight. Kennedy is seen here in the Los Angeles Superior Court making remarks at the sentencing hearing for Robert Rizzo. Mark Boster, Copyright © 2014, *Los Angeles Times*, Reprinted with Permission.

Former Assistant City Administrator Angela Spaccia is remanded to custody on December 9, 2013, after being convicted on eleven out of the thirteen counts for which she was standing trial for her role in the corruption within the City of Bell. In April 2014, Spaccia was then sentenced to serve eleven years and eight months in prison. Lawrence K. Ho, Copyright © 2013, *Los Angeles Times*, Reprinted with Permission.

Robert Rizzo standing beside his attorney addressed the court at his sentencing April 16, 2014. Rizzo had pleaded no contest to sixty-nine felony counts against him, he was sentenced to twelve years in prison and ordered to pay back $8.8 million in restitution to Bell. Rizzo's statement at the hearing was one of the few time he had spoken publicly about his role in the Bell corruption scandal. In his brief statement Rizzo admitted some fault, he stated, "I breached the public's confidence by starting to look at the position more towards myself than towards the community. I'm very, very sorry for that. I apologize for that." Al Seib, Copyright © 2014, *Los Angeles Times*, Reprinted with Permission.

Chapter Four

Whispers of a Scandal

BASTA & The Whistle Blowers

"Laws can embody standards; governments can enforce laws—but the final task is not a task for government. It is a task for each and every one of us. Every time we turn our heads the other way when we see the law flouted—when we tolerate what we know to be wrong—when we close our eyes and ears to the corrupt because we are too busy, or too frightened—when we fail to speak up and speak out—we strike a blow against freedom and decency and justice."
—Robert F. Kennedy[1]

When, on July 15, 2010, the *Los Angeles Times* published a front-page article entitled "Is A City Manager Worth $800,000?," it was for most southern Californians the first public revelation of the massive corruption that had thrived in Bell under the leadership of Robert Rizzo.[2] But the newspaper's investigation was not the first.

Indeed, at a public discussion of the scandal in August of 2010, reporter Ruben Vives recounted that, while investigating an issue in nearby Maywood in June, his partner, Jeff Gottlieb, had asked a contact in the Los Angeles County district attorney's office "if there were any investigations going on in Maywood."[3] The response, Vives said, was "no we're not, but we're inquiring about Bell."[4]

"What's going on in Bell?" Gottlieb asked. The response: "Well, we're inquiring about their salaries; they're pretty high up there."[5]

This prompted Vives and Gottlieb to visit Bell City Hall and request the salaries of the city's councilmembers and administrators. At the end of June, the reporters published a story about the D.A.'s probe of Bell Councilmembers' salaries. Then, after meeting with Rizzo, they wrote of his grossly inflated salary, starting the process that would end in scandal, resignations, and prosecution.

The day the story broke, Cristina Garcia, then a math teacher in neighboring Bell Gardens, met a Bell businessman named Ali Saleh, who had failed at previous attempts to win election to the council.[6] The two discussed the scandal and decided to organize some residents to take action. Saleh, a respected member of the Bell community, set about gathering a group of citizens to fix a broken city.

But an organization needs a name. The next day, Garcia was discussing the scandal with a friend and found herself wanting to call the corrupt officials bastards. Bastards! Garcia hit on the name BASTA as an approximate acronym for Bell Association To Stop The Abuse.[7] BASTA is also a common Spanish phrase for stating an impassioned "enough!" and would be recognized by Spanish speakers as a statement of contempt for the current state of political affairs.[8] During the 1990s the related phrase "¡Ya Basta!," or "enough already," was popularized in Mexico by the Zapatista revolutionary group and became associated with leftist and anti-globalization activists. In other words, the selection of BASTA was sure to inspire a response from Bell's angry, primarily Latino residents.

Even before BASTA, a new group called the Bell Residents Club (BRC) had already begun holding meetings about citizens' problems with obtaining public records from the city.[9] BRC was led by its founder, Nestor Valencia, today a Councilmember.[10] But despite their common aims, relations between the two groups have been rocky. Accusations of ulterior motives and secret funding from outside interest groups have been flung back and forth.[11] [12]

Bell residents looking into goings-on at City Hall were met with obstruction and delay at every turn; public-records requests went unfulfilled. In frustration, some residents reached out to Garcia, who was making a name for herself from her success at obtaining public records in Bell Gardens that revealed corruption in that city's government. In September of 2009 Garcia began meeting with Bell residents and attending council and community meetings. Garcia quickly became passionate about uncovering the problems in Bell—whose residents were paying the second-highest property tax rates in the county while city officials were talking about cutbacks and combining some services with other cities.

Garcia first began working with the BRC, but decided to form her own group—BASTA—because the leadership of the BRC "were unorganized, motivated by goals I could not support, and their structure didn't fit with how I worked."[13] Garcia claims that the BRC was driven by "ulterior motives, which included electing a slate of three to the council to get a majority, and getting them to appoint the club's president to the city manager position." In other words, Garcia claimed, the BRC was attempting "to replace one corrupt city manager with one inexperienced one"—BRC leader Valencia.[14] Garcia said the BRC turned out to "be the biggest and most constant barrier to BASTA's success."[15]

According to each group's leadership, the other has had ties to the Bell Police Officers Association (POA). Garcia charged that the POA funded the BRC recall campaign aimed at gaining a majority on the council.[16] She tried to convince the POA leadership that the recall campaign was poorly run and would not succeed, but the POA decided to pursue it anyway. After gathering only five hundred signatures in a month, many of them ineligible, the campaign failed.[17]

For his part, Valencia, himself a failed Bell Council candidate, alleged that BASTA was created by and is run by the POA. At a BRC meeting on August 19, 2010, he said, "BASTA is a well, well run structured organization; they are coming initially from the police officers' association and they have hired consultants to do that."[18] In a press release sent out to members of the BRC in September of 2010, Valencia further questioned BASTA's legitimacy, asking "Who gave BASTA the authority to lobby under the cloak of representing the citizens of Bell?"[19] Valencia even charged that BASTA's apparent success in promoting cooperation between Latino and Lebanese residents was artificial, saying, "It was fabricated for the purpose of the police department."[20]

There was in fact a relationship between BASTA and the POA, which Garcia has acknowledged. BASTA reached out to the POA for community contacts and for funding of the recall campaign. The common goal of BASTA and POA, she said, presented "a means of getting around the cost hurdle."[21] In reference to Valencia's persistent allegations, Garcia said, "BASTA would constantly get attacked as a puppet of the Bell POA, but really we were partners in need of each other for a common goal—ending the Rizzo regime."[22]

Political maneuvering and the trading of allegations clearly persisted among some Bell Councilmembers. During the course of an interview about the scandal, Valencia indicated that he was cooperating in some form of surveillance by wearing a recording device to catch further perpetrators of corruption in the city.[23] He has also alleged that some of his fellow councilmembers may have ties to corrupt attorneys in neighboring cities.[24] No further information has surfaced about ongoing investigations in Bell. And the track record of agencies that uncovered the prior scandal does not inspire confidence for the future.

Despite their differences, BASTA and the BRC both successfully worked to recall the corrupt Bell Councilmembers. The leaders of both organizations won election to public office. Garcia was elected to the California State Assembly representing District 58, while both Ali Saleh and Nestor Valencia have been elected to the Bell Council, and have each has been chosen by the rest of the council to serve at least one term as mayor.

Bell residents were not the only ones unhappy with the city's leadership. As noted above, police Sgt. James Corcoran began investigating allegations of corruption in Bell and providing information to state and federal investigators as early as January of 2009.[25] After Chief Randy Adams took no action on his allegations, Corcoran and two other officers contacted the L.A. district attorney's office.

After meeting at length with District Attorney's Office investigator, Corcoran said, the officers were told, "You got a good story, but we can't take it unless you get a public official to come forward."[26] There was only one person Corcoran had in mind: Councilmember Victor Bello.[27]

Victor Bello immigrated to the United States in 1987 with only a high-school education, and after only a decade in the country began serving on the Bell Council.[28] [29] He also worked as a building inspector and a phone-jack installer.[30] Eventually, however, Bello began clashing with his colleagues, and as early as 2006 reached out—in vain—to the L.A. District Attorney's Office.[31] It is unclear why Bello's allegations of corruption were not officially followed up. In testimony during the 2011 trial of Bell officials, the D.A.'s senior investigator revealed that Bello told the office in 2006 that Clifton Albright offered him $200,000 to step down from his council seat.[32] A 2005 *Los Angeles Times* article cited Deputy District Attorney Anthony Colannino as saying the DA's Public Integrity Division was investigating Albright's law firm for ties to corrupt Southgate official Albert Robles.[33] Still, Bello could not raise official interest in his bribery allegations against Albright.

But Corcoran was on the case. Shortly after the sergeant was interviewed by the D.A.'s investigators, he asked Bello if he would write to the District Attorney about the problems in Bell. When Bello expressed uncertainty that he was capable of doing so,[34] Corcoran told him, "You tell me what you want to say, I'll write it for you."[35] Bello agreed, and Corcoran immediately composed a letter on Bello's behalf to James Fontenette, the D.A.'s investigator who had interviewed Corcoran and the other two Bell officers. Bello signed the letter alleging widespread corruption in Bell; it was sent to the D.A.'s office on May 6, 2009, the same day that office first opened an investigation into the city.[36]

Bello's letter stated that he had personally witnessed abuses of power, specifically "public corruption, bribery, underhanded real-estate deals, unethical retirement arrangements, and police misconduct, including civil-rights violations."[37] However, Bello's attorney, Stanley L. Friedman, later claimed that Bello actually had no direct knowledge of corruption, but had only signed the letter because "he wanted to be a good citizen and representative on the city council."[38]

The letter also mentioned concerns over the most recent city elections, and stated that Bello was aware that "several police officers are willing to come forth as witnesses in these matters."[39] Yet one concern that Bello's letter did not mention were the high salaries of the councilmembers, perhaps because he was one of those receiving $100,000 for the part-time, elected position. Most of the councilmembers had rationalized that they deserved such generous compensation; Bello apparently had also. On the other hand, Corcoran seemed to not know about the council salaries; the letter he wrote for Bello indicated that he was primarily aware only of the issues concerning Rizzo and his associates.

The success of Rizzo's schemes depended upon the cooperation of many others. Bello, like many of the councilmembers and the mayor at the time, had limited English skills as well as low levels of education. Once a Councilmember was brought into the circle and rewarded with a high salary, their silence was expected. None of the other highly paid councilmembers attempted to contact authorities, likely due to varying measures of both willful ignorance and active collusion. Even Bello's own attempts to come forward seemed at times to lack serious concern for the situation—especially for the degree of his own involvement.

An L.A. County D.A.'s investigator, David Demerjian, wrote back to Bello on May 19, 2009.[40] "Before I can determine whether a criminal investigation is warranted," he wrote, "I will require more detailed information."[41] Demerjian gave Bello thirty days to supply evidence to substantiate the allegations against Rizzo.[42] Nearly a month later, on June 17, 2009—again writing as Bello—Corcoran charged in a letter to Demerjian[43] that, acting under Rizzo's authority, Eric Eggena "was possibly accepting bribes in return for approving building permits," as well as confiscating merchandise from illegal vendors and selling it for personal gain.[44] The letter also claimed that Eggena may have been using his position as election commissioner to falsify ballots during the March 3, 2009 municipal election. Finally, the letter said Rizzo interrupted Corcoran's investigation into corruption and ordered him to "cease any further action."[45]

In August 2009, three months after Bello's first letter to the D.A., he abruptly resigned his council seat[46] and took a job created specifically for him: assistant to the coordinator of the city food bank,[47] although he performed the exact same duties as the volunteers at the food bank. Bello continued to receive the same $100,000 salary he had enjoyed on the council.[48] [49] Not even the coordinator knew it.

Following Bello's response to Demerjian's request for more information, the D.A.'s office did not contact Bello again until more than ten months later, in March of 2010.[50] On March 24, Bello was interviewed at his home by investigators Maria Grimaldo and Mike Holguin.[51] Later, during the trial against Bello and the other officials, Grimaldo said one reason for the long delay in interviewing Bello was "difficulty getting ahold of Mr. Bello." She did not elaborate.[52]

In the course of the taped interview, Bello mentioned that he wanted to retire and collect his monthly $3,900 city pension.[53] He said the council created the food bank job at the same salary so he could serve in that position until his council term expired in March of 2011, at which time he could begin collecting on his pension.

Holguin asked, "Your monthly salary as councilmember is how much? You said $3,900." Bello replied, "No, no, no, no, it's about $100,000 a year." Grimaldo: "$100,000 a year?"[54] This and Bello's subsequent statements would be used to bring corruption charges against him and the other current and former councilmembers who were receiving salaries in violation of state laws restricting the salaries of elected councilmembers.

Bello kept talking. He went on to elaborate about the benefits of being a Bell councilmember under Rizzo. He noted that Rizzo had advocated for Bell to become a charter city because it would allow councilmembers to be paid more than legally permitted as a general law city.[55] Throughout, Bello seemed woefully unaware of the gravity of what he had admitted. For the first time, the D.A.'s office had first-hand information about inappropriate salaries in Bell. The investigation slowly ramped up following Bello's admissions and culminated in the charges brought against Bello and the rest of the Bell 8 after the *Los Angeles Times* broke the story.

At the same time that Corcoran wrote the first Bello letter, he also composed a letter to the Election Fraud Investigation Unit (EFIU) of the California Secretary of State's office. In this letter, dated May 6, 2009, Corcoran recorded his suspicions about voter fraud in Bell.[56] He wrote that he had contacted an investigator with the EFIU as early as February 2008 concerning Bell's municipal elections.[57] Corcoran claimed that absentee ballots were being used to ensure that Rizzo's handpicked array of councilmembers stayed in office. He added that a confidential informant could vouch for the fact that at least sixteen individuals who had submitted absentee ballots were actually deceased, incarcerated, or no longer in the United States.

Corcoran appealed to the EFIU for help. The agency contacted him by May 18, 2009, and provided some information to allow him to continue his own investigation; but little other action was taken by anyone other than Corcoran to investigate voter fraud.[58] In August of 2010, after the scandal had already broken and the D.A.'s office had announced that it was investigating, the EFIU wrote to Corcoran stating that they had forwarded the findings of his investigation to the District Attorney's Office.[59]

Corcoran was not one to wait around. During the rest of 2009 and into 2010, he continued to investigate voter fraud in Bell. He claimed that, under Rizzo's auspices, several Bell police officers were dispatched to hand out absentee ballots and instruct voters how to vote. Corcoran said he also had uncovered cases of officers filling out ballots in the names of deceased voters.[60] Through his persistent efforts, Corcoran began to make somewhat of a name for himself. Among Rizzo's circle, he was a nuisance—or worse. But some staff members and residents began to consider him the only man in Bell they could trust. In 2009, a secretary, Angela Ruiz, who had worked under Rizzo then moved to the Bell Police Department, approached Corcoran and, as he recalled, said "hey, this guy Rizzo a few years ago sexually assaulted me."[61] Corcoran told her to speak to her captain. Ruiz spoke with Lourdes Garcia, then director of administrative services. According to Corcoran, Ruiz said she had gone to Rizzo's condominium one night to babysit, but Rizzo was there and had been drinking. Rizzo was watching a History Channel show about Adolf Hitler and, she said, started talking about how he admired Hitler and then tried to sexually assault her. Ruiz never filed charges against Rizzo, but Corcoran said he reported the incident to the attorneys contracted with the city to give advice and provide ethics training, Ken White and Tom Brown of the firm Brown, White & Newhouse.[62]

About a week later, Corcoran met with White and went over the issues he had emailed about. When White attempted to brush Corcoran off, Corcoran said he told him that Rizzo was the subject of the sexual harassment incident. Soon afterwards, Corcoran said, "word got back to Rizzo, and that was the beginning of the end for me."[63] Rizzo and Spaccia had recently hired Randy Adams to take over as police chief. According to Corcoran, Spaccia later remembered a conversation in which Rizzo told Adams, "Get rid of this guy. Do it by the numbers, but get rid of him."[64] Shortly afterwards Adams placed Corcoran on administrative leave for insubordination; he would then face an internal affairs review and likely be dismissed. Corcoran consulted with his attorney and decided that his best course of action was to resign.[65]

On July 26, 2010, a few weeks after the initial *Los Angeles Times* stories about Bell began to run, Corcoran sued Bell for being wrongfully placed on administrative leave and being forced to resign.[66] The very next day the L.A. County District Attorney's Office announced that it had been investigating voter fraud and other corruption allegations in Bell since March of 2010.[67] This corresponded with the date of Bello's interview and his revelation of the unusually high council salaries. The D.A. had in fact had an open investigation in Bell since May of the prior year, and had already been tipped off about corruption issues going back to at least 2006 and Bello's bribery allegation. It is unclear why the D.A. did not conduct a full investigation sooner, and instead repeatedly required informants provide more evidence before it would even begin an in-depth look at Bell. Had the D.A.'s office acted earlier, it might have uncovered the corruption sooner and saved Bell residents a great amount of money.

Corcoran was not the only whistleblower to come out of Bell before the *Los Angeles Times* story broke and D.A.'s investigation launched. After hearing rumors about the high official salaries in August 2008, a citizen, Roger Ramirez, appeared at council meetings in August and September.[68] Ramirez filled out a speaker comment slip each time with a question about the rumors of Rizzo's making a salary of $400,000 a year. At the August meeting, Ramirez listed two questions. One was about the timeline for the building of a park. The second was, "Rizzo $400,000 annually salary?" Ramirez remembers seeing Mayor Oscar Hernandez and Councilmember George Mirabal discussing his speaker slip after his first question had been answered. But they failed to answer the second question, and Ramirez did not press the matter. "I just felt I wasn't going to get really a good answer or truthful answer," he said, "so I didn't really feel like I wanted to bring it up."[69]

But he changed his mind. Ramirez returned to the next council meeting, in September, and filled out a speaker slip with a direct question about rumors of Rizzo's making $400,000 a year and the councilmembers making $80,000. Later, during Bell trial testimony Ramirez recounted that Rizzo replied, "You know, Mr. Ramirez, if I could be making $400,000 a year, I wouldn't be working here. You're hearing too many rumors…and the rumors about the police officers being laid off, now you come back with this rumor. There's no truth to that."[70] Unsatisfied, Ramirez then asked the councilmembers about rumors they were making $80,000 a year.[71] Councilmember George Mirabal did not deny the amount, but instead referred Ramirez to his right to request the information under the Public Information Act and Brown Act.[72]

Ramirez subsequently visited City Hall and requested information about the salaries of the councilmembers and city manager. A response was not forthcoming. A secretary told him she would speak with Valdez, the city clerk and that the response would take three to five days. Ramirez returned several days later and was told he had to fill out a form again and then wait another ten to fifteen days; he did so.

Later, both Valdez and Lourdes Garcia testified that they were told to provide incorrect information about Rizzo's salaries.[73] After Rizzo had them compile the information, they said, Rizzo asked Lourdes how much he made and she gave him the global amount. "No," he responded, "that is not what I make. . . . What is my . . . what . . . how much do I make?" When Garcia repeated the total amount, he said "NO, that's is not what I make. What I meant is my salary as CAO, is what is being charged to the general fund." Garcia was then instructed to only include Rizzo's salary from the general fund, not from the other agencies that were paying him.[74]

On September 17, Ramirez was given a memo with several monthly salary amounts for different positions in the city. He later stated in court that he had repeatedly asked for annual salaries of the city manager and councilmembers but that the document provided had only monthly amounts. He remained suspicious that the figures he was given were not correct, and the memo and his account would be used in 2010 in the case against Rizzo and his colleagues for knowingly providing false information about their salaries. The letter to Ramirez stated that the mayor made $673 (monthly); councilmembers ($673 monthly); city attorney—Best Best & Krieger LLP—$13,125 (monthly retainer); Brown, White & Newhouse LLP, attorneys for labor negotiations/personnel attorney ($8,500 monthly); and Rizzo, the chief administrative officer $15,478 (monthly). [75]

The $185,736 base salary reported for Rizzo was significantly less than his actual base salary of $787,637—or $1.5 million a year when the components of computation and benefits are added in. Likewise, the $8,076 annual salary for the mayor and council was not close to the actual salaries of more than $100,000.

In 2011 testimony, Garcia admitted that she prepared the memo at Rizzo's explicit direction and felt guilty that the information was false. [76] She said the city's records showed that councilmembers received $150, a figure she told Rizzo was too low to be given out publicly. He then instructed her to list the salary as $673 per month. [77]

The Ramirez case shows the level of collusion that took place among multiple Bell officials to hide the truth from residents. Ramirez knew the numbers he received weren't accurate, but did not have the resources or ability to put the evidence together against Bell's corrupt officials. Indeed, the Bell case highlights the delicate role that public servants play in maintaining public trust. Had any of the offices that were made aware of improprieties done even just a little more digging, they might have uncovered more of the corruption sooner. Time and time again, however, the public were left to fend for themselves.

The officials upon whom Rizzo's grand scheme depended notably included Dennis Tarango, director of building and planning. Tarango maintained an outside business relationship with Rizzo as a co-owner of Rizzo's horse ranch in Washington state, while also performing contracted work for Bell through his firm, D&J Engineering. [78] The audit conducted after the scandal broke indicated that Tarango's businesses had received $10.4 million since 1994, despite an expired contract. The audit showed that Rizzo approved monthly invoices from Tarango. [79]

There had been previous rumors that Tarango was up to no good in other parts of California. D&J Engineering was a fictitious name for the real company, D&J Municipal Services, which had contracted with Yorba Linda to provide building inspection services. [80] In February 2010, Yorba Linda residents Brian and Cherie Wink sued everyone involved in a massively failed remodel of their home: After spending $700,000 on renovations, they learned that it was unlivable and had to be torn down. The Winks claimed that an inspector from D&J Municipal Services was accepting bribes from the general contractor for approving unacceptable work.[81] The fact that Tarango and his business were accused of bribery should have set off alarms, especially as Bell was already the subject of multiple investigations for bribery. The fact that Tarango and Rizzo were in a joint business venture was another warning sign that should have alerted investigators. Tarango's problems in Yorba Linda resulted in his company losing that contract and his company having to pay the Winks $610,000.[82]

Tarango also consulted with Rizzo in computing the excessive business fees levied on Bell residents,[83] and Corcoran cited other affiliations between the two, such as being in the race horse business together. Corcoran filed a complaint with the California Fair Political Practices Commission (FPPC) about conflict of interest, and was not alone in doing so. In April of 2010, a similar FPPC complaint was filed against Tarango by a citizen, William Fick. The FPPC's response was that Fick's complaint lacked evidence to substantiate the conflict-of-interest claim. Tarango was never charged in connection with any questionable activities during his employment in Bell.

The Tarango case would prove to be just another lead that was not properly followed up. While there were systemic breakdowns, the people who made up those systems were those who were ultimately responsible for ensuring that functioning systems of checks and balances were in place. Hopefully, scandals such as in Bell will help curb the propensity for this type of widespread corruption.

Rizzo and Spaccia had both made arrangements for retirement accounts with a partner agency of the International City/County Management Association (ICMA), the premiere professional organization of local government leaders and managers whose stated mission is "to create excellence in local governance by developing and fostering professional management to build better communities."[84] Although Rizzo and Spaccia were reaping large sums of money in retirement contribution in line with their exorbitant salaries, officials at ICMA's partner agency, ICMA-RC—like those in CALPERS—have continued to assert that there were no red flags raised before the D.A.'s investigation had begun.

A source with firsthand knowledge inside the ICMA has stated that, when its officials were asked about the salaries in Bell, they said that the situation there seemed to be in line.[85] In fact, the extremely high retirement contributions—well beyond the norm for city manager and assistant city manager positions in municipalities of Bell's size and wealth—should have raised immediate red flags in ICMA. Yet there were no attempts by the organization to follow up. It seems that, in several cases, individuals in positions of power throughout the entire Bell saga willfully turned a blind eye to the highly questionable goings-on.

NOTES

1. Robert F. Kennedy, attorney general, remarks before the Joint Defense Appeal of the American Jewish Committee and the Anti-Defamation League of the B'nai B'rith, Chicago, Illinois, June 21, 1961.—*A New Day: Robert F. Kennedy,* ed. Bill Adler, p. 26 .1968.

2. Gottlieb, J. & Vives, R. "Is a City Manager Worth $800,000?" *Los Angeles Times.* July 15, 2010. Retrieved from http://www.latimes.com/local/la-me-bell-salary-20100715,0,3275417.story#axzz30rdIU3Zb.

3. Gottlieb, J. & Vives, R. "Discussion of Bell at the Los Angeles Press Club. How I Got That Story Series." *Los Angeles Press Club.* Uploaded August 29, 2010. Retrieved from https://youtu.be/6c_qW_HNRmU.

4. Ibid.

5. Ibid.

6. Garcia, C. & Saleh, A. "Discussion of Bell Scandal at Chapman University Conference, Panel #1 – Origins & Chronology, The City of Bell Revisited. Chapman University, Wilkinson College of Arts, Humanities, and Social Sciences." February 19, 2015. Retrieved from http://ibc.chapman.edu/Mediasite/Play/aaec6c3312674b7a9151d60f8a5722cf1d.

7. Ibid.

8. Garcia, C. "Building BASTA." (white paper at the City of Bell Scandal Revisited Conference, Chapman University, 2015). p. 5.

9. Ibid, p. 4.

10. City of Bell. "Biography of Councilmember Nestor Enrique Valencia." N.D. Retrieved from http://www.cityofbell.org/?NavID=237.

11. Garcia, Building, pp. 4–5.

12. Knoll, C. "Bell Residents Question City's Grass-Roots Organization." *Los Angeles Times.* September 18, 2010. Retrieved from http://articles.latimes.com/2010/sep/18/local/la-me-basta-20100918/2.

13. Garcia, Building, p. 4.

14. Ibid.

15. Ibid.

16. Ibid.

17. Ibid.

18. Valencia, N. "Comments at Bell Residents Club Meeting." August 19, 2010. Retrieved from https://www.youtube.com/watch?v=j513gO_oKqM.

19. Knoll, Bell Residents.

20. Moodian, M. "Unity Through Crisis: How a Latino and Lebanese American Coalition Helped Save Democracy in the City of Bell." (white paper at the City of Bell Scandal Revisited Conference, Chapman University, 2015). p. 15.

21. Garcia, Building, p. 9.

22. Ibid.

23. Nestor Valencia, Interview with author, February 12, 2015.

24. Ibid.

25. James Corcoran, Interview with author, February 12, 2015.

26. Ibid.

27. Ibid.

28. Knoll, C. "Final Bell Council Member Sentenced." *Los Angeles Times.* August 1, 2014. Retrieved from http://www.latimes.com/local/politics/la-me-0802-bell-finale-20140802-story.html.

29. Lloyd, J. & Wire Reports. "Last of Ex-Bell Officials Sentenced to Jail in Corruption Scandal." *NBC4 Los Angeles- KNBC.* August 1, 2014. Retrieved from http://www.nbclosangeles.com/news/local/Bell-City-Council-Corruption-Scandal-Victor-Bello-269596251.html.

30. Gottlieb, J. "Accused Bell Councilman Had Contacted D.A. About Misconduct in City." *Los Angeles Times.* February 6, 2013. Retrieved from http://articles.latimes.com/2013/feb/06/local/la-me-0207-bell-trial-20130207.

31. Knoll, Final Bell.

32. People v. Hernandez, Jacobo, Mirabel, Cole, Bello, & Artiga. BA376025. Testimony of Maria Grimaldo. S.C. CA 2011.

33. Becerra, H. "South Gate Chases Legal Firms." *Los Angeles Times*. January 23, 2005. Retrieved from http://articles.latimes.com/2005/jan/23/local/me-southgate23.

34. Corcoran, interview.

35. Ibid.

36. Davis, C. "Tipster in Bell Scandal Waited Months for D.A., Then Was Arrested." *Californiawatch.org*. October 11, 2010. Retrieved from http://californiawatch.org/dailyreport/tipster-bell-scandal-waited-months-da-then-was-arrested-5508.

37. Bello, V. Letter to James Fontenette, LA County DA Investigator. May 6, 2009.

38. Davis, Tipster.

39. Bello, Letter to Fontenette, May 6, 2009.

40. Demerjian, D. Response Letter to Victor Bello. May 19, 2009.

41. Ibid.

42. Ibid.

43. Bello, V. Letter to LA DA David Demerjian. June 17, 2009.

44. Ibid.

45. Ibid.

46. Ibid.

47. Knoll, C. Gottlieb, J. & Goffard, C. "Blame Flies as Bell Trial Begins." *Los Angeles Times*. January 24, 2013. Retrieved from http://articles.latimes.com/2013/jan/24/local/la-me-0125-bell-trial-20130125.

48. Ibid.

49. Knoll, Final Bell.

50. Davis, Tipster.

51. Ibid.

52. BA376025, Testimony of Grimaldo, 2011.

53. Gottlieb, Accused Bell.

54. Ibid.

55. "Bell Trial: After 10 Days, Jurors Say They Hope to 'Speed Up'." *Los Angeles Times*. March 7, 2013. Retrieved from http://latimesblogs.latimes.com/lanow/2013/03/bell-trial-after-10-days-jurors-say-they-hope-to-speed-up.html.

56. Corcoran, J. Letter to Mark Loren. May 6, 2009.

57. Ibid.

58. Election Fraud Investigation Unit. Letter to James Corcoran. August 25, 2010.

59. Ibid.

60. Ravindhran, S. "Voter Fraud Alleged in Troubled City of Bell." *ABC7 Los Angeles KABC*. July 27, 2010. Retrieved from http://abc7.com/archive/7578966/.

61. Corcoran, interview.

62. Ibid.

63. Ibid.

64. Ibid.

65. Ibid.

66. Ravindhran, Voter Fraud.

67. Ibid.

68. People v. Rizzo, Spaccia, Artiga, and Hernandez. BA376026. Testimony of Roger Ramirez. S.C. CA 2011.

69. Ibid.

70. Ibid.

71. Ibid.

72. Ibid.

73. People v. Rizzo, Spaccia, Artiga, and Hernandez. BA376026. Testimony of Lourdes Garcia. S.C. CA 2011.

74. Ibid.

75. People v. Spaccia. BA376026. People's Exhibits 101 to 156. Exhibit 101. N.D.

76. Ibid.

77. Ibid.

78. Saavedra, T. "Yorba Linda Case Linked to Bell Figure." *The Orange County Register.* September 30, 2010. Retrieved form http://www.ocregister.com/taxdollars/strong-477694-city-winks.html.

79. Ibid.

80. Saavedra, T. "Building Inspectors Took Bribes, Left New House Unlivable, Suit Says." *The Orange County Register.* February 12, 2010. Retrieved from http://www.ocregister.com/taxdollars/strong-477324-wink-building.html.

81. Ibid.

82. Saavedra, Yorba Linda.

83. Esquivel, P. & Lopez, R. "Bell Demanded Extra Fees From Some Businesses." *Los Angeles Times.* November 2, 2010. Retrieved from http://www.latimes.com/local/la-me-1102-bell-fees-20101102-m-story.html#page=1.

84. International City/County Management Association. "About: Overview." N.D. Retrieved from http://icma.org/en/icma/about/organization_overview.

85. Confidential source in discussion with the author. February 2015.

Chapter Five

The Corruption Hearings

With Gregory D. Coordes

"In questions of power, let no more be heard of confidence in man, but bind him down from mischief by chains of the constitution."
—Thomas Jefferson [1]

It was in the summer of 2010 that Bell unraveled. After the *Los Angeles Times* exposé [2] of Rizzo and other officials on July 15, the city government erupted in turmoil as many top officials resigned and agencies at all levels of government launched investigations. Bell residents flooded city council meetings [3] over the coming months and protested in the streets. [4]

On September 21, Los Angeles County District Attorney Steve Cooley authorized felony criminal charges against Rizzo, Spaccia, and six current and former councilmembers. As the charges were being announced, police went to each of the eight officials' homes and took them into custody. While most of the "Bell 8" submitted quietly, Mayor Oscar Hernandez put up some resistance. After he failed to respond quickly to officers pounding on his door, they took a battering ram and broke it down. [5] [6]

The arrests were just the beginning of a long process of accounting. Investigations and court hearings would go on for years, and in some instances still are. The corruption hearings would have a profound impact on their targets, but also on how Bell would clean up and move forward.

After the corruption scandal went public in July 2010, the city's immediate problem was that most of the officials implicated were mostly still in office, including the chief administrative officer, assistant chief administrative officer, chief of police, and most councilmembers. Over the next few months, most of the appointed leadership would be forced out.

On July 23, about a week after the *Los Angeles Times* story, the council met in special session to decide upon a response to the dramatic allegations. After a session lasting nearly eight hours, it announced that Rizzo, Spaccia, and Adams had agreed to resign. According to the council, Rizzo and Adams would quit in August, and Spaccia would step down at the end of September. The three would receive no severance pay.[7]

They would later dispute that they had actually resigned, claiming that the council had fired them. Adams said the first he heard of his "resignation" was after the public announcement, when Brown called to tell him that the council had "decided in closed session to announce that [Adams] had resigned without severance."[8] Rizzo's version of events was more dramatic. He also denied that he'd resigned, insisting that he'd been fired. Rizzo also said councilmembers didn't inform him directly, but instead simply locked him out of his office and stopped paying his salary.[9]

The implicated councilmembers proved much more difficult to remove from office. As elected officials, they could not be fired or forced to resign. Being convicted of a crime like four of the five councilmembers were charged with in September 2010 would automatically disqualify them from office. But that could not take effect unless or until a criminal judgment was entered against them.[10] The councilmembers could conceivably remain in office for years waiting for their trials to conclude.

But Bell residents were unwilling to wait that long. As soon as the scandal broke, many began clamoring for the implicated councilmembers to step down. Even though the council voted on July 27 to dramatically reduce member salaries to $673 per month—the amount paid to Lorenzo Velez—they initially refused to resign.[11] Only Luis Artiga voluntarily left office, and that was only after he and three of the other members were indicted.[12] Adding to this bizarre and awkward situation was the fact that the indicted councilmembers refused to attend council meetings after the arrests.[13] Without a quorum at meetings, the city government essentially shut down.[14]

Lacking a functioning government, Bell residents had to find a way to replace the councilmembers more quickly than simply waiting for criminal convictions. That method would be a recall election which was provided for in the California Constitution.[15] Grassroots organizations, particularly BASTA, were able to collect more than 16,000 voter signatures to schedule a recall vote on Mayor Hernandez and Vice-mayor Teresa Jacobo for March 2011, the date of the regular election faced by Councilmembers Artiga, Velez, and Mirabal.[16]

It was a landslide. In a city where voter participation was historically under 10 percent,[17] more than a third of registered voters went to the polls. They chose overwhelmingly to oust all five councilmembers, including Velez, who had no apparent involvement in the corruption.[18] The new council included three former members of BASTA.[19]

Following the March 2011 recall, the criminal proceedings against of Hernandez, Jacobo, Mirabal, Cole, and Bello began picking up speed. When the Bell 8 were originally arrested in September 2010, all were charged together under one complaint listing all of the charges. On March 18, 2011, however, the District Attorney's Office filed an amended criminal complaint that focused on the six former councilmembers. Specifically, the complaint alleged that they violated California Penal Code Section 424(a), which prohibits public officials from "receipt, safekeeping, transfer, and distribution of public moneys . . . [in a] manner not incidental and minimal without authority of law, appropriate the same, and a portion thereof, to personal use and the use of another" at various time periods between January 1, 2006 and July 26, 2010.[20] These charges related to councilmembers' pay and other alleged misappropriations since the City Charter was enacted.

All six pleaded not guilty to the charges in the amended complaint, and were tried together in a jury trial beginning in January 2013. During this trial, the defendants sought to shift the blame for the corruption to Rizzo and, to a lesser extent, City Attorney Edward Lee.[21]

After a trial lasting several weeks, the jury began deliberations. After eighteen days, it still had yet to reach a verdict on many of the counts. However, they had agreed on a verdict on Luis Artiga. On March 20, 2013, they voted to acquit Artiga of all twelve charges against him.[22]

Like most of his former colleagues, Artiga had a long history in Bell, having worked in the city since the late 1980s as a Baptist church pastor. Unlike the other defendants, however, he only joined the council in 2008, after many of the major council votes to raise salaries. He also did not serve on any of the boards that Rizzo created to boost salaries. His attorney, George McDesyan, said "[h]e was not aware, he didn't vote on any of them, he was not there when the authorities were created, he was not there when the raise was given."[23]

Indeed, claiming ignorance of the level of council salaries prior to joining, Artiga called his first paycheck a "miracle from God."[24]

After his arrest, his reaction was less ebullient: "I thought God had answered my prayers, but it was a trap from the devil."[25]

Many Bell residents held a higher opinion of Artiga than of the other councilmembers and did not believe he belonged in jail. This may have been due in part to his efforts as a church leader; he claimed, for example, to have used about half his salary to pay off his church's mortgage.[26] Further, Artiga appeared contrite in public, admitting in a 2010 interview that "[i]t was my job to know, and not knowing is not an excuse. I should have demanded answers, and, for that, I failed."[27]

However, not everyone believed in Artiga's innocence. Corcoran claimed he was a former gang member and considered him a "thug." He claimed that eyewitnesses told him that Artiga helped orchestrate the 2005 Bell Charter voter fraud, triaging ballots in the church basement before the election.[28] In any case, Artiga clearly escaped the fate of many of his council colleagues.

On the same day that Artiga was acquitted, his fellow defendants received less positive news. The jury acquitted four of the five remaining former councilmembers on the charges related to their Public Finance Authority Board pay. But each was found guilty on charges concerning their compensation for supposedly serving on the Solid Waste and Recycling Authority Board.[29] With only about half of the charges decided, Judge Kennedy ordered the jury to continue deliberations until reaching a verdict on all counts. However, the end of the trial came just one day later.

Acrimony within the jury reached such a level that a juror anonymously sent a note to the judge asking her to "remind the jury to remain respectful and not to make false accusations and insults to one another."[30] This note and other factors led Kennedy to conclude that "all hell has broken loose" in the jury room. She declared a mistrial on the remaining charges. However, the judge refused to reconsider the guilty verdicts handed down the previous day.[31]

The mistrial meant that a new trial would be needed and a new jury selected to decide the remaining criminal charges. But it never happened. About a year after the mistrial, in April 2014, the five defendants struck a plea bargain with prosecutors. The agreement required them to plead no contest to the remaining charges; in exchange, the maximum sentence any of them could receive was four years in prison. Kennedy would decide the exact sentences at a separate hearing.[32]

The sentences Kennedy imposed varied widely. The longest prison term went to Teresa Jacobo. Jacobo was appointed to the council in 2001 as the first Latina councilmember in Bell's history. She was subsequently elected as mayor in the 2003 election. Her platform emphasized helping Bell's large and growing Hispanic community. Born in Mexico, Jacobo came to the United States with her father as an infant. An active community member, she served on the boards of several organizations, such as the American Cancer Association and Salvation Army. In addition to her role on the council, she was also a real-estate agent.[33]

During the trial, Jacobo tried to justify her increasingly high salary by testifying that Rizzo told her he was increasing her salary—legally—so she could quit her real-estate job.[34] She also testified that she "thought [she] was doing a very good job to be able to earn" almost $100,000 a year for a part-time position.[35] The prosecutor, on the other hand, recommended the maximum allowed four-year sentence. In the his sentencing memorandum, Assistant District Attorney Hassett argued that Jacobo "abused the trust of the people of Bell, and left the city deeply in debt, all to serve her own greedy self-interest."[36] Corcoran also urged Kennedy to impose the maximum, describing Jacobo as "very culpable," and claiming that the Bell police chief had once had to intervene when Jacobo got caught trying to illegally bring a family member across the Mexican-American border.[37]

Jacobo also provided Kennedy with the results of a lie-detector test, but the judge was unmoved. "I mean, lie detector tests of course are not admissible in a court proceeding," Kennedy said. "And it seems, even yet [the fact] that it's being attached as an exhibit is a further effort on the part of the defendant to not take responsibility because the essence of this lie detector test is I didn't think I did anything wrong, and I passed that lie detector test."[38]

Jacobo also directly sought mercy from the court, saying, "I'd just like to express my apologies and to mention that I have accepted my responsibility and I am very sorry for my negligence . . . I intended to serve with all my heart. And just like that, with all my heart, I apologize to the city of Bell."[39]

Jacobo's efforts were in vain. The judge sentenced her to two years in prison and ordered her to pay the city of Bell $242,000 in restitution.[40] Kennedy ultimately thought Jacobo deserved more time, at least in part because she had a more "sophisticated" occupation as a real-estate agent and should have recognized the unfair increases in Bell's property taxes.[41]

Jacobo, the vice-mayor when the scandal broke in 2010, ended up receiving a harsher sentence than the mayor, Oscar Hernandez. After being elected mayor in 2006 and serving through 2007, he was appointed to the position in 2009. Like many other councilmembers, Hernandez was a Mexican immigrant, coming to the United States as a teenager. During the criminal proceedings, he said he lacked a formal education and had only a limited understanding of English.[42] His lawyer emphasized that Hernandez was too uneducated to understand the documents Rizzo gave him to sign.[43]

Prosecutors did not believe it. They portrayed Hernandez as Rizzo's "go-to" man, since his signature appeared on a variety of complicated documents, particularly those that helped to cover up the many avenues through which Rizzo was drawing a large salary.[44] Nor did he question when his own salary rose from $673 a month to $62,000 a year in only two years. Hernandez's served on the council for eight years, with three terms as mayor, suggesting that he could have picked up more education along the way than his lawyer let on. In addition, he owned a grocery store and several rental properties in Bell; he may not have been as unsophisticated as he wanted the court to believe.[45]

Hernandez did not try to defend his actions on the council. When arrested, he said he was a lousy mayor and a lousy politician and that Bell suffered because he failed to question and stand up to Rizzo.[46] During the trial, he admitted that he and his colleagues delivered "lousy service," such as getting paid to hold meetings that only lasted a few minutes.[47] At his sentencing hearing, he apologized for his role in the scandal, pleading to the judge, "I just want to say I am sorry for not being so aggressive in my questions to the people, the one who was in charge in the office. And I take all the blame. I blame myself. My . . . probably poor English, that's why. It was so poor when I asked questions, I am sorry."[48]

Kennedy said she did not believe that Hernandez had obtained adequate English skills, "and Mr. Rizzo took advantage of that, and so did others by having Mr. Hernandez sign documents that he obviously didn't read. Made no attempt to read. All these matters were on the consent calendar. They weren't debated. They weren't read."[49] While acknowledging that Hernandez was not "the absolute worst of the worst," the judge said he had "a disincentive to upset the apple cart because he was receiving a very good salary . . . so there was a disincentive for [him] to look and question."[50] She sentenced him to four years in prison, but suspended the sentence and ordered him to serve one year in the county jail, pay $241,000 in restitution, and perform 1,000 hours of community service.[51]

George Mirabal received a similar sentence. A funeral director and long-time civil servant in Bell, Mirabal began serving on the council in 1986, then worked as city clerk for a year. He rejoined the council as an appointee in 1993 after an incumbent died.[52] Instead of expressing an oral plea for mercy, Mirabal wrote a long letter to the court. He blamed Rizzo and Lee for the corruption, writing, "I never dreamed that any one person could create such havoc as Rizzo did but I was wrong. In another time, another ethic, I would have fallen on my sword; my disappointment was that all encompassing." He was sentenced to one year in jail and five years' probation, and ordered to pay $242,000 in restitution.[53]

The sentencing of the remaining two former councilmembers, George Cole and Victor Bello, presented somewhat different issues in that they were no longer serving on the council when the corruption scandal broke. Their personal developments during the corruption hearings also made their punishments different than the others'.

While Rizzo took most of the heat, with Spaccia a close second, some have theorized that Cole, who ran as a reformer during the California Bell Club corruption scandal in the early 1980s, was actually the mastermind. First elected to the council in 1984, Cole was part of Bell's "Old Guard" and had even been referred to as the "Godfather of Bell politics." This was due in part to his long tenure in public service, but also to his philanthropic and other longtime ties to elected officials and community alike. At one time he was running four different nonprofits.[54]

Most notably, Cole was at the helm of the Oldtimers Foundation, which had a contractual relationship with the city. This created an inherent conflict of interest, as Cole was paid both by the foundation and the city. Cole's salary as foundation chief executive hovered around $95,000. The foundation's purpose, according to its federal tax filings, is "to promote the welfare of needy elderly and handicapped families." It had revenues of $7.5 million last year, and salaries and compensation totaling $3.4 million. The latter includes Cole's $95,000 salary as chief executive.[55]

Cole served on the council for twenty-four years, including rotations as mayor, then abruptly announced his retirement in October 2008. He said that he had not participated in the council vote to give his foundation a contract to provide transportation to senior citizens. But the fact that Cole's charity was largely financed by the city while he was on the council gave the appearance of a conflict of interest.[56] The foundation ended up being sued by the city for contracts that were obtained illegally.[57] The foundation also came under scrutiny for falsely claiming that it did not receive any government funds from June 2006 to June 2009, while records from Bell, Norwalk, Fontana, and Huntington Park showed otherwise.

Still, Cole was reported to have boasted that he was so connected in Bell that no one could touch him. This self-aggrandizement did not go ignored among other key community stakeholders, including former mayor and current Councilmember Nestor Valencia. Valencia called Cole the mastermind of a history of scandals in and around Bell, and emphasized Cole's propensity for securing contracts: "he was big on contracts . . . any contract he can get, he will get." Valencia also claimed that Cole's work with the Oldtimers Foundation and Meals on Wheels might have been at least partially done to secure votes, noting that Bell's older residents, like older people elsewhere, were typically more likely to vote. Valencia further claimed that Cole told the media that, "I'm untouchable; I have high connections."[58]

One of Cole's rumored connections was with Steve Cooley, the L.A. district attorney. Cole suggested they were good friends. However, in an interview with a local CBS affiliate in Bell, a reporter asked why Cole was bragging so much about being well-connected. Cooley responded: "I don't know a George Cole."[59]

Perhaps Cole was right about his political invincibility; he did end up receiving a relatively forgiving sentence of five years' probation with 180 days of home confinement and one thousand hours of community service. The sentence also included the requirement of wearing a GPS ankle bracelet and an order to pay more than $77,000 in restitution to the city.

There were several reasons for this relatively light sentence. The prosecutor recommended the maximum four-year sentence, because Cole collected almost $75,000 in one year for serving on two "sham boards" the city council created. Even after he stopped getting paid, prosecutors said, he "continued to play an active part, voting for additional unearned and illegal raises for his co-defendants, although he did not personally benefit from them."[60] Cole did not accept a salary for his service on the city council from November 2007 to October 2008, presumably due to the conflict-of-interest issue generated by his affiliation with both the city and his nonprofit, which was being paid by city funds.

His attorney, Ronald Kaye, had a different opinion. Kaye asked for probation in lieu of jail time because of his client's health and Cole's declining payment, which Kaye said was prompted by Cole's realization that city employees had been laid off and that a "huge rift" was occurring with Rizzo.[61]

During the hearing, Hassett, the prosecutor acknowledged that Cole and possibly Bello were the only members of the Bell 8 who seemed actually remorseful. However, he claimed that greed drove all of them from 2001 onwards. He contended that special blame should be placed on Cole as "the elder statesman from Bell. He was there for twenty-four years. He predated everyone," and could have—should have—stopped them. Hassett also noted the irony in Cole's having been elected to the council on an anti-corruption platform.[62] He said Cole betrayed his campaign promises "every month when all of the items now appeared on the consent calendar, when all of the resolutions bore misleading titles, when all of the agendas did not accurately reflect what was happening at city hall. Month after month after month, when all of these were approved without discussion, without objection, he betrayed the people of Bell."[63]

Cole was sentenced to home confinement instead of jail due to his health, which had deteriorated further since his arrest in 2010. His attorney said Cole had suffered several heart attacks and strokes, and also struggled with kidney problems.[64]

Like Cole, Victor Bello was also off of the council by 2010. While on it, he enjoyed the same exorbitant salary as the others. However, Bello said that by 2009 he had to resign due to stress, and that he was on the verge of a nervous breakdown. He said stress came from his increasing anxiety about the way the city was being run and worry about rampant corruption. Before he left the council, Bello had begun to ask uncomfortable questions and voted against the other members. This did not endear him to them, or to Rizzo. Valdez, the city clerk, testified that Bello was effectively banned from City Hall toward the end of his tenure except to attend council meetings. If Bello showed up, she was to tell the police chief and her supervisor. Twice a week, Valdez said, she took Bello's mail to his home, accompanied by code enforcement officers.[65]

Bello's attorney, noting that his client had cooperated with Corcoran in writing letters to the D.A.'s office about corruption, wrote in his sentencing memorandum that Bello "assisted greatly as a whistleblower in bringing to light the corruption in the city of Bell," but found himself a criminal defendant instead of being offered immunity for having come forward against Rizzo. Judge Kennedy took this into account, commenting during the hearing:

I guess Mr. Bello was not exactly in lockstep with all of these other council-men all the time. And if there is one thing that is true about Robert Rizzo, it is that he did everything possible to make sure that everybody was on the same page about everything. And so this defendant was a bit of a thorn in his side . . . I think that what motivated Mr. Bello to come forward to the DA's office as motivated a lot by his personal animus with certain members of the council and perhaps Rizzo. [66]

The judge sentenced Bello to one year in jail and five years' probation, in addition to completing five hundred hours of community service and paying $177,600 in restitution to Bell. [67] This sentence is even less harsh than it first may seem. Unlike the rest of the Bell 8, Bello could not afford to post bond when he was arrested, and as a result spent 340 days, almost a full year, locked up awaiting trial. This confinement was counted toward his punishment, reducing his actual sentence to just two days in jail. [68]

Bello was the final former councilmember to be sentenced. [69] His August 1, 2014 hearing thus marked the close of the council corruption hearings after four years.

Rizzo and Spaccia, were initially scheduled to be tried together. However, as the criminal cases unfolded, the combined trial never happened. And while both defendants ended up with long prison terms, their respective routes through the justice system diverged before the trial could begin.

Among the Bell 8, Rizzo bore the brunt of the criminal charges. He eventually faced trial on sixty-nine felony charges [70] stemming from his tenure as Bell's chief administrative officer from 2003, about the time Spaccia was hired, through 2010. The charges included allegations that he falsified public records, misappropriated public funds, engaged in conflicts of interest, committed perjury, and engaged in a conspiracy to commit those felonies. [71] [72] [73] Most of the felony charges were related to the loans to city employees that Rizzo authorized. [74]

One of the primary distinctions that set Rizzo and Spaccia apart from the councilmembers was the quality of their legal representation. Both retained highly respected criminal lawyers. Rizzo's lawyer was James Spertus, a founding partner at Spertus, Landes & Umhofer, LLP, a Los Angeles-area criminal defense firm. Prior to starting the firm, Spertus was a federal prosecutor. [75] Since switching to criminal defense in 2006, he has gained a substantial degree of respect in the legal community; he's been named a "Southern California Super Lawyer" [76] every year since 2009 and one of the "Best Lawyers in America" every year since 2012. [77]

Rizzo and Spaccia, despite being tried together, mounted divergent legal arguments in their defense. One of Rizzo's main defenses was a separation-of-powers argument. During opening statements in the February 2011 preliminary hearing on Rizzo and Spaccia's criminal charges, Spertus declared that "everyone was agreed that it's not a crime to be paid too much," and that the city council legally approved the city budgets and delegated decision-making authority to Rizzo.[78] Rizzo, in other words, was simply acting according to decisions made by the city's legislative branch. The principle of separation of powers maintains that the three branches of government have distinct responsibilities and powers that should not conflict with one another. Spertus argued that the Los Angeles County District Attorney, part of the executive branch, was violating the principle by asking the court, a part of the judicial branch, to tell the Bell Council, a legislature, what it can and cannot do in setting salaries and delegating authority.[79]

Spertus never got to try the argument on a jury. In a surprise move, on October 3, 2013, Rizzo accepted a plea bargain. In exchange for pleading "no contest" to all sixty-nine felony counts against him, his punishment would be limited to ten to twelve years in state prison. Rizzo also agreed to testify against Spaccia at her trial.[80]

About two months later, he also struck a deal with federal prosecutors. Despite not having yet been charged with a federal crime, Rizzo pleaded guilty to the felony charges of conspiracy and "conspiracy and filing a false federal income tax return with the Internal Revenue Service" by creating a dummy "corporation to fraudulently claim losses on his income tax return" to reduce the tax liability from his Bell salary.[81]

In April 2014, merely days before his sentencing hearing before Kennedy, Rizzo was sentenced for his IRS convictions to serve thirty-three months in federal prison and pay $250,000 in restitution to the IRS. Importantly, the federal judge recommended that his sentence would run consecutively with any state court sentence he would receive; however, Judge Kennedy allowed the federal and state terms to run concurrently.[82]

Rizzo's state court sentencing hearing before Kennedy two days later was one of the very few times he spoke publicly about his role in the corruption. His statement, however, was not as strong, detailed, or remorseful as many may have hoped.

Judge Kennedy was apparently unmoved. "[I]t is a good thing to hear that he is sorry," she replied, "but it doesn't change the fact that Mr. Rizzo, you did some very, very bad things for a very long time."[83] She further called him a "kind of godfather-like character," and that he "was controlling everything" in Bell.[84] Rizzo was sentenced to the maximum twelve years in state prison and was ordered to pay almost $9 million in restitution.[85]

Spaccia traveled a different path to conviction. She faced thirteen felony counts, many fewer than Rizzo. But they were familiar ones: misappropriation of public funds, conspiracy to misappropriate public funds, conflict of interest, and secretion of the public record.[86]

Spaccia's high-caliber legal team was led by Harland Braun, who like Spertus had also received recognition from the legal community for his defense work.[87] However, his colorful career perhaps prepared him better than Spertus for the media attention surrounding the Bell 8. Braun had been involved in many famous cases: He represented a doctor accused of over-prescribing painkillers to Elizabeth Taylor,[88] one of the police officers acquitted of beating Rodney King,[89] and many celebrities.[90] He was perhaps most famous for the 1980s "Twilight Zone" manslaughter case, when he won acquittal of director John Landis and producer George Folsey, Jr. over the deaths of two child actors after a helicopter crashed on the set.[91]

Much of Spaccia's defense rested on her subordinate position in Bell's government. She argued that her position as assistant chief administrative officer gave her no authority comparable to other executive positions. The City Charter did not give her broad powers, and only empowered her to act for the chief administrative officer when he was absent. Thus, she argued, she could not control or appropriate the city's money.[92] Lacking official control over what went on under Rizzo, she could not be held responsible.

Unlike Rizzo, Spaccia did not accept a plea bargain. Her trial opened on October 24, 2013, three weeks after Rizzo pleaded no contest.[93] In December 2013, after four weeks of testimony and more than two weeks of deliberation, the jury found Spaccia guilty of eleven of the thirteen counts. She was acquitted of one count of secretion of funds, and the judge declared a mistrial on one count of misappropriation of funds after the jury could not make a decision.[94]

Strangely, Rizzo did not participate in Spaccia's trial. As part of his plea bargain, he agreed to cooperate with prosecutors to testify truthfully against Spaccia. But Rizzo was never called to the stand by either side during Spaccia's trial.[95] And when Braun subpoenaed Rizzo to testify at Spaccia's sentencing hearing, the judge quashed it, arguing that there was little he could add in support of a lighter sentence for his former assistant.[96] Braun would later argue that Rizzo's whole plea bargain was invalid, and that the District Attorney's Office was under a lot of political pressure to win the case that forced them into a deal they should not have made.[97]

At her sentencing hearing on April 10, 2014, Spaccia fared little better than Rizzo. Kennedy said, "Miss Spaccia likes to portray herself as somehow a victim of Mr. Rizzo. She is no victim."[98] Playing on the infamous "pigs and hogs"email from Spaccia to Adams, Kennedy concluded, "[i]t was all about the money. And it was about greed. And ultimately what happened is that both Rizzo and Spaccia were not content with being pigs; they were hogs. And they basically got slaughtered because you can't keep these kinds of things hidden forever."[99]

Spaccia was sentenced to serve eleven years, eight months in state prison and ordered to pay $8.2 million in restitution.[100]

The court proceedings did not stop with the convictions of the Bell 8. Their punishment provided little practical relief for a city reeling from the theft of millions of dollars from its coffers. The fight to recover that money spawned a series of civil suits by and on behalf of Bell, and reciprocal lawsuits by the ousted officials. The cases dragged on for years, though Bell was eventually able to recover some of the lost money as well as relieve much of the potential future liabilities against it.

The first court case was not the criminal complaint. On September 15, 2010, a week before the criminal complaints were filed, the California Attorney General had filed a civil complaint on behalf of Bell against Rizzo, Spaccia, and Councilmembers Hernandez, Jacobo, Cole, Bello, and Mirabal. Former Police Chief Randy Adams, who was not criminally charged, was also named. [101]

The Attorney General brought six claims against the defendants, though only Rizzo was charged with all six. The first was for waste of public funds and illegal expenditure of public funds. All of the defendants were named in this claim, as each had excessive salaries and collaborated in the wasteful expenditure of public funds. Rizzo and the councilmembers were also charged with negligence for failing to exercise the necessary duty of care and due diligence required by their positions in authorizing employment and other contracts.

They were also alleged to have committed fraudulent deceit in relation to the Council's misrepresenting facts in meeting minutes related to Ordinance No. 1158 in order to mislead the public about their salaries; this ordinance would become known as the "misleading ordinance." Related to the "misleading ordinance," the Attorney General claimed that Rizzo also committed fraudulent deceit by deliberately misleading Bell residents about his and councilmembers' salaries by distributing a memo containing false and incomplete salary information, a document referred to as the "misleading memorandum." Rizzo and Spaccia were charged with violating Government Code section 1090, which is essentially a public employee conflict-of-interest law, prohibiting public officials and employees from entering into contracts in their official capacities in which they have a personal financial interest. The sixth claim, brought against all of the defendants, was for breaching their fiduciary duties and violating the public trust as city officers and employees for their excessive salaries and efforts to deceive Bell residents about the extent of their compensation. [102]

Finally, the Attorney General named Bell itself as a defendant, even though at the same time it was acting on behalf of the city. In September 2010, the councilmembers and other Bell officials involved in the scandal still held positions of power in Bell. Unsurprisingly, they did not agree to pursue litigation against themselves. Further, the city was still paying many defendants the salaries and benefits that the Attorney General was alleging were excessive and wasteful. With the city still under their control, these officials were still causing harm to the city and its finances. [103]

As the lawsuit moved through the courts, there was a changing of the guard in Bell. The 2011 municipal elections replaced all of the councilmembers who were in power during the scandal. The city then became more willing to cooperate with the Attorney General and to act on its own behalf to sue. The new councilmembers also brought on new legal counsel, namely David Aleshire and his firm Aleshire and Wydner, LLP. The firm first became involved with Bell by volunteering services to the grassroots organization, BASTA. Aleshire was appointed Bell city attorney in July 2011. The city immediately switched from opposing the Attorney General's lawsuit to supporting it. In the time between the Attorney General's filing its suit and the new elections, the case had developed into a convoluted morass that threatened to bog down entirely. Aleshire and his firm began working with the Attorney General to obtain restitution from the other defendants. [104]

The complications plaguing the Attorney General's lawsuit started soon after it was filed. Rizzo, eventually followed by the other defendants, filed a demurrer with the court—essentially a motion to dismiss the suit for failing to state a valid claim against him. Judge Ralph Dau, who presided over the civil case, had been skeptical of the complaint from the beginning, and doubted the Attorney General's ability to bring it. In a November 2010 hearing, less than two months after the complaint was filed, Dau stated, "There is a real question of authority here. You say they're looting the city and you can enforce it, but where is the case that says the attorney general can enforce it?" In the same hearing he wondered aloud whether this was "just a political lawsuit" coinciding with then-Attorney General Jerry Brown's campaign for governor. [105]

Seven months later, in May 2011, Dau granted Rizzo and the other defendants' demurrers and dismissed the Attorney General's complaint. Specifically, the court ruled that the Attorney General lacked standing to sue the defendants. Moreover, the court dismissed the case because the Bell officials had legislative immunity under the separation-of-powers doctrine from being judged by the court for their legislative acts. The council could vote to pass excessive salaries for its members and for city employees, and even though that "may be remiss, it is not actionable in civil court." The court dismissed all of the causes of action against the defendants, except for one against Rizzo and Spaccia, "with prejudice," meaning that those claims could never again be brought against the defendants. [106] [107]

The Attorney General's Office, working with Bell's attorneys, appealed the decision. Almost two years after Judge Dau's ruling, the California Court of Appeals for the Second District ruled on the appeal. As will be noted later, this decision is likely to have a larger impact than the Bell case alone on civil suits regarding public municipal corruption in California. On the merits of the case, the decision was mixed for the Attorney General, though the court mostly ruled in its favor.

First, the appeals court held that the Attorney General did in fact have standing to sue on behalf of the Bell and its taxpayers to seek restitution from the former officials. This reversed the heart of the trial court's ruling concerning separation of powers and legislative immunity. Specifically, the appeals court held that the alleged *ultra vires* actions by Rizzo and the councilmembers were not protected. This means that actions or decisions outside the scope of the officials' authority—such as a council action not granted by the city charter, or Rizzo's entering into a contract that was not authorized by the Council—can expose the officials to liability.

The excessive salaries that Rizzo bestowed upon himself and other officials were therefore not protected actions. The "misleading ordinance" was protected by legislative immunity, the court ruled, but not the "misleading memorandum."

The appellate court's ruling had differing impacts on the various defendants. The court allowed all of the causes of action for restitution to be refiled against Rizzo and Spaccia. The former councilmembers were granted some legislative immunity, though their excessive salaries and duty of care owed to the people of Bell still exposed them to liability before the Attorney General.

Adams received perhaps the most favorable ruling. As with the other defendants, the appellate court ruled against him on the issue of his liability for excessive pay. But it ruled in his favor on the only other claim brought against him, breach of fiduciary duty. The court held that Adams did not owe Bell a fiduciary duty when negotiating his contract because he did not become a city employee until after the contract was executed.[108] The court of appeals' argument paralleled the Assistant District Attorney's argument to Judge Kennedy a year and half prior as to why Adams was never criminally prosecuted.

Almost two years later, in March 2015, the Attorney General filed a new complaint based on the court of appeals decision to proceed with the litigation. The amnded complaint notably does not include either Rizzo or Adams as defendants.[109] Both Rizzo and Adams settled their civil claims with the city and returned the money that they owed. With these settlements, there was no need for the Attorney General to proceed in a lawsuit against them on behalf of Bell. However, the second amended complaint is proceeding against the other Bell 8 defendants who have not resolved their civil claims with Bell. The new case is still awaiting trial.

Some of the complexity of the Attorney General's case arose not from the complaint itself, but from the related cases that it spawned between the defendants and the city. One of the most important and potentially expensive set of cases involved the issue of the city's indemnification of its former employees as provided in their employment contracts.

As with the demurrers to dismiss the Attorney General's case, Rizzo was the first defendant to file an action against the city to indemnify him for the legal costs he incurred from the defending his civil as well as criminal cases. The clause in Rizzo's employment contracts provided that:

> City shall defend, hold harmless and indemnify Employee against any claim, demand, judgment or action, of any type or kind, arising out of any act or failure to act, by Employee, if such act or failure to act was within the course and scope of Employee's employment. City may compromise and settle any such claim or suit provided City shall bear the entire cost of any such settlement. [110]

Rizzo used this clause as well as state statutory provisions providing for a government employer to indemnify and defend officials and employees for criminal and civil cases against them in their official capacity. He filed his indemnity claim against the city in October 2010, scarcely a month after the Attorney General commenced its suit against him and his former colleagues. [111] Within the next year, all of the defendants would file similar lawsuits against Bell to recover their litigation fees. [112]

The indemnification claims presented an especially thorny issue for the city. The claims brought by the former officials and employees represented a huge liability for Bell, with potential costs running into several million dollars if they lost all of the indemnification suits. For example, Randy Adams was claiming $500,000 in legal fees for defense against the Attorney General lawsuit alone through October 2011. And the Bell 8 clearly had legal fees for the criminal defense case on top of the civil matters, which would compound legal fees beyond what Adams was claiming. On top of all this were the eventual lawsuits by the former employees to recover unpaid wages and the wrongful termination suits that many of them would file against Bell. [113]

Beyond the direct costs of this litigation was the potentially negative effect that indemnification would have on Bell's efforts to reclaim the money taken by the former employees and officials. Bringing a suit against them to recover lost money would mean that the city would have to pay not only for the prosecution but also for the defense. Doing so would be prohibitively expensive and would dramatically change the calculus about which lawsuits the city could bring. In short, Bell desperately needed to end its indemnity obligations.

Relief was a long time coming. Rizzo, as the first to file a claim for indemnification, was the first case to be definitively decided. Due to the complex procedural nature of the case, intertwined as it was with the Attorney General's suit, civil cross-complaints between Rizzo and Bell, two criminal prosecutions and an indictment, the case had still not been heard on the merits by January 2013, nearly two years later. In March, Bell filed a petition for a writ of mandate from the court of appeals on whether Rizzo was entitled to a jury trial for the indemnification case. The court of appeals issued a decision about six months later, in October 2013. The court did not actually decide the jury trial issue, but instead, issued a decision that was very favorable for Bell as well as for other cities seeking restitution in the future from corrupt former employees. The appellate court concluded that, as a matter of law, the indemnification clause in Rizzo's employment contract, as well as applicable statutory provisions, did not compel Bell to pay Rizzo's legal expenses for any of the criminal or civil cases arising out of his alleged corruption.[114]

The court of appeals decision only directly decided the issue of Bell's indemnifying Rizzo's claims, which itself was a major win for the city. The other former officials and employees seeking indemnification had similar contract language and arguments as Rizzo, meaning that the appellate decision could be used to dismiss their suits as well. As a result, Bell's litigation costs and potential liability declined substantially.

As the litigation dragged on through the years, Bell and its former employees continued to file civil cases against each other. In particular, Rizzo, Spaccia, and Adams each filed complaints against Bell for wrongful termination of employment and sought for the city to pay for unpaid wages and benefits they had accrued since July 2010. In November 2011, Rizzo, the highest-paid former official, made the largest claim. He sought approximately $1.5 million in damages as a "severance payment" for the salary he should have received from Bell.[115] Rizzo claimed that he did not get a thirty-day written notice of termination, as required by his contract. He further alleged that he was entitled to severance pay if the city terminated him unless he was *first* convicted of a felony or a crime involving moral turpitude. Around the same time, Spaccia filed a similar, albeit smaller wrongful-termination claim against Bell, seeking $800,000, including indemnification costs. Approximately a year later, Adams also sued the city, seeking over $500,000 in unpaid wages, leave, and benefits. In all three cases, Bell countersued, seeking restitution for the money taken by the former employees.[116]

None of these cases turned out well for the former Bell employees. Rizzo's lawsuit went nowhere. After stipulating with Bell to postpone hearing the case until after the conclusion of the criminal case against him, Rizzo withdrew his claim.[117] Spaccia pursued her claim, but the judge granted the city's motion to dismiss her case for breach of contract as a matter of law.[118] Adams's case likewise never made it to trial; instead, he settled with the city to dismiss both their claims. As part of the settlement, Adams agreed to pay Bell approximately $214,000 to make his compensation as Bell police chief commensurate with his previous salary as Glendale chief, as well as with the salary of the prior Bell chief.[119]

The civil suits were not limited to members of the Bell 8 being criminally prosecuted by the L.A. District Attorney or civilly prosecuted by the Attorney General. The sheer scope of the scandal meant that there were many more people involved than could be brought to justice. And Bell's recovery efforts were resisted by former Bell officials who were never criminally charged. In particular, the director of general services, Eric Eggena, waged a familiar suit-countersuit battle with the city.

Like Adams, Eggena was never criminally prosecuted, but he was fired from his positions as city prosecutor and director of general services without notice in October 2010. Two years later, he filed a complaint against Bell alleging that his termination breached his employment contract, and he sought compensation for severance pay, unpaid wages, leave benefits, and health benefits. He also asked for punitive damages and attorney's fees. [120]

Specifically, Eggena claimed he was owed 192 vacation days and 137 sick days accrued over his eight years as a Bell employee. He also sought eighteen months' salary as severance at his final annual compensation of $421,000. In total, Eggena claimed Bell owed him $837,000. [121] [122] As with the other lawsuits from former officials, Bell filed a countersuit against Eggena, claiming that Eggena violated the False Claims Act and sought as damages all compensation he received pursuant to employment contract addenda that were not approved by the council. [123] From his hiring in 2002 to 2010, Eggena's salary rose by over 500 percent; beginning in 2006, Rizzo amended his employment agreement several times without council approval. Eggena's benefits also increased dramatically during this period. In its lawsuit, Bell asked for more than $2 million from Eggena. [124]

This case did not make it to trial. In December 2013, Bell settled the case and paid Eggena $50,000 to satisfy all of his claims. [125]

Not all of the wrongful-termination claims brought against Bell went so smoothly for the city. James Corcoran, in particular, had a strong case. Corcoran was the Bell police sergeant who was demoted and later put on administrative leave by former chief Adams after Corcoran and other officials contacted the District Attorney and Attorney General in 2009. Learning that Rizzo wanted him fired, [126] Corcoran resigned in April. [127]

In July 2010, about a month after the *Los Angeles Times* broke the scandal, Corcoran filed a whistleblower lawsuit against Bell. [128] He had served as a Bell officer for more than eighteen years "with an essentially clean record," as City Attorney David Aleshire put it. The case went to mediation with retired federal Judge Dickran Tevrizian as mediator. Tevrizian advised the city that Corcoran could win more than $3 million from a jury if the case went to trial, in part because the ongoing corruption cases would cast Bell officials in a negative light. Tevrizian recommended that Bell settle Corcoran's lawsuit for $1.6 million. [129]

But the ultimate settlement was for much less. After receiving an initial offer, Corcoran decided that he would rather resume his job in Bell than get paid for damages.[130] In August of 2012, the council agreed to reinstate Corcoran as a sergeant, pay him $240,000 in compensation for lost wages along with two years' purchased CALPERS retirement credit, and pay $160,000 in legal fees.[131] In all, it was about $1.1 million less than the mediator's recommendation.

The court cases clearly had a tremendous impact at the local level. They punished Rizzo, Spaccia, and the former councilmembers, recovered some misappropriated city funds, and perhaps more importantly relieved some of Bell's potential future pension and other liabilities. However, the Bell litigation will also have great implications for future California municipalities dealing with public corruption. These implications arise from two important appellate court decisions: *People ex rel. Harris v. Rizzo*[132] and *City of Bell v. Superior Court.*[133]

In a common-law legal system like California's, judges have to follow legal precedent in deciding a case. Most court decisions are unpublished, meaning that they have no precedential value, and bind only the parties to that particular case. When a higher-level court decides a case important enough to have impacts on other cases, the court will "publish" the decision and give it precedential authority on future lower-court decisions. The court of appeals published both of these decisions.

The first, *People ex rel. Harris v. Rizzo*, was decided in March 2013. This appellate decision dealt with whether the state Attorney General could file a civil lawsuit on Bell's behalf. In September of 2010, the Attorney General sued Rizzo, Spaccia, the councilmembers, Randy Adams, and Bell.[134] All of the defendants filed a demurrer, a motion challenging the sufficiency of the Attorney General's complaint. The trial court granted the defendants' demurrers and dismissed the complaint.[135]

The Attorney General's appeal raised many issues, ranging from procedural questions to separation-of-powers concerns. But the one with the greatest implications for future corruption cases was whether the Attorney General had "standing" to sue the defendants. To have standing to sue, a party must have suffered harm or otherwise have a connection to the issues over which it is bringing the lawsuit. At first glance, it is not obvious that the Attorney General, as a state-level agency, should have standing to sue over what were municipal-level harms. In the complaint, the Attorney General did not allege any specific harm to the agency or the state. Instead, the agency was bringing the complaint on behalf of Bell.

In a forty-three–page decision, the court of appeals ruled that the Attorney General indeed did have standing in the case. The Attorney General draws its authority from the California Constitution, which provides that "the Attorney

General shall be the chief law officer of the state. It shall be the duty of the Attorney General that the laws of the state are uniformly and adequately enforced."[136] This constitutional duty, the court found, includes bringing civil lawsuits "necessary for the enforcement of the laws of the state, the preservation of order, and the protection of public rights and interests."

As part of this duty, the Attorney General could sue on behalf of Bell to bring order to the city in the wake of the corruption. Furthermore, the Attorney General could sue on behalf of the city while at the same time naming the city as a defendant. The appeals court reasoned that the city could not consent to sue on its behalf because at the time the complaint was filed the city "was still under the control of [the] defendants" and "[continued] to pay defendants their excessive and wasteful salaries."[137] The court of appeals ultimately reversed the trial court decision and reinstated the Attorney General's.

This decision sets a powerful precedent for future public corruption cases. Municipalities suffering from public corruption and that have lost a significant amount of their treasury are in a poor position to recover stolen funds. This is particularly true for small, already low-income cities like Bell, which spent almost $4.5 million on litigation between 2011 and 2014. Being able to partner with the Attorney General to pursue civil litigation to recover misappropriated funds and other damages gives municipalities a greater ability to recover after the corruption ends. In instances when corruption is still ongoing, the Attorney General can litigate on the city's behalf.[138]

The second published decision was handed down by the same panel of appellate judges later that year, in October 2013. *City of Bell v. Superior Court* arose from the same Attorney General's complaint as *People ex rel. Harris v. Rizzo*. After Rizzo was sued by the Attorney General on Bell's behalf, Rizzo cross-sued the city to indemnify him for the costs of defending himself in the suit. He didn't stop there. Over time, Rizzo sought city indemnification for two civil cases and three criminal cases.

Rizzo had both a contractual and a statutory basis for these efforts. First, his employment contract contained an explicit indemnification clause. Second, California law generally requires municipalities and other public entities to indemnify their employees for civil cases that arose within the employee's scope of employment.[139] However, an important exception allows public entities to refuse to indemnify employees if the act or omission that led to the suit falls outside the employee's scope of employment; the employee's actions or omissions were the result of fraud, corruption, or actual malice; or defending the employee would create a conflict of interest between the entity and the employee.[140]

Public entities are allowed, but not required, to indemnify employees in criminal cases.[141] Following several adverse rulings at the trial court level, Bell filed to have this issue heard by the court of appeals.

In a thirty-seven–page decision, the court of appeals held that Bell did not have to indemnify Rizzo in any of his civil or criminal cases. The court interpreted the indemnity agreement as not to include civil or criminal claims made by or on behalf of the city. Furthermore, the court determined that the statutory provisions on indemnification prohibited Bell from providing a defense for Rizzo in his civil and criminal cases. Lastly, the court looked at the public policy implications of Bell indemnifying Rizzo. Reviewing the allegations against him, the court found it "difficult to believe that any expenditure of City funds to defend Rizzo would not constitute an impermissible waste of public funds," and that "the idea that the City must pay Rizzo additional funds in order to provide him a defense against the very actions seeking to obtain justice for the City is unacceptable."

The court rejected the "concept that a public entity allegedly victimized by a corrupt employee must provide that employee with a defense to those charges."[142]

This decision has profound implications for public corruption cases. Previously, the law had effectively barred victimized municipalities from trying to recover stolen money from their corrupt employees. Not only were indemnity clauses very common in public employment contracts, but statutory provisions created a barrier as well. If a city did seek restitution, the employee could seek indemnification from it, making the restitution case a useless exercise. This ruling meant that a municipality seeking to recover funds from a corrupt employee would not have to pay for a defense against its own efforts.[143]

NOTES

1. Thomas Jefferson, "10 Nov. 1798, Writings 17:385–91," in *The Writings of Thomas Jefferson*, eds. Andrew A. Lipscomb and Albert Ellery Bergh (Washington: Thomas Jefferson Memorial Association, 1905), http://press-pubs.uchicago.edu/founders/documents/v1ch8s41.html.

2. Gottlieb, J. & Vives, R. "Is a City Manager Worth $800,000?" *Los Angeles Times*. July 15, 2010. Retrieved from http://articles.latimes.com/2010/jul/15/local/la-me-bell-salary-20100715.

3. "Bell City Council Meeting Postponed." July 23, 2010. Retrieved from https://www.youtube.com/watch?v=7hYCWy2ueO0.

4. "Protests in Bell: City Residents Say 'Enough!'" July 27, 2010. Retrieved from https://www.youtube.com/watch?v=v1effEnDsrM.

5. Ibid.

6. "Bell Officials Arrested." September 21, 2010. Retrieved from https://www.youtube.com/watch?v=x1Zj5MjFFo0.

7. Vives, R. & Gottlieb, J. "3 Bell Leaders to Quit in Pay Scandal." *Los Angeles Times.* July 23, 2010. Retrieved from http://articles.latimes.com/2010/jul/23/local/la-me-bell-council-20100723.

8. Adams v. Bell. BC489331. Deposition of Randy Adams. May 1, 2013. p. 34.

9. Rizzo v. Bell. BC472566. Complaint for Damages. October 31, 2011; *see also* Martinez, M. "Former Bell, California, Administrator Sues City for His $11,000 Monthly Salary." *CNN.* November 1, 2011. Retrieved from http://www.cnn.com/2011/11/01/us/california-bell-lawsuit.

10. CA. Government Code § 1770(h).

11. Vives. R. & Gottlieb, J. "Bell councilmembers Cut Salaries 90 percent; Some Will Forgo Pay." *Los Angeles Times.* July 27, 2010. Retrieved from http://articles.latimes.com/2010/jul/27/local/la-me-bell-salaries-20100727.

12. "Pay Scandal, Resignation Deflate City Council in Bell, California." *CNN.* October 5, 2010. Retrieved from http://www.cnn.com/2010/CRIME/10/05/california.bell.council/.

13. Ali Saleh, interview with author, February 12, 2015, pp. 27–28.

14. Hogen-Esch, T. "Predator State: Corruption in a Council-Manager System – The Case of Bell, California." (white paper at the City of Bell Scandal Revisited Conference, Chapman University, 2015). p. 14.

15. CA. Const. art.II §§ 13–19.

16. Garcia, C. "Building BASTA." (white paper at the City of Bell Scandal Revisited Conference, Chapman University, 2015). p. 11.

17. Hogen-Esch, Predator State, p. 18.

18. Goffard, C. & Esquival, P. "Bell Voters Cast Out the Old and Opt for the New." *Los Angeles Times.* March 9, 2011. Retrieved from http://articles.latimes.com/2011/mar/09/local/la-me-bell-elections-20110308.

19. "Bell Election: Newly Elected Pledge to Sweep Out City Hall; Interim Administrator likely to be Fired [Updated]." *Los Angeles Times.* March 9, 2011. Retrieved from http://latimesblogs.latimes.com/lanow/2011/03/bell-rizzo-fire-carrillo-casso-police-disband-corruption.html.

20. People v. Hernandez, Jacobo, Mirabal, Cole, Bello, and Artiga. BA376025. Amended Complaint. March 18, 2011.

21. Knoll, C., Gottlieb, J., & Goffard, C. "Blame Flies as Bell Trial Begins." *Los Angeles Times.* January 24, 2013. Retrieved from http://articles.latimes.com/2013/jan/24/local/la-me-0125-bell-trial-20130125.

22. Knoll, C., Vives, R. & Winton, R. "Five of 6 Ex-Bell Council Members Found Guilty in Corruption Trial." *Los Angeles Times.* March 20, 2013. Retrieved from http://articles.latimes.com/2013/mar/20/local/la-me-bell-verdict-20130321-1.

23. Granda, C. "Bell Corruption Trial: Luis Artiga Acquitted on All Charges." *ABC 7 News.* March 20, 2013. Retrieved from http://abc7.com/archive/9035318/.

24. Gottlieb, J. "Bell: A Total Breakdown." (white paper at the City of Bell Scandal Revisited Conference, Chapman University, 2015).

25. Ibid.

26. Gottlieb & Vives, Is a City Manager.

27. Tasci, C. "Former Bell Councilman Luis Artiga's House in Chino Quiet After Verdict." *Daily Bulletin News.* March 20, 2013. Retrieved from http://www.dailybulletin.com/general-news/20130320/former-bell-councilman-luis-artigas-house-in-chino-quiet-after-verdict.

28. James Corcoran, interview with author, February 12, 2015.

29. Knoll, Vives, & Winton, Five of 6.

30. Knoll, C., Winton, R., & Vives, R. "Bell Trial Ends in Chaos." *Los Angeles Times.* March 21, 2013. Retrieved from http://articles.latimes.com/2013/mar/21/local/la-me-0322-bell-jury-20130322.

31. Ibid.

32. Keith, T. "5 Former Bell City Council Members Accept Plea Deal, Face Maximum 4 Years in Prison." *Los Angeles Daily News.* April 9, 2014. Retrieved from http://www.dailynews.com/government-and-politics/20140409/5-former-bell-city-council-members-accept-plea-deal-face-maximum-4-years-in-prison.

33. Knoll, C. "Former Bell Councilwoman Teresa Jacobo Gets Two-Year Prison Sentence." *Los Angeles Times.* July 25, 2014. Retrieved from http://www.latimes.com/local/la-me-bell-sentence-20140726-story.html.

34. Rogers, J. "Ex-Officials Convicted in California Corruption Case." *The Big Story.* March 20, 2013. Retrieved from http://bigstory.ap.org/article/verdicts-reached-bell-calif-corruption-case.

35. Knoll, Former Bell Councilwoman.

36. Ibid.

37. Corcoran, interview.

38. Ibid, p. 52.

39. Knoll, Former Bell Councilwoman.

40. Knoll, C. "Ex-Bell Council Member Gets 2 Years in Prison for Role in Pay Scandal." *Los Angeles Times.* July 25, 2014. Retrieved from http://www.latimes.com/local/lanow/la-me-ln-ex-bell-council-member-sentenced-20140725-story.html.

41. Ibid.

42. People v. Jacobo. BA376025-02. Sentencing Minutes. July 25, 2014.

43. "Ex-Bell, Calif., Mayor Oscar Hernandez Too Uneducated to Know His Actions Were Illegal, Lawyer Says." *The Associated Press.* February 21, 2013. http://www.cbsnews.com/news/ex-bell-calif-mayor-oscar-hernandez-too-uneducated-to-know-his-actions-were-illegal-lawyer-says/.

44. Goffard, C. "How Bell Hit Bottom." *Los Angeles Times.* December 28, 2010. Retrieved from http://www.latimes.com/local/la-me-bell-origins-20101228-story.html#page=1.

45. People v. Hernandez. BA376025. People's Sentencing Memorandum. July 24, 2014, at p. 17.

46. Ibid.

47. Hernandez, M. "Ex-Bell Mayor Oscar Hernandez Sentenced in Corruption Scandal." *ABC 7 News.* July 31, 2014. http://abc7.com/news/ex-bell-mayor-oscar-hernandez-sentenced/230499/.

48. People v. Hernandez. BA376025-01. Sentencing Minutes. July 31, 2014.

49. Ibid.

50. Ibid.

51. Knoll, C. "Former Bell Mayor Gets a Year in Jail For Salary Scandal." *Los Angeles Times.* July 31, 2014. Retrieved from http://www.latimes.com/local/lanow/la-me-ln-former-bell-mayor-sentenced-20140731-story.html.

52. Gottlieb, J. "Bell Corruption: Former Councilman Gets One Year in Jail." *Los Angeles Times.* July 11, 2014. Retrieved from http://www.latimes.com/local/lanow/la-me-ln-ex-bell-councilman-sentenced-corruption-20140711-story.html.

53. Ibid.

54. Ibid.

55. Ibid.

56. Ibid.

57. Sprague, M. "Bell Sues Ex-Councilman, Construction Company, Foundation for $3.4 Million." *Whittier Daily News.* June 25, 2014. Retrieved from http://www.whittierdailynews.com/general-news/20140625/bell-sues-ex-councilman-construction-company-foundation-for-34-million.

58. Ibid.

59. Ibid.

60. Lloyd, J. "Ex-Bell Councilman Sentenced to Home Confinement in Corruption Scandal." *NBC Los Angeles.* July 23, 2014. http://www.nbclosangeles.com/news/local/Bell-City-Corruption-Scandal-George-Cole-268307752.html.

61. Ibid.

62. People v. Cole. BA376025-04. Sentencing Minutes. July 23, 2014.

63. Ibid.

64. Ibid.

65. Gottlieb, J. & Knoll, C. "Bell City Clerk Says: 'I Couldn't Ask Any Questions.'" *Los Angeles Times.* January 29, 2013. Retrieved from http://articles.latimes.com/2013/jan/29/local/la-me-0130-bell-trial-20130130.

66. People v. Bello. BA376025-05. Sentencing Minutes. August 1, 2014. p. 27.

67. Lloyd, J. & Wire Reports. "Last of Ex-Bell Officials Sentenced to Jail in Corruption Scandal." *NBC4 Los Angeles-KNBC.* August 1, 2014. Retrieved from http://www.nbclosangeles.com/news/local/Bell-City-Council-Corruption-Scandal-Victor-Bello-269596251.html.

68. Knoll, C. "Final Bell Council Member Sentenced." *Los Angeles Times.* August 1, 2014. Retrieved from http://www.latimes.com/local/politics/la-me-0802-bell-finale-20140802-story.html.

69. Ibid.

70. *See, for example,* Grad, S. & Yoshino, K. "Bell's Robert Rizzo Pleads No Contest, To Get 10 to 12 Years in Prison." *Los Angeles Times.* October 3, 2013. Retrieved from http://articles.latimes.com/2013/oct/03/local/la-me-ln-bell-robert-rizzo-pleads-no-contest-prison-20131003.

71. Ibid

72. People v. Rizzo, Spaccia, Artiga, and Hernandez. BA376026. Amended Felony Complaint. February 7, 2011.

73. People v. Rizzo, Spaccia. BA382701. Criminal Indictment. March 29, 2011.

74. "The City of Bell Scandal Revisited." Conference Transcript. February 19, 2015. p. 6.

75. Spertus, Landes & Umhofer, LLP. "James W. Spertus – Managing Partner." N.D. Retrieved from http://www.spertuslaw.com/attorney/james-w-spertus/.

76. Super Lawyers. "James W. Spertus." N.D. Retrieved from http://profiles.superlawyers.com/california-southern/los-angeles/lawyer/james-w-spertus/bd14c9fc-cadb-4fca-82cd-bc44567fa1f4.html.

77. Best Lawyers. "James W. Spertus." N.D. Retrieved from https://www.bestlawyers.com/lawyers/james-w-spertus/128574/.

78. People v. Rizzo, Spaccia, Artiga, and Hernandez. BA376026. Preliminary Hearing. February 22, 2011. p. 9.

79. The City of Bell, Conference Transcript, p. 5.

80. Grad & Yoshino, Bell's Robert.

81. U.S. Attorney's Office. "Former Chief Administrative Officer for City of Bell Agrees to Plead Guilty to Conspiracy and Tax Charges in Plot to Avoid Income Taxes." December 12, 2013. Retrieved from https://www.fbi.gov/losangeles/press-releases/2013/former-chief-administrative-officer-for-city-of-bell-agrees-to-plead-guilty-to-conspiracy-and-tax-charges-in-plot-to-avoid-income-taxes.

82. "Robert Rizzo Sentenced to 33 Months in Prison for Tax Evasion." *Abc7.com.* April 14, 2014. Retrieved from http://abc7.com/archive/9503371/.

83. Ibid, p. 30.

84. Ibid, p. 28.

85. Gottlieb, J., Knoll, C., & Goffard, C. "Bell's Rizzo Sentenced to 12 Years in Prison." *Los Angeles Times.* April 16, 2014. Retrieved from http://www.latimes.com/local/la-me-0417-rizzo-prison-20140417-story.html#page=1.

86. Pamer, M. "Jury Finds Angela Spaccia Guilty of Multiple Counts in Bell Corruption Trial." *KTLA5.* December 9, 2013. Retrieved from http://ktla.com/2013/12/09/verdict-reached-in-corruption-trial-of-ex-bell-administrator-angela-spaccia/.

87. Super Lawyers. "Harland W. Braun." N.D. Retrieved from http://profiles.superlawyers.com/california-southern/los-angeles/lawyer/harland-w-braun/2946e2d6-c0e0-4644-a040-16e25d7145d8.html.

88. Lee, J. & Ellis, V. "Taylor Doctors Are Accused of Prescription Violations." *Los Angeles Times.* September 8, 1990. Retrieved from http://articles.latimes.com/1990-09-08/local/me-466_1_elizabeth-taylor.

89. Decker, T. "Braun's Defense is Aggressive Defense." *Los Angeles Times.* May 12, 2001. Retrieved from http://articles.latimes.com/2001/may/12/local/me-62610.

90. O'Neill, A. "Harland Braun is Unfazed by His Clients' Fame." *CNN.* October 4, 2010. Retrieved from http://www.cnn.com/2010/CRIME/10/04/celebrity.lawyer.braun/.

91. Ibid.

92. BA376026, Preliminary Hearing, February 22, 2011, pp. 14–15.

93. Holguin, R. & Gregory, J. "Bell Corruption Case: Angela Spaccia in Hot Seat." *Abc7.com.* October 24, 2013. Retrieved from http://abc7.com/archive/9298404/.

94. Pamer, Jury Finds.

95. People v. Spaccia. BA376026, BA382701. Sentencing Minutes. April 10, 2014. pp. 2–3.

96. Ibid, pp. 4–14.

97. The City of Bell, Conference Transcript, pp. 11–12.

98. BA376026, BA382701, Sentencing Minutes, April 10, 2014, p. 64.

99. Ibid, p. 68.

100. Orzeck, K. "Ex-Calif. Official Gets Nearly 12 Yrs. For Corruption." *Law360.* April 10, 2014. Retrieved from http://www.law360.com/articles/527227/ex-calif-city-official-gets-nearly-12-yrs-for-corruption.

101. State of California Department of Justice Office of the Attorney General. "Brown Sues to Recover Bell Officials' Excessive Salaries and Cut Their Pensions, And Announces Other Steps on Public Pay and Benefits." September 1, 2010. Retrieved from http://oag.ca.gov/news/press-releases/brown-sues-recover-bell-officials-excessive-salaries-and-cut-their-pensions-and.

102. People ex rel Brown v. Rizzo, Spaccia, Adams, Hernandez, Jacobo, Cole, Bello, and Mirabal. BC445497. First Amended Complaint. November 15, 2010.

103. Ibid.

104. Aleshire, D. & Taylor, A. "Corruption on Steroids: The Bell Scandal from the Legal Perspective." (white paper at the City of Bell Scandal Revisited Conference, Chapman University, 2015).

105. Winton, R. "Attorney General's Lawsuit Against Bell Officials Could be in Jeopardy." *Los Angeles Times.* November 5, 2010. Retrieved from http://articles.latimes.com/2010/nov/05/local/la-me-bell-ag-20101105.

106. People ex rel Brown v. Rizzo, Spaccia, Adams, Hernandez, Jacobo, Cole, Bello, and Mirabal. BC445497. Order on Demurrers and Motions to Strike Directed to First Amended Complaint. May 2, 2011.

107. Knoll, C. "Judge Tosses California's Civil Suit Against Ex-Bell Leaders." *Los Angeles Times.* May 6, 2011. Retrieved from http://articles.latimes.com/2011/may/06/local/la-me-bell-attorney-general-20110506.

108. People ex rel Harris v. Rizzo. 214 Cal.App.4th 921 (App. 2013).

109. People ex rel Harris v. Spaccia, Hernandez, Jacobo, Cole, Bello, and Mirabal. BC445497. Second Amended Complaint. N.D.

110. City of Bell v. Superior Court. 220 Cal.App.4th 236 (App. 2013).

111. Heller, M. "Calif. City Can't Escape Defense Costs for Ex-Manager." *Law360.* November 28, 2012. Retrieved from http://www.law360.com/articles/397162/calif-city-can-t-escape-defense-costs-for-ex-manager.

112. Aleshire & Taylor, Corruption.

113. Aleshire, D. "Bell Staff Report RE: Report on Status of Litigation: Conclusion of FY 2011-2012." November 7, 2012.

114. 220 Cal.App.4th 236 (App. 2013).

115. Romero, D. "Robert Rizzo Sues City of Bell for $1.5 Million." *LA Weekly.* November 11, 2013. Retrieved from http://www.laweekly.com/news/robert-rizzo-sues-city-of-bell-for-15-million-2388051.

116. Aleshire, Bell Staff, November 7, 2012.

117. Rizzo v. Bell. BC472566. Superior Court of California County of Los Angeles – Case Summary. July 5, 2015. Retrieved from http://www.lacourt.org/casesummary/ui/casesummary.aspx?.

118. Lopez de Haro, A. "Judge Dismisses Allegations of Past Assistant to Ex-Bell City Manager." *City News Service.* June 28, 2013. Retrieved from http://patch.com/california/southgate-lynwood/judge-dismisses-allegations-of-assistant-to-exbell-city-manager.

119. Adams, R. Settlement Agreement and Release of Claims. April 11, 2014.

120. Aleshire, Bell Staff, November 7, 2012.

121. Broder, K. "Fired Bell Official Joins Parade of Ex-Officials Suing the City." *All Gov California.* August 31, 2012. Retrieved from http://www.allgov.com/USA/CA/news/where-is-

the-money-going/fired-bell-official-joins-parade-of-ex-officials-suing-the-city-120831?news= 845169.

122. Gottlieb, J. "Ex-Bell Official Seeks $837,000 Payout." *Los Angeles Times.* August 28, 2012. Retrieved from http://articles.latimes.com/2012/aug/28/local/la-me-bell-20120829.

123. Aleshire, Bell Staff, November 7, 2012.

124. "Bell City Council Sues Eric Eggena for Damages in Excess of $2 Million." *Latino California.* October 1, 2012. Retrieved from http://latinocalifornia.com/home/2012/10/bell-city-council-sues-eric-eggena-for-damages-in-excess-of-2-million/.

125. Eggena, E. Settlement Agreement and Release of Claims. December 18, 2013.

126. Corcoran, interview, p. 5.

127. Gottlieb, J. "Former Bell Cop Who Blew Whistle on Alleged Corruption Gets Job Back." *Los Angeles Times*. August 3, 2012. Retrieved from http://latimesblogs.latimes.com/lanow/2012/08/former-bell-cop-who-blew-whistle-on-alleged-corruption-gets-job-back.html.

128. Winton, R. "Lawsuit Against Bell Suggests Voter Fraud in 2009 Election." *L.A. Now.* July 27, 2010. Retrieved from http://latimesblogs.latimes.com/lanow/2010/07/bell-lawsuit-suggests-voter-fraud.html.

129. Gottlieb, Former Bell.

130. Corcoran, interview, p. 32.

131. City of Bell. "Minutes of the Bell City Council/Bell Community Housing Authority/Successor Agency to the Bell Community Redevelopment Agency/Bell Public Finance Authority." August 1, 2012.

132. 214 Cal.App.4th 921 (App. 2013).

133. 220 Cal.App.4th 236 (App. 2013).

134. People ex rel Brown v. Rizzo et al.

135. 214 Cal.App.4th, pp. 934-935 (App. 2013).

136. CA. Const. art. V § 13.

137. 214 Cal.App.4th 921 (App. 2013).

138. Aleshire & Taylor, Corruption.

139. CA. Government Code § 995.

140. CA. Government Code § 995.2.

141. CA. Government Code § 995.8.

142. 220 Cal.App.4th 236 (App. 2013).

143. Aleshire & Taylor, Corruption.

Chapter Six

The Aftermath

With Gregory D. Coordes

"Sunlight is said to be the best disinfectant."
—Justice Louis D. Brandeis [1]

One of the most daunting tasks Bell faced in the wake of the corruption scandal was cleaning up the resulting legal mess. The city's former leaders had saddled it with legal liabilities for loans, pensions, and contracts that they entered into on Bell's behalf. Even though Rizzo, Spaccia, and many former councilmembers were convicted for their actions, this did not automatically absolve Bell from its obligations.

Indeed, from the initial *Los Angeles Times* exposé in July of 2010, Bell faced investigations by federal agencies such as the Securities and Exchange Commission and the Internal Revenue Service, as well as by state agencies, including the Attorney General, the State Controller, and CALPERS. The city was even named as a defendant in the civil suit filed by the Attorney General on behalf of its Bell residents. [2]

Beyond this government scrutiny, the city faced numerous lawsuits and threats of lawsuits from parties seeking the money promised them by former Bell officials with whom they entered into obligations. Even the disgraced former officials sued to enforce their illegal contracts and pension obligations. Since 2010, the city has faced more than $70 million in liability claims stemming from the scandal. [3]

Bell has also gone to court as a plaintiff. In order to recover as much as possible of the estimated $12 million dispensed in illegal compensation to former Bell officials, as well as the millions more in illegal payments to third parties authorized by the officials, the city needed to aggressively pursue the recipients in court. Bell could also seek restitution from the professional entities, such as the former city attorney's law firm and the independent accounting firm that failed in their duties to spot the corruption.[4]

This all meant that Bell needed a legal team capable of effectively handling the high volume of complex cases. This task was taken on by David Aleshire and his law firm, Aleshire & Wynder, LLP. Aleshire had almost forty years of legal experience prior to becoming the city attorney for Bell, and much of his practice had focused on municipal law. During his career, he filled the role of city attorney for thirteen southern California municipalities. For some, he has held that position for a long time, including fifteen years serving Palm Springs, seventeen years serving Lawndale, and thirty years serving Signal Hill.[5]

Aleshire also had a personal connection to the council-manager form of government that existed in Bell. His father had been city manager in several cities for thirty-five years. Through him, Aleshire learned early how municipal governments should function and how things can go wrong.[6] This background enabled him to tackle Bell's myriad legal problems.

Aleshire was not alone in representing Bell. Even though he was appointed Bell city attorney, much of the legal work was done by other members of Aleshire & Wynder, LLP. The firm was formed in 2003 by Aleshire and other lawyers specializing in public law and representing cities like Bell.[7] Anthony Taylor, a partner in the firm, acted as the lead litigator for the Bell cases.[8] Most notably, Taylor argued Bell's appeals before the California Court of Appeals in the precedent-setting cases of *People ex rel. Harris v. Rizzo*[9] and *City of Bell v. Superior Court.*[10]

Prior to being appointed city attorney, Aleshire and his firm provided free services to BASTA, one of the grassroots organizations formed in response to the *LA Times* story exposing Rizzo's large salary. He had met Christina Garcia while attending the first council meeting held after the corruption allegations became public in 2010. Garcia and the other BASTA organizers then retained Aleshire to assist them in the 2011 recall election of the councilmembers implicated in the scandal.[11] Aleshire & Wynder, LLP volunteered their time eventually performing $70,000 worth of services to help BASTA gather the four thousand signatures necessary to get the recall measure placed on the March 2011 ballot.[12]

The 2011 recall election was a resounding success for BASTA, as all of the councilmembers who were in office during the corruption were replaced.[13] Three of the newcomers, Ali Saleh, Violeta Alvarez, and Danny Harbor, were BASTA members. One of the new council's first priorities was to find a city attorney who could handle Bell's crippling legal issues.[14]

The council held a special meeting on June 6, 2011 to choose a new city attorney. Aleshire was one of three attorneys who competed for the job, and was ultimately chosen by three-two vote. His three supporters were the same three councilmembers who belonged to BASTA. The two members who voted against Aleshire, Nestor Valencia and Ana Maria Quintana, expressed concern that his work for BASTA created a conflict of interest if he were to become city attorney. However, the work done for BASTA by Aleshire and his firm was limited to the recall campaign, and it was decided that any potential conflicts connected to that work could be dealt with by the council as they arose.[15] Saleh dismissed the issue, stating, "As far as a conflict with Aleshire & Wynder, it is my understanding that all his firm did was to perform a much needed service for all of our community; they helped make sure the recall was done as efficiently and correctly as possible."[16]

Aleshire's and his firm then had to decide how to tackle the mountain of litigation facing Bell. More than sixty cases were pending in various courts and administrative proceedings, and the lawyers had to figure out how to obtain the best outcomes using the least amount of money. Bell could not afford to pursue all of the potential claims by and against the various actors in the scandal; each had to be evaluated on the likelihood of success, the probable litigation costs, the length of time the litigation would take, and the relative position of the opposing party. Aleshire and Taylor used these criteria to decide whether to litigate a case at trial, settle the case with terms the council found acceptable, or defer taking any action.[17]

One of the major cases they faced was the claim by Dexia Credit Local against Bell for the unpaid balance and interest on $35 million in taxable lease revenue bonds that the city had issued in 2007. The bonds were secured by a 23.4-acre parcel of land that was supposed to be leased by BNSF, a railroad company. At the closing of the bond sale to Dexia on October 31, 2007, former city attorney Ed Lee asserted that there was no existing litigation that would threaten the deal. This, it turned out, was not true. Five days before the closing of the bond sale, a California Environmental Quality Act petition was filed against the city and BNSF seeking to stop the latter from using the land as it intended under the lease. A court granted the petition, and BNSF was unable to use the property. The Dexia bonds went into default.[18]

In 2010, Bell missed the final interest payment and the scheduled repayment of the $35 million principal. Dexia declared the transaction to be in default and sued Bell for $38 million.[19] Dexia also sought to foreclose on the parcel securing the bond issuance. If Dexia was successful in this effort, Bell would face a major dilemma: Under a forced sale, the property was expected to bring in some $12 million to $15 million less than Bell owed. In its lawsuit, Dexia sought to collect the deficiency out of Bell's general fund.[20] [21] This would likely force the city to file for municipal bankruptcy.[22]

After four mediation sessions and a mandatory settlement conference, Dexia and Bell reached a settlement in April of 2013, less than a week before the trial date. Bell had until December 1, 2013, to sell the 23.4-acre property for at least $28.7 million, to be paid to Dexia. If it did, Dexia would be

limited to a maximum $2 million of potential deficiency against Bell. [23] [24]
Fortunately for Bell, it had found a buyer for the parcel as well as an adjacent
15-acre plot in April 2013. The developer paid $29 million for the 23.4-acre
parcel and another $15.5 million for the 15-acre plot. The sale closed prior to
the deadline, eliminating Bell's liability to Dexia, and Bell took in an additional $15.5 million. [25]

The Dexia lawsuit intersected with another suit that Bell pursued but
eventually settled. After Ed Lee, the city attorney throughout the years of
corruption, misrepresented the existence of the adverse litigation affecting
the bond sale in 2007, Dexia filed suit against his former firm, Best Best &
Krieger (BB&K). Bell also had a claim against Lee for inaction relating to
the Dexia sale but initially waived its claim so that Dexia could pursue its
claim against Lee and BB&K. [26] In the April 2013 settlement of the Dexia
claim, however, Bell agreed to receive $250,000 in entitlement costs from
BB&K in exchange for releasing it from malpractice liability connected to
the bond sale. [27]

This was not the only malpractice lawsuit against BB&K for Lee's role in
the corruption scandal. Lee had been Bell's city attorney for fifteen years,
before resigning after the corruption became public in July 2010. For most of
that period, he worked for the firm of Oliver Sandifer & Murphy, though for
the last four years Lee was a partner at BB&K. [28]

BB&K was one of the first litigation targets that the City of Bell chose to
pursue. Bell's malpractice claims went beyond the Dexia bond transaction.
Their main elements were what Aleshire called "asleep at the switch" claims
related to Lee's giving Bell bad legal advice and simply allowing the corruption to occur. Specifically, the malpractice complaint included allegations
that Lee failed to prevent the former officials' illegal compensation and loan
schemes, that he had conflict of interest in representing both Bell and Maywood when Bell took over Maywood's government services, that he allowed
tax fee increases without Bell voter approval, and that he failed to establish
an environment of fair process in the city. [29]

After extensive mediation, the suit was settled before trial. BB&K's attorney remarked that it was a "a financial decision to get the case settled." [30] The
parties agreed that the BB&K would pay Bell $2.5 million to settle all of its
malpractice claims. [31]

Aleshire also pursued a malpractice claim against Mayer Hoffman
McCann (MHM), the accounting firm that acted as Bell's auditor from 1994
to 2010. Even though MHM and a private audit firm they acquired audited
the city during nearly Rizzo's entire tenure, it failed to discover his or other
officials' corrupt financial dealings. In December 2010, after the *L.A. Times*
story brought the corruption to light, and following a subsequent audit of
Bell, the California State Controller conducted an audit of MHM's perfor-

mance as Bell's auditor. That probe concluded that, during MHM's fiscal year 2009 audit of Bell, it committed ninety-seven audit violations, and

> did not comply, to varying degrees, with the majority of the fieldwork auditing standards and OMB Circular A-133 requirements in its audit of the City of Bell[,] . . . did not comply with the Guidelines for Compliance Audits of California Redevelopment Agencies (RDA Audit Guide) [,] . . . and did not comply with section 5097 of the California Business and Professions Code.[32]

These findings gave Bell a viable malpractice claim against MHM. But in May 2012, before the city acted, the Attorney General filed a disciplinary action against the firm before the State Board of Accountancy.[33] On the next day, the Attorney General and MHM entered into a settlement in which the firm would pay a $300,000 fine plus $50,000 in investigation fees, and serve two years of probation. Bell was not a part of the settlement and shared no part of the fine.[34]

As with the BB&K malpractice suit, this case was settled after mediation. MHM agreed to pay Bell $3 million to drop the claims against it.[35]

Although the Bell Council approved both the BB&K and MHM settlements, not everyone was happy with the outcomes. The settlements together brought in more than $5 million in guaranteed payments that the city would not have been able to count on if the cases went trial. Critics thought that the city could have gotten more money out of the firms. In particular, when the settlements were approved in 2013, then-mayor Violeta Alvarez stated that the firms "should be able to pay more," and that the city only settled the cases because it couldn't afford to fully litigate them.[36] This sentiment was likely true, particularly considering Bell's precarious financial footing during the first few years after the corruption was exposed. But the settlement decisions fit in with Aleshire's overall plan to "litigate, settle, or defer" cases. Any settlement payout had to be weighed against the money, time, and risk incurred when litigating complex malpractice cases against sophisticated defendants.

This was demonstrated in one of Bell's malpractice suits that did not go as well for the city. In October 2012, Bell filed a malpractice claim against Nixon Peabody, LLP, which acted as the city's bond counsel from 2002 through 2008. During this time, Bell issued more than $100 million in bond debt, including $35 million for the Dexia bond transaction. The City of Bell alleged that none of the issuances were approved by voters as required by the California Constitution and the Bell City Charter. Further, the Nixon Peabody attorney hired by Bell, Edsell Martindale Eady, charged up to $615 per hour for services, rates that that the City of Bell alleged had not been approved by the council. In fact, the rates Nixon Peabody charged Bell were much higher than those the firm charged other Los Angeles-area public entities. For example, the firm charged a maximum rate of $395 per hour for partners in the Los Angeles World Airports in 2010, two years after the firm ceased representing Bell.[37]

Nixon Peabody filed a motion to dismiss the city's malpractice complaint, arguing in part that the city had waited too long to file, and was on notice from at least July 2011 when it filed the malpractice suit against BB&K.[38] The judge ruled against dismissal, but the city eventually dropped the suit. Aleshire and Taylor considered this a "disappointment," but said Nixon Peabody's "high cost" defense turned the suit into the city's "most expensive case."[39]

Despite this setback, Bell was able to clean up part of the mess created by the city's issuance of $100 million in general-obligation bonds. By March 2012, the city had hired KNN Public Finance[40] for financial services consulting and Fulbright & Jaworski, LLP as bond counsel[41] to help restructure $50 million in bonds Rizzo issued for the sports complex and community facilities that were never built. If left unmodified, the bonds would have required Bell's property taxes to increase by 70 percent in order to keep up with payments. However, the council approved an offer to the bondholders to buy back about 50 percent percent of the outstanding bonds, using $20 million in proceeds from the bond issuances that Bell had not yet spent.[42]

Another avenue of potential litigation for Bell stemmed from the federal investigations into the practices of the city's former officials. These were conducted primarily by the IRS and the SEC, and ultimately stemmed from Bell's various bond issuances in the early 2000s. The IRS got involved because the $50 million in general obligation bonds were issued as tax-exempt obligations under the Internal Revenue Code. If the IRS found that the bonds did not comply with code, it could declare them taxable. That would require Bell to start collecting taxes from bondholders who thought they were buying tax-exempt bonds, or to refinance the bonds as taxable; that would likely result in the need to raise property taxes.[43] Bell's liability could have been as high as $6 million, along with the cost of subsequent litigation with the bondholders.[44]

The IRS ultimately closed its audit of the $15 million in bonds issued in 2004 without changing their tax status. For the $35 million in bonds issued in 2007, Bell settled with the IRS in 2014, agreeing to pay $257,000 to preserve their tax-exempt status.[45] The fine was relatively small compared to Bell's potential liability if the tax-exempt status had been revoked.

The SEC also investigated Bell's bond issuances in search of possible violations of securities law. In particular, the city's sales of the bonds seemed likely to have defrauded investors, particularly in light of evidence found during the investigation by the State Controller. Unlike the IRS, however, the SEC was less open about the progress of the investigation and its likely outcome.[46] As it turned out, the investigation ultimately led nowhere. In February 2015, the SEC concluded that "we do not intend to recommend an enforcement action by the Commission against the City of Bell."[47]

Aleshire's litigation strategy turned out well for the city. From 2011 through 2015, Bell was able to recover more than $12 million for the city treasury to help stave off financial disaster. Just as important, Bell has so far been able to avoid almost $70 million in potential liability that had accrued during the corruption scandal through court victories and settlements. The court also awarded Bell approximately $10 million in restitution from the seven convicted former officials.[48] Even though this restitution money has not been paid—and may never be paid—such high awards serve as a symbolic victory over those who had breached the public trust.

The criminal cases against the Bell 8 were a significant victory for the city and its finances. As part of the sentencing of each defendant, Judge Kennedy ordered each of the convicted officials to pay restitution to the city. The largest restitution awards naturally were levied against Rizzo and Spaccia, who were each ordered to pay more than $8 million to the city of Bell for their crimes.[49] However, the total amount that Bell could receive from its former chief administrative officer and his assistant was capped because almost all of the restitution amount was joint, or shared between the two of them.[50] Additionally, their restitution liabilities would be offset by any amount that Adams paid to the city as part of a civil settlement of its claims against him, which eventually amounted to $214,000.[51] Judge Kennedy handed down individual restitution orders to the former counsel members that were an order of magnitude smaller than the multimillion dollar orders against Rizzo and Spaccia. Their restitution amounts were largely based on their tenure on the city council while the corruption was taking place.[52] However, their individual amounts added up to just shy of a million dollars for the city of Bell.

Being awarded about $10 million in restitution is one thing, but actually benefiting from those orders is another. Collection proved to be tricky for Bell, particularly since the people ordered to pay restitution were unemployed, mostly in jail, and facing their own litigation defense costs. In order to collect restitution, Bell went after the former officials' assets being allocated for the future—the retirement benefits that were the focus of much of the corruption of the previous decade. The process of clawing back those former city officials' exorbitant pensions started even before the Bell 8 were ordered to pay restitution. Bell's first recovery victory against a criminally charged former official came in December 2012, when Rizzo settled a federal civil suit against his ICMA retirement account by having more than $240,000 in retirement funds in his name be returned to the City of Bell.[53] This settlement became a model of sorts for collecting restitution, as turning over ICMA retirement account funds to the city was specifically written into the restitution orders of four of the five councilmembers.[54] The city was able to collect almost a quarter of a million dollars in restitution from those councilmembers' ICMA accounts.[55] Bell has also been credited back almost $600,000 it made to CALPERS after the state retirement system adjusted the Bell 8's retirement accounts.[56] By the end of 2015, Bell had received more than $1 million in restitution from the former officials through their retirement accounts. With pension sources exhausted, it is unclear how much more in restitution payments the City will receive from the Bell 8.

Bell's financial recovery in the aftermath of the corruption scandal was not limited to criminal restitution. In fact, most of the money Bell has recovered to date has come from settlements with parties who were not criminally charged. Much of the recovered money also came from various city employee retirement accounts. The largest chunk of money came from a settlement between the city and many of its employees concerning the supplemental retirement plan administered by Wells Fargo. As part of the settlement in March 2014, the supplemental retirement plan was invalidated for those employees, and almost $4.8 million in undistributed funds was returned to Bell.[57] Those undistributed funds are needed by the City to cover the substantial unfunded liabilities under the supplemental retirement plan for the Bell 8. However, the criminal restitution orders for Rizzo and Spaccia subsequently allowed the City to collect on the over $2 million contributions to the fund on their behalf to be forfeited, effectively freeing that money up for the city to put to other uses.[58]

Bell was even more successful in recovering money on its various malpractice lawsuits. As part of settlement agreements with BB&K, the law firm of the former city attorney Ed Lee, and MHM, the former accounting firm in charge of city audits, Bell recovered $5.5 million.[59] The biggest single source of money recovered by Bell, however, involved its settlement with Dexia in which the city was able to sell an extra fifteen-acre plot of land to a developer for $15.5 million.[60] Including this land sale, Bell has received over $28 million in revenue in the aftermath of the corruption scandal.[61]

Another problem the city faced as a result of the corruption was the prospect of enormous future financial liabilities. Though the nature of the corruption makes it difficult to measure the extent of Bell's potential future liabilities, city attorney David Aleshire estimated them to be about $75 million.[62] However, by 2015, almost all of this liability had been avoided through settlements or court victories. The largest potential liability was from Dexia for $38 million in unpaid principal and interest on their bond issuance that went sour. However, in 2013 Bell was able to reach a settlement in which all of its liability was erased.[63] The city was also able to reduce its liability in another land deal undertaken during Rizzo's tenure. In 2008, the city issued a ten-year, $4.6 million bond at six percent interest to the Pete Werrlein Children's Private Annuity Trust for the purchase of the former

Table 1. Total Amount of Money Successfully Recovered by the City of Bell

Amount Paid	Party	Fund Source
$242,719.56	Robert Rizzo	Robert Rizzo ICMA Retirement Account Settlement
$229,241.09	Robert Rizzo	CALPERS Retirement Account Readjustment credit back to Bell
$71,085.39	Angela Spaccia	CALPERS Retirement Account Readjustment credit back to Bell
$23,316.87	Victor Bello	Court-ordered restitution from ICMA Retirement Account
$27,525.55	Victor Bello	CALPERS Retirement Account Readjustment credit back to Bell
$103,763.36	George Cole	Court-ordered restitution from ICMA Retirement Account
36,648.80	George Cole	CALPERS Retirement Account Readjustment credit back to Bell
$61,007.91	Oscar Hernandez	Court-ordered restitution from ICMA Retirement Account
$120,495.94	Oscar Hernandez	CALPERS Retirement Account Readjustment credit back to Bell
$56,725.82	Theresa Jacobo	Court-ordered restitution from ICMA Retirement Account
$61,072.79	Theresa Jacobo	CALPERS Retirement Account Readjustment credit back to Bell
$36,772.92	George Mirabal	CALPERS Retirement Account Readjustment credit back to Bell
$4,788,758.41	Bell Employees	Undistributed funds returned to Bell as part of Wells Fargo Supplement Retirement Account
$112,797.97	Eric Eggena	CALPERS Retirement Account Readjustment credit back to Bell
$86,458.75	Annette Perertz	CALPERS Retirement Account Readjustment credit back to Bell
$52,624.09	Lourdes Garcia	CALPERS Retirement Account Readjustment credit back to Bell
$214,714.12	Randy Adams	Settlement for all claims between Adams and City of Bell
$1,000,000	Alliant Crime Insurance Program	Settlement of all claims alleging loss due to employee dishonesty
$3,000,000	Mayer Hoffman McCann	Settlement of all malpractice claims against audit firm

$250,000	Best Best & Krieger	Settlement of malpractice claims against law firtm arising from Dexia Bond sale
$2,250,000	Best Best & Krieger	Settlement of all other malpractice claims
$15,233,868	Land Developer	Sale of 15 acre parcel related to Dexia bond land deal
$242,719.56	Robert Rizzo	Robert Rizzo ICMA Retirement Account Settlement
$229,241.09	Robert Rizzo	CALPERS Retirement Account Readjustment credit back to Bell

Total Money Recovered = $28,059,597.34

Source: Kratzer, Michael. Personal correspondence with Thom Reilly. December 14, 2015.

Western Auto property, for a total liability of seven million dollars.[64] However, in 2013 the city settled with the Trust to reduce the bond to $2.5 million at 5 percent interest, reducing the city's total liability by about three million dollars.[65]

The Bell 8 and other former city employees also had millions of dollars in claims against Bell. A major part of this potential liability came from pensions and unpaid wages. Fortunately for Bell, the court and CALPERS rejected most of the Bell 8's claims against the city. Other city officials also ended up settling with the city for substantially less than what they originally claimed.[66] By 2015, Bell's estimated potential liabilities had been reduced by almost 95 percent.[67]

But the victories did not come free. From Aleshire's appointment as city attorney to halfway through the 2014–2015 fiscal year, Aleshire & Wynder charged Bell nearly $5.5 million in fees. A large portion of the fees was racked up in corruption-related litigation. For an average city of Bell's size, this would be an unimaginable sum of money to spend on legal representation in only three and a half years. After 2010, however, Bell was not a normal city.

Still, Councilmember Ana Maria Quintana in particular voiced concerns about the costs, and in November 2013, alleged that Bell was paying more in legal fees than was being officially reported. She calculated that, for the fiscal year 2012–2013, "the city council has approved warrants indicating that $1,847,934.96 was spent on legal services when in actuality the figure was $2,770,320.96." She equated Aleshire & Wynder's deferred billing arrangement with the city with the corruption under Rizzo.[68]

Aleshire & Wynder's 2011 bid for the city attorney position included charging the city between $155 and $215 per hour for legal services.[69] This was about one-third of the rate former bond counsel charged during the Rizzo era. And soon after starting work for Bell and discovering that the city had no real budget in 2011, the firm dropped its hourly rate by $10 and held its monthly bills to $100,000. In the firm's second year representing Bell, the level of litigation increased dramatically, leading to over $2 million in expected legal fees. Since that figure represented about a quarter of Bell's budget, there was no way that the city would be able to pay for it without deferring other projects or services.

In order to continue the litigation, Aleshire & Wynder agreed to defer $1.08 million in legal fees until Bell received enough money to pay for them.[70] [71] By 2013, Bell had received several million dollars in settlement money, enough to pay the deferred fees.

During its representation of Bell, Aleshire & Wynder also wrote off several hundred thousand dollars in legal fees and more than $1 million in other write-downs.[72] However, even with such a discount, $5.5 million was a significant amount of money for a city in Bell's situation. Considering the results of the litigation, this looks like a bargain compared to the money directly received by the city and the avoided potential liability. Litigation is expensive. Handling over sixty active and prospective cases at once would cost a lot of money no matter which firm Bell chose.

Despite Quintana's criticism, most people seemed pleased with the work that Aleshire & Wynder was doing in Bell. One indication was that, in March 2015, Aleshire and Taylor were recognized by *California Lawyer* magazine as *California Lawyer* Attorneys of the Year in the category of municipal law for their work representing Bell.[73]

After Rizzo's resignation and the subsequent recall of councilmembers, there were no immediate applications for the city manager position. This prompted the International City/County Management Association (ICMA) to help provide interim administrators before Doug Willmore came on full time. "Partnering with the League of California Cities and the California City Management Foundation, ICMA arranged for Ken Hamplian, the retired city manager of San Luis Obispo, to step in for thirty days, without compensation. Arne Croce, a retired city manager of San Mateo, who agreed to serve for nine months, followed him. Pam Easter, another retired city manager stepped in, as a volunteer, to assist Ken Hamplian and then Arne Croce. Over two dozen local government professionals worked with the City of Bell over the next several months providing needed technical assistance."[74]

In the summer of 2012, Doug Willmore became Bell's first permanent city administrator since Rizzo left the position in July 2010. Willmore's task: Rebuild a city with a legacy of mismanagement that was on the brink of insolvency. He signed a three-year contract at $175,000 a year, saying he was impressed by the new Council's "commitment to progress" and claiming that a lot of great things could be done. There were seventy-two applicants for the job; Willmore was chosen because his expertise and knowledge would help move the community forward. [75]

Perhaps one of the reasons Willmore seemed like a good fit was his prior experience as city manager in El Segundo—even though he ended up being fired. Willmore took on a powerful business in the city, Chevron, which he discovered owed several million dollars in back utility-users' taxes. For decades, he found, Chevron had paid millions of dollars less in taxes than other refineries in the state. Some El Segundo residents took preliminary steps to place a measure on the ballot to increase Chevron's tax, but found they lacked the four council votes needed to send it to voters. Instead, the council and Chevron agreed to negotiate. [76]

Wilmore and others believed that city officials fired him in retaliation for going after the business giant. He ended up settling with the city, and was honored with the Ethics Award from California's state affiliate of ICMA. [77]

When Willmore started in Bell, the city hadn't reconciled bank statements in three years and was behind in audits. It was facing fifty-five lawsuits. The State's Controller had published a report on Bell's accounting controls in September 2010, but Willmore deemed it "virtually useless as a roadmap for the urgent problems Bell faced." He developed a one hundred-day plan and, together with the council and new city attorney, addressed several urgent priorities including the hiring of new department heads, completing the three years of past financial audits, and bringing financial transactions current. They refunded the citywide debt that Rizzo had issued but not paid for, and which raised the need for massive tax increase.

The council then passed the first rational and transparent annual budget Bell had seen in years. [78] Under Rizzo, there was a five-year budget document that made it impossible to understand what expenses were being incurred or what the city was doing. Costly budget items were rolled up into this document and placed before the council for approval with confusing, misleading and/or missing backup documentation. Willmore instead initiated an annual budgeting process that included workshops for the public and the posting of budget documents on the city's website.

Willmore also worked on making the city's governance process more transparent. One way he did this was to work with the Sunlight Foundation, a nonprofit organization that advocates using technology to make governments more transparent. The resulting website overhaul earned Bell a grade of A- in the foundation's 2013 "Sunny Awards," the highest mark given that year. [79]

In May 2013, the State Controller's Office (SCO) came back with a follow-up report that was extremely critical of Bell for not following up with their recommendations, stating:

The City of Bell has made some progress since it ejected a corrupt city management two years ago. But many of the same fiscal management and internal control lapses that allowed Bell to fail its citizens in the past remain unaddressed today. This review does more than point out problems. It serves as a blueprint to preventing the return of unlawful taxation, abusive spending and backroom deal-making.[80]

Willmore contends that the SCO missed the point. "In my assessment," he said, "spending our time at that moment trying to implement and correct the SCO recommendations would have been akin to rearranging the deck chairs on the Titanic. The ship was sinking and following their recommendations would not have kept the ship afloat." He said the SCO recommendations did not address steps to ensure Bell would not fall into insolvency, and that the report would be useful later in the process.[81] [82] Willmore was widely credited with restoring good governance in Bell and made great strides ensuring the process was open and transparent to residents. However, he began looking for another job after some friction with current mayor, Saleh. Saleh was critical of Willmore's economic development plan to implement a "managed structural deficit" in favor or building up the city's administration, community development, and recreation. Saleh worried that Bell would end up doing worse economically, and his relationship with Willmore soured. Willmore ended up getting hired for significantly more money as city manager for Rancho Palos Verdes, where officials praised him for his time in Bell, asserting that he "was responsible for implementing significant changes to enhance transparency and accountability, institute better governance, and restore Bell's fiscal health."[83] Indeed, Bell's general fund balance grew to $22.5 million in Willmore's three years at the helm.

The court system has had a huge impact on the aftermath of the Bell corruption scandal. Not only were Rizzo, Spaccia, and several of the former councilmembers convicted and punished, but the city was also able to recover some of the millions they and others stole. However, the judiciary was not the only branch that responded to the crisis in Bell. Since 2010, the California legislature has enacted laws that have helped Bell recover and has worked to prevent similar corruption happening in other California municipalities.

The first bill concerning Bell corruption was A.B. 900, introduced in the state Assembly in August 2010. The bill sought to address the excessive and illegal property taxes that had been assessed on Bell property owners while Rizzo was in charge. Specifically, it made an exception to the requirement that excessive property taxes collected be allocated to local public school districts. Instead, any excess property taxes collected by the city for fiscal years 2007–08, 2008–09, and 2009–10 would be refunded directly to the property owners.[84] A.B. 900 was enacted into law in September 2010. Starting the next month, Bell property owners started receiving refunds.[85]

The next piece of legislation passed was targeted at a problem unique to Bell. Prior to the March 2011 recall election, the court had ordered the three sitting councilmembers who had been criminally charged to stay at least one hundred yards away from City Hall and to refrain from conducting any official business. Unfortunately, this meant that the council could not comply with the city charter requirement that it officially declare election results and install the new members.[86] To solve this problem, Assemblyman Ricardo Lara of nearby Bell Gardens sponsored A.B. 93, which created an alternative procedure enabling the Los Angeles County clerk and Bell clerk to certify the election results and allowing the Bell clerk to install the new council.[87] Lara swore in the five new councilmembers on April 7, 2011.[88]

Later legislation aimed at preventing future Bell-style corruption from arising in California cities. A.B. 23, signed by Governor Jerry Brown in July 2011, strengthened the Brown Act provisions requiring public meetings. The bill added Government Code Section 54952.3, requiring the clerk or a member of the legislative body to verbally announce the amount of compensation legislative members will receive for attending any simultaneous or sequential meetings.[89] The purpose was to prevent future municipal legislatures from surreptitiously increasing their pay as Bell Councilmembers did, by holding simultaneous meetings that paid generous stipends.[90]

A.B. 1344, signed by the governor in October 2011, addressed several legal gaps that allowed corruption in Bell to fester.[91] It put new limits on contracts for employment that no longer allowed executive employees like Rizzo and Spaccia to receive more than eighteen months of salary and benefits as a settlement for termination. Automatic increases in salary for executives are now limited to cost-of-living adjustments, and local legislative bodies, such as city councils, can no longer hold special sessions to consider salary, salary schedule, or any other form of compensation for executive employees.[92] [93]

A.B. 1344 also strengthened the punishment for public employees who abuse their power in office. Any official or employee convicted of such abuse are now required to fully reimburse the municipality or agency for the wrongdoing. The bill also addressed government transparency concerns: For the first time, municipalities are required to post notice and agendas of any legislative meetings.[94]

Not all statutory changes happened at the state level. One important transformation took place at the hands of Bell voters: reform of the 2005 charter. The charter was infamously enacted in an election in which fewer than five hundred voters participated, and was widely blamed for enabling the corruption that followed. In the years following the scandal, Bell has modified the charter to make corruption less instead of more likely.

The move for charter reform started in earnest with the adoption of Resolution No. 2014-45 in August 2014.[95] The resolution set up a charter-reform committee to review various reform possibilities and recommend changes that would protect against the self-interest of city officials, increase government transparency and financial soundness, promote economic growth, and make Bell a better place to live and work.[96]

Residents had mixed feelings about charter reform and what form it should take. At one extreme were those who believed that the 2005 charter arose from corruption and only served to enable it. As such, they said, the charter should be repealed. Repeal would return Bell to a general-law city bound by the limitations on compensation set by the state. One problem with this argument is that the 2005 charter had set limits on Bell officials, limits that Rizzo regularly violated.[97] This suggests that the corruption happened in spite of the charter, not because of it.

At the other extreme were those, such as Councilmember Ana Maria Quintana, who do not believe a council-created committee can truly reflect the will of the people. Since the Charter is the city's governing document, these residents said, it should be modified only "through processes that allow for Bell community participation."[98]

By October 2014, the charter-reform committee had made its recommendations to the council. One was to eliminate the position of assistant city administrative officer, which was not a common position in a city the size of Bell, and which had been left vacant since Spaccia left in 2010.[99] Many of the other recommendations concerned councilmembers' pay and benefits. The reformed charter, if approved by voters, would limit the council's ability to increase their pay and prohibit them from receiving compensation for sitting on boards or committees unless explicitly allowed by state law. Indemnification of councilmembers by the city for legal defense would also be severely curtailed. Automatically renewed franchise agreements would be outlawed, and every council-approved franchise would have to be re-approved at least once every ten years. Finally, the conflict-of-interest standard would be made much more stringent, with all public officials and employees required to "adhere to the highest ethical standards."[100]

The council adopted these recommendations, and set charter reform as Measure C in the March 2015 election.[101] More than 1,700 people voted on the issue, more than three times the turnout for the 2005 election. However, turnout was still low, with only about 15 percent of registered voters participating. Measure C won by a landslide, with more than 80 percent of voters supporting it.[102]

NOTES

1. Louis D. Brandeis, *Other People's Money and How the Bankers Use It*, (New York: Frederick A. Stokes Company, 1914), 92.

2. *See* People ex rel Brown v. Rizzo, Spaccia, Adams, Hernandez, Jacobo, Cole, Bello, and Mirabal. BC445497. First Amended Complaint. November 15, 2010.

3. Aleshire, D. & Taylor, A. "Corruption on Steroids: The Bell Scandal from the Legal Perspective." (white paper at the City of Bell Scandal Revisited Conference, Chapman University, 2015).

4. Ibid.

5. City of Bell. "City Attorney. David Aleshire." N.D. Retrieved from http://cityofbell.org/?NavID=251.

6. The City of Bell Scandal Revisited. "Conference Transcript." February 19, 2015. p.16.

7. Aleshire, & Taylor, Corruption.

8. Aleshire & Wynder, LLP. "Anthony R. Taylor." N.D. Retrieved from http://www.awattorneys.com/our-team/attorneys/anthony-r-taylor#.

9. People ex rel Harris v. Rizzo. 214 Cal.App.4th 921 (App. 2013).

10. City of Bell v. Superior Court. 220 Cal.App.4th 236 (App. 2013).

11. "SH City Attorney Working Pro Bono to Help Bell Citizens Recall Their Controversial Officials." *Signal Tribune.* November 10, 2010. Retrieved from http://www.signaltribunenewspaper.com/?p=8410.

12. Aleshire, & Taylor, Corruption.

13. Garcia, C. "Building BASTA." (white paper at the City of Bell Scandal Revisited Conference, Chapman University, 2015).

14. "Bell Election: Newly Elected Pledge to Sweep Out City Hall; Interim Administrator likely to be Fired [Updated]." *Los Angeles Times.* March 9, 2011. Retrieved from http://latimesblogs.latimes.com/lanow/2011/03/bell-rizzo-fire-carrillo-casso-police-disband-corruption.html.

15. City of Bell. "Special Minutes of Bell City Council." June 6, 2011. *See also* "City of Bell Hires a Permanent City Attorney: The Bell City Council Has Approved David Aleshire as its Permanent City Attorney." *Los Angeles Times.* June 7, 2011. Retrieved from http://latimesblogs.latimes.com/lanow/2011/06/city-of-bell-hires-a-permanent-city-attorney.html.

16. City of Bell Hires, Los Angeles Times.

17. Aleshire & Taylor, Corruption.

18. Willmore, D. "City of Bell Agenda Report RE: November 13, 2013. Consideration of Stipulation for Settlement with Dexia Credit Local Including Limited Settlement Terms with BB&K." April 3, 2013.

19. Aleshire & Taylor, Corruption.

20. Ibid

21. Willmore, City of Bell, April 3, 2013.

22. Gottlieb, J. "A Mountain of Lawsuits Weighs Heavily on Bell." *Los Angeles Times.* February 2, 2013. Retrieved from http://articles.latimes.com/2013/feb/02/local/la-me-bell-challenges-20130203.

23. Willmore, City of Bell, April 3, 2013.

24. Aleshire, D. "Report on the Status of Litigation Sept 2011–June 2013." N.D.

25. Aleshire & Taylor, Corruption.

26. Aleshire, Report Sept 2011–June 2013.

27. Willmore, City of Bell, April 3, 2013.

28. Gottlieb, J. "Bell Sues Its Former City Attorney, Claiming Faulty Legal Advice." *Los Angeles Times.* July 29, 2011. Retrieved from http://latimesblogs.latimes.com/lanow/2011/07/bell-sues-its-former-city-attorney-for-faulty-legal-advice.html.

29. Aleshire, Report Sept 2011–June 2013.

30. Gottlieb, J. "Corruption-Scarred Bell Finds Itself on Better Financial Footing." *Los Angeles Times.* December 22, 2013. Retrieved from http://articles.latimes.com/2013/dec/22/local/la-me-bell-settlements-20131223.

31. Aleshire & Taylor, Corruption.

32. California State Controller. "Mayer Hoffman McCann, P.C. (Irvine Office) Review Report Quality Control Report For the Firm's Audits of City of Bell and Bell Community Redevelopment Agency for the Fiscal Year Ended June 30, 2009." December 21, 2010.

33. Aleshire & Taylor, Corruption.

34. Aleshire, D. "Bell Staff Report RE: Report on Status of Litigation: Conclusion of FY 2011-2012." November 7, 2012.

35. Aleshire & Taylor, Corruption.

36. Gottlieb, Corruption-Scarred.

37. Aleshire, Bell Staff, November 7, 2012.

38. Heller, M. "Nixon Peabody Remains in Scandal-Plagued City's Crosshairs." *Law360.* March 28, 2013. Retrieved from http://www.law360.com/articles/428320/nixon-peabody-remains-in-scandal-plagued-city-s-crosshairs.

39. Aleshire & Taylor, Corruption.

40. City of Bell. "First Amendment to Contract Services Agreement for Financial Advisor Services." March 6, 2012.

41. City of Bell. "Contract Services Agreement for Bond Counsel Services." March 20, 2012.

42. City of Bell. "Resolution No. 2012-46: Resolution of the City Council of the City of Bell, California to Approve the Form of an Offer to Purchase and Related Documents and an Escrow Agreement and Providing For Matters Related Thereto." June 6, 2012.

43. Aleshire, Bell Staff, November 7, 2012.

44. Aleshire & Taylor, Corruption.

45. Webster, K. "Bell, Calif. Pays $257,000 IRS Fine, Retains Tax Exempt Status on $35M GOs." *The Bond Buyer.* November 26, 2014. Retrieved from http://www.bondbuyer.com/news/regionalnews/bell-calif-pays-257000-irs-fine-retains-tax-exempt-status-on-35m-gos-1068302-1.html.

46. Aleshire, Bell Staff, November 7, 2012.

47. Reid, T. "SEC Closes Investigation into Bell, Calif. Bond Debt." *Reuters.* February 24, 2015. Retrieved from http://www.reuters.com/article/2015/02/24/usa-municipals-bell-idUSL1N0VY3EF20150224.

48. Aleshire, Bell Staff, November 7, 2012.

49. People v. Rizzo. BA276026, BA377197, BA382701. Sentencing Minutes. April 16, 2014. at p. 41; People v. Spaccia. BA376026, BA382701. Sentencing Minutes. April 10, 2014. at pp. 76–77.

50. Ibid.

51. Adams, Randy. Settlement Agreement and Release of Claims. April 11, 2014.

52. See Table 1.

53. Rizzo v. ICMA Retirement Corporation, et al. CV 12-02690-RGK (VBKx). Order.

54. People v. Cole. BA376025. Notice of Entry of Order for Restitution to the City of Bell from Defendant George Wendell Cole, Jr. December 16, 2014; People v. Bello. BA376025. Notice of Entry of Order for Restitution to the City of Bell from Defendant Victor Bello, December 16, 2014; People v. Hernandez. BA376025. Notice of Entry of Order for Restitution to the City of Bell from Defendant Oscar Hernandez, December 16, 2014; People v. Jacobo. BA376025. Notice of Entry of Order for Restitution to the City of Bell from Defendant Theresa Jacobo. December 16, 2014. *See* Table 1.

55. Ibid.

56. Kratzer, Michael. Personal correspondence with Thom Reilly. December 14, 2015.

57. Aleshire, D. & Taylor, A. "Corruption on Steroids: The Bell Scandal from the Legal Perspective." 2015.

58. People v. Rizzo. BA276026, BA377197, BA382701. Notice of Entry of Order for Restitution to the City of Bell from Defendant Robert Rizzo. April 16, 2014. People v. Spaccia. BA376026, BA382701. Notice of Entry of Order for Restitution to the City of Bell from Defendant Pier'Angela Spaccia. April, 10, 2014.

59. Aleshire, D. & Taylor, A. "Corruption on Steroids: The Bell Scandal from the Legal Perspective." 2015.

60. Ibid.

61. See Table 1.
62. Aleshire, D. & Taylor, A. "Corruption on Steroids: The Bell Scandal from the Legal Perspective." 2015.
63. Willmore, D. City of Bell Agenda Report RE:. November 13, 2013. Consideration of Stipulation for Settlement with Dexia Credit Local Including Limited Settlement Terms with BB&K. April 3, 2013. Aleshire, D. Report on the status of litigation Sept 2011–June 2013. (N.D.).
64. Aleshire, D. & Taylor, A. "Corruption on Steroids: The Bell Scandal from the Legal Perspective." 2015.
65. Pete Werrlein Children's Private Annuity Trust Dated August 28, 1991. Settlement Agreement and Full Release of Claims. September 19, 2013.
66. *See, for example,* Adams, Randy. Settlement Agreement and Release of Claims. April 11, 2014; Eggena, Eric. Settlement Agreement and Release of Claims. December 18, 2013.
67. Aleshire, D. & Taylor, A. "Corruption on Steroids: The Bell Scandal from the Legal Perspective." 2015.
68. Quintana, A. Press Release. September 27, 2013.
69. Aleshire, D. "City of Bell Agenda Report RE: Attorney Report on Client No-Pay Arrangement." November 11, 2013.
70. Ibid.
71. Aleshire & Taylor, Corruption.
72. Ibid.
73. California Lawyer. "California Lawyer Attorneys of the Year." March 2015. Retrieved from https://ww2.callawyer.com/Clstory.cfm?eid=939885&wteid=939885_California_Lawyer_Attorneys_of_the_Year.
74. Frederickson, H. G. & Meek, J. W. Presentation. "Searching for Virtue in the City: Bell and Her Sisters." (white paper at the City of Bell Scandal Revisited Conference, Chapman University, 2015).
75. Nestor Valencia, interview with author, February 12, 2015.
76. Agostoni, K. "Former El Segundo's Manager's Firing Leads to Messy Lawsuit." *Daily Breeze News.* March 23, 2013. http://www.dailybreeze.com/general-news/20130323/former-el-segundo-managers-firing-leads-to-messy-lawsuit.
77. Barnes, M. "Rancho Palos Verdes Hires City Manager Who Helped Repair Scandal-Plagued Bell." *Daily Breeze News.* January 1, 2015. http://www.dailybreeze.com/government-and-politics/20150129/rancho-palos-verdes-hires-city-manager-who-helped-repair-scandal-plagued-bell.
78. Willmore, D. "City of Bell – Reformed and Reborn." (white paper at the City of Bell Scandal Revisited Conference, Chapman University, 2015).
79. Center for the Advancement of Public Integrity at Columbia Law School. "The City of Bell Scandal Revisited." N.D. Retrieved from http://web.law.columbia.edu/public-integrity/city-bell-scandal-revisited.
80. Willmore, City of Bell – Reformed and Reborn.
81. Ibid.
82. Doug Willmore, interview with author, February 12, 2015.
83. Barnes, M. "Rancho Palos Verdes Hires City Manager Who Helped Repair Scandal-Plagued Bell." *Daily Breeze.* January 29, 2015. Retrieved from: http://www.dailybreeze.com/government-and-politics/20150129/rancho-palos-verdes-hires-city-manager-who-helped-repair-scandal-plagued-bell.
84. Assem. Bill 900, 2009–2010 Reg. Sess (Cal. 2010).
85. Casso, J. & Williams, J. "Bell – What Happened and How It Happened: The Role of the New Administration and the City Attorney." *League of California Cities.* May 6, 2011. Retrieved from http://www.cacities.org/getattachment/6202b6ac-a488-4df1-9653-65a16bb3b2ae/5-2011-Spring-James-Casso-Jayne-Williams-Crisis-Ma.aspx.
86. Vives. R. "Bell Seeks Emergency Legislation to Certify Election Results." *Los Angeles Times.* March 16, 2011. Retrieved from http://latimesblogs.latimes.com/lanow/2011/03/bell-emergency-legislation-election-results.html.
87. Assem. Bill 93, 2011-2012 Reg. Sess (Cal. 2011).

88. Barboza, T. "New Bell City Council Sworn in Amid Promises to Rebound from Corruption Scandal." *Los Angeles Times*. April 7, 2011. Retrieved from http://latimesblogs.latimes.com/lanow/2011/04/city-council-sworn-in-bell.html.

89. Assem. Bill 23, 2011-2012 Reg. Sess (Cal. 2011).

90. "AB 23 Assembly Floor Analysis." June 9, 2011.

91. Assem. Bill 1344, 2011-2012 Reg. Sess (Cal. 2011).

92. Ibid.

93. Aleshire & Taylor, Corruption.

94. Ibid.

95. City of Bell. "Resolution No. 2014-45: A Resolution Establishing a Charter Review Committee to Evaluate and Make Recommendations to the City Council of the City of Bell for Amendments to the City Charter." August 13, 2014.

96. Ibid.

97. Willmore, interview, pp. 1–2.

98. Quintana, A. "Argument Against Measure C." N.D. Retrieved from http://www.cityofbell.org/home/showdocument?id=5732.

99. Willmore, interview, p. 1.

100. City of Bell. "Resolution No. 2014-60: A Resolution of the City Council of the City of Bell, California, Calling an Election and Requesting Placement of a Ballot Measure on the General Municipal Election Ballot for the City of Bell on Tuesday March 3, 2015, to Consider an Amendment to the Bell City Charter to Revise Councilmember Candidate Residency Requirements to 30 Days, Limit Councilmember Compensation and Indemnification, Create a Citizen Planning Commission, Revise Recall Election Procedures, Eliminate the Assistant Chief Administrative Officer Position, Prohibit Financial Conflicts of Interests, and Limit the Term of City Franchises, All Consistent with State Law." October 29, 2014.

101. Ibid.

102. Los Angeles County Registrar-Recorder/County Clerk. "March 03, 2015 – Consolidated Elections: Final Official Election Returns." March, 10, 2015. Retrieved from http://rrcc.co.la.ca.us/elect/15032316/rr2316p01.htm#3754.

Chapter Seven

Postscript

"You must first enable the government to control the governed; and in the next place, oblige it to control itself."
—James Madison, *The Federalist Papers No. 51*[1]

Steve Cooley was first elected District Attorney for Los Angeles in November 2000 and served until 2012, leading the largest prosecutor's office in the country. During that time, he oversaw the prosecution of Rizzo, Spaccia, and five former Bell councilmembers. When asked to describe the Bell corruption case, Cooley issued his now famous description of the scandal as "well, it is corruption on steroids."[2] That stuck as the label for the case. And Cooley said that, if you want to prevent, deter, and expose public corruption, four elements are required: an engaged and informed electorate, a robust media, transparency, and effective and skilled investigators and prosecutors.[3] The lack of the first three certainly were core factors contributing to Bell's woes. But there were other elements present (or lacking) in the city that deserve attention: an organizational culture that tolerated, or even supported, the pursuit of self-interests over public interests; a complete breakdown of a city government's traditional system of checks and balances; and an absence of ethical leadership. All of these have become part of the post-scandal narrative voiced by politicians, academics, and the media as they attempt to explain how such large-scale corruption occurred in such a small town. However, two other questions deserve equal if not more exploration: How did such rampant corruption emerge in a system—the council-manager form of government—that had been designed specifically to prevent municipal corruption and promote good governance? And how did so many officials and employees collectively conspire to participate in or at least tolerate the ongoing corruption?

During the century following the adoption of the U.S. Constitution in 1789, the new nation went through a massive social restructuring of its population. From its founding up into the twentieth century, a nation established largely upon agrarian principles transformed from a predominantly rural society to an urban one. In the 1790 Census, the U.S. population was nearly 95 percent rural and just more than 5 percent urban.[4] The population as a whole grew by no less than 15 percent in each decade from 1790 until 1920; the rate stood above 30 percent from 1790 to 1860.[5] The urban population grew at a rate at or near double that of the nation as a whole, hitting a peak of just more than 93 percent in 1850.[6]

At the same time, the rural population declined steadily, sinking to a growth rate of just above 3 percent in the 1920 Census.[7] That was the year in which the U.S. population first became more urban than rural, if barely: More than 51 percent lived in urban areas.[8]

Throughout the nineteenth century and the early decades of the twentieth, cities evolved into the nation's main financial, commercial, and industrial centers. Economic centers were particularly concentrated on the Eastern seaboard, in the older cities of New York, Boston, Philadelphia, and Baltimore, which "attracted huge volumes of capital investment and cheap immigrant labor."[9] Newer cities located along waterways, such as Chicago, Cincinnati, New Orleans, and St. Louis, also rose in economic importance.[10]

As immigrants began to stream into the urban centers of the East and Midwest, large city governments began to take shape to keep up with the ever-growing demand for services. The first- and second-generation immigrants who settled into the largest cities were often disenfranchised and left out of state and national politics, so they gravitated toward the politics of the cities where they lived. They developed ways of obtaining necessary services for their ethnic enclaves, a process that evolved into the "machine style" of political organization. A political machine is "a hierarchical organization controlled by a single leader, a 'boss,' or tightly organized clique."[11]

For a century, machine-type local governments—which evolved into what we call the "strong mayor-council" form—were the dominant structures in the nation's industrial cities. New York City was famously run by the Democratic Party's Tammany Hall machine, whose Irish-immigrant-based spoils system was headed by William "Boss" Tweed.[12] Longtime Chicago Mayor Richard J. Daley, who died in 1976, was among the last of the "bosses."

Another important historical figure was Enoch "Nucky" Johnson, whose appointment to lead New Jersey's Atlantic County Republican Executive Committee effectively made him boss of Atlantic City during the "Roaring 20s." Prohibition was in full swing and organized crime operated smoothly with public officials. Johnson oversaw the continued growth of Atlantic City's "vice" industry, including speakeasies, gambling halls, and prostitution. He would be paid by the operators of such pursuits in exchange for redirecting police away from investigating certain venues. His reign also included kickbacks on government contracts and other types of organized corruption.

In his thirty-year rule, Johnson became known as the most powerful New Jersey Republican, even though he never ran for office. Asked once why he wouldn't run for governor, Johnson said that he didn't think a "real boss" was dignified in running for election. [13]

Some urban residents felt that the political machine got the job done, but in many cases its corrupt officials, bribery, and nepotism nurtured widespread urban corruption during the late-nineteenth and early-twentieth centuries. In direct reaction to this, the Progressive Movement emerged around the turn of the century to urge reform. As the field of public administration took shape following the work of Woodrow Wilson, Max Weber, and Frederick Winslow Taylor, reformers wanted to transform government service into a profession with standards of conduct and expectations of ethical behavior.

Progressive reformers introduced new approaches to the way city governments were formed and governed that stripped away the power of the political machines. Machine politics in the mayor-council form has traditionally depended upon council elections from strategically drawn districts that assumed party loyalty from their dominant ethnic enclaves. The reform movement brought about the idea of at-large council elections that diluted the impact of heavily immigrant districts on filling council seats. Another element Progressive reformers introduced was having the council appoint a nonpartisan, professional city manager to oversee the running of the city. The reformers envisioned a format similar to a for-profit corporation, where an appointed administrator implemented policies developed by an elected body, like a CEO and its board of directors. Citizens of a community would be similar to stockholders of a corporation. These reforms created the council-manager form of local government, which was presumed to be less politicized and more business-like than the strong mayor type. Staunton, Virginia, hired the first professional manager in 1908; in 1913, Dayton, Ohio, became the first city of substantial size to adopt the council-manager form. [14]

Large older cities on the Eastern seaboard and in the Midwest have traditionally had mayor-council forms of government (usually of the strong-mayor type), while large Western cities as well as most smaller cities and county governments have operated with council-manager forms. The popularity of the latter approach in the West reflects the fact that many Western cities, towns, and counties were established or organized into local governments during the Progressive era.

The reforms seem to have worked. Local governments in the last half of the twentieth century and the first years of the twenty-first century have suffered from significantly less corruption than existed at the time of the

Progressive movement. Still, by the end of the twentieth century, problems with local government corruption began to reemerge. [15]

The two forms of local government, mayor-council and council-manager, are often thought of in stark terms of machine versus reform. Under the strong mayor (or mayor-council) form, an elected mayor holds overall authority to appoint and dismiss department heads. Serving as CEO of the city's executive branch, the mayor prepares and administers the budget, which is approved by the council, the legislative branch. Strong-mayor governments have increasingly been appointing a chief administrative officer, who performs activities similar to city managers, but reports to the mayor instead of to the council as a whole. City administrative officers are perceived as having less authority than their city-manager counterpart and occupying a secondary position in the executive chain of command. [16]

Under the council-manager form, as noted above, elected officials form the council or commission and hire a professionally trained manager, chosen on the basis of education and experience, to oversee the delivery of public services and daily operations of the community. The manager serves at the pleasure of the elected body.

This machine-versus-reform view has been popular among scholars of public administration for the past century. Council-manager government has come to be considered the best system for preventing the local-government corruption that was rampant in the past. On the other hand, the mayor-council form is thought of as the more politically responsive form, and as a result has gained favor in growing cities. And while the council-manager form emerged as a solution to corruption, there is no evidence to confirm that it is in fact better at combating corruption than the strong-mayor system. Surprisingly, even decades of research have failed to confirm that that there are systematic differences between these two forms in how they respond to powerful constituencies, in their levels of citizen participation, the quality of public services they offer, or in operational effectiveness. [17]

Some cities, particularly larger ones, have in recent decades abandoned the council-manager form of government in favor of the mayor-council type in order to become more accessible to their residents. [18] The council-manager form remains the most common. But while it is employed in 57 percent of municipalities with populations between 5,000 and 249,999, 67 percent of cites over 500,000 operate as strong-mayor governments. [19] Colorado Springs, Colorado; San Diego, California; Oakland, California; and Spokane, Washington, are examples of cities that have recently switched from council-manager to strong-mayor forms, while El Paso, Texas, and Topeka, Kansas, have gone the opposite way. Research suggests that communities suffering some type of problem or disturbance look to change their structure of governance as a response. [20] The emergence of corruption in either form raises questions about the effectiveness of the other type to prevent it. In addition, the differences between the two forms have increasingly become less clear, especially as many cities adopt various hybrid approaches.

Many mayor-council governments, for example, have hired what are essentially city managers under a different title to lead day-to-day operations. Some council-manager forms have abandoned non-partisan, at-large elections in favor of district-elected councilmembers who retain party affiliations.

A middle way has emerged between the two once clearly delineated forms of government. In the traditional view, the mayor-council form exists in politically run cities, while the council-manager type appears in administratively run cities. However, the new dominant form of local government now found in most major American cities can most appropriately be called "the adapted city."[21] The nation's largest cities borrow aspects from both forms; in many places, the two are now largely fused.

Both machine/political and reform/administrative approaches, when implemented in orthodox fashion, can lead to problems. Jessica Trounstine, in *Political Monopolies in American Cities,* found that either side of this traditional divide could be used to form "political monopolies" that benefit the leaders and constituents of one side or the other.[22] She suggests that the council-manager form is less a barrier to corruption than simply a alternate power structure. The major challenge facing practitioners of both forms is that of reelection. In fact, elections—though rife with their own problems—are actually what tends to keep the local government leadership honest. As Trounstine found, "When politicians cease to worry about reelection, they become free to pursue government policy that does not reflect constituent preferences. They acquire the ability to enrich themselves and their supporters or pursue policies that would otherwise lead to their electoral defeat."[23]

Using the system to remain in office without worrying about reelection is a common practice in both major forms of American local government, which may explain how corruption can arise in both.

The "political monopolies" concept is a key to understanding what happened in Bell. During Rizzo's tenure, he controlled who came onto the council; candidates ran unopposed or were appointed.[24] When vacancies occurred, Rizzo would interview and select who would fill them.[25] [26] He essentially removed the threat of losing elections or of having to contend with councilmembers who might challenge him. Thus he, his assistant, and the council were free to disenfranchise the public and place self-interest over the public interest.

Rizzo's two main techniques were to remove those who opposed him and co-opt those around him. He then diluted and dismantled the checks and balances built into the council-manager form. It is worth noting that, while the council as a whole was not highly educated, Rizzo and his senior staff were well schooled and trained. He and several others held master's degrees in public administration. And although Rizzo generally discouraged Bell officials from participating in professional organizations and attending conferences, many were members of professional organizations like the International County Management Association (ICMA) and the Los Angeles County Police Association; such memberships require loyalty to a professional code of ethics.

Rizzo carefully drew others into the of web corruption. He rewarded those who played along and removed those who got in his way. He did so by placing certain individuals in key positions, and ensuring that other individuals and groups became complicit in illegal activities. One example was his weakening of the union presence for police and other municipal employees. When the scandal broke, the three bargaining units in Bell had no memorandum of understanding (MOU); two of the three units never had one. [27]

Rizzo made many municipal workers at-will employees, and removed their civil service status so they could be terminated easier. The only active union in Bell was the that of the police. But sergeant and whistleblower James Corcoran claimed that the MOU between the union and the city was seven years out of date but there were never any negotiations. "Rizzo would befriend the head of the union, would take him under his wing, show him how to invest money . . . pretty soon they'd be a team," Corcoran said. "Rizzo was very generous—with others people's money, the taxpayer." [28] Doug Willmore echoed this sentiment, saying he'd "never seen anything like it."

Willmore said that Rizzo had cultivated substantial power over the police union, and that the lieutenants and captains were afraid of him. [29] Police unions are usually among the most powerful organizations in a city; they tend to be well funded and respected by the community. Rizzo's dominance over the one in Bell simply further underscores how exceptional his tenure was.

Rizzo created loyalty among his top officials by means of pay and perks. He paid them high salaries, allowed them to buy credits in the retirement system with taxpayer dollars, and accrue sick and vacation leave at extraordinarily high amounts. He then oversaw a loan program in which the majority of city employees benefited from using their sick and vacation leave accruals as collateral for the loans. Forty-four of the sixty-nine employees were participating in the program, as were Mayor Hernandez and Councilmember Artiga. [30] He tied the council to the corruption by paying the (part-time) members more than $100,000 from phantom agencies that rarely if ever met. When he was not getting the legal advice he wanted, Rizzo hired additional counsel, even though Ed Lee, the city attorney, took direction from Rizzo instead of the council.

In these and other actions, Rizzo preyed on Bell's largely low-income, undereducated residents by operating in a non-transparent matter and ensuring that, even when they tried to understand what was occurring, they could not. He and the council did everything they could to suppress communication, including holding meetings in the middle of the workday.[31] Attendance at council meetings was consistently low, averaging seven to ten persons.[32] [33]

Rizzo also broke down the council-manager systems traditional checks and balances. *Los Angeles Times* reporter Gottlieb said, "Council members were either part of the scam or too dumb to realize Rizzo worked for them, not the other way around."[34] The gaps in checks and balances began with Rizzo's ability to conceal his former misdeeds in other cities. Former Councilman George Bass said seventeen years later that he regretted that he and his fellow councilmembers did not diligently investigate Rizzo's background before hiring him.[35] However, due to Rizzo's aptitude for manipulating systems and gaining loyalty, very little negative information was available. Looking more closely at those past assignments, one finds the same predispositions toward cultivating, accumulating, and wielding political power for personal gain.

Rizzo sought to increase his authority by converting Bell to a charter city and attempting to get his legal consultants to draft a resolution granting him authority without a check-and-balance system. He took advantage of an uneducated, inactive populace by introducing a deceptive ordinance that, instead of limiting council salaries, actually increased them. *Los Angeles Times* reporter Gottlieb commented that, "Ed Lee probably goofed when he wrote the charter, and neither Rizzo nor the councilmembers read it closely enough, if at all, to understand that it actually kept their pay at the state limits. Had the charter been worded differently, councilmembers might not have faced criminal charges."[36]

The council granted Rizzo authority to execute business documents on behalf of the city, but placed no dollar limits on that authority. Typically, there is a cap ($25,000 or $50,000) on such expenditures, with council approval required for exceeding it—another typical—check-and-balance. Rizzo cited the charter as justification for increasing his and other top officials' salaries without council approval. Defense attorneys later attempted to get charges dropped against councilmembers, claiming they did not know the salary increases were illegal. Judge Kennedy was not moved. Councilmembers should have known their salaries were unjustified, she said. "The city of Bell charter," she wrote, "did not make Bell a sovereign nation not subject to the general penal laws of the State of California."[37] What permeated the city's decision-making process, she said, was simply unchecked greed.[38] Rizzo also took care to cripple legal and audit oversight of city policies. He ensured that the city attorney and any legal consultants reported directly to him, and did not rotate auditors, keeping the same one for ten years. Thus further critical components of a check-and-balance system were essentially eliminated.

In addition to intimidation and deception, Rizzo also used confusion, creating a system for approving city business that was completely incomprehensible. He manipulated council meeting agendas, choosing items for the consent agenda and often listing items with misleading titles, incorrect back-up, or no backup at all. When he needed attorney approval, Rizzo would often use a cover sheet bearing the city attorney's signature, and place it on items—or simply switch signatures with different items. This combined created a totally indecipherable process for conducting city business.

Rizzo and his staff also went to great lengths to hide many of his actions from the public. One way was to keep minimal or poorly documented records. Whether it was a lack of recorded minutes from council meeting or non-existent documentation of business transactions, there were almost no written policies and procedures, contrary to how documentation is supposed to occur in city governments.[39] Rizzo intentionally avoided a paper trail for many of his activities, and created an elaborate scheme of phantom agencies in order to hide his and the Council's salaries.

In order to finance these salaries and benefits, Rizzo used multiple techniques to extract revenues from the city and its residents. He raised property taxes and issued bonds for imaginary capital improvements, imposing a huge burden of debt on Bell residents. He also used the police force and city code inspectors to drain more money from individuals and businesses. McGuire and Olson's theory of "stationary and rover bandits" provides insight into how Rizzo corrupted various fiscal systems.[40]

Under their theory, a stationary bandit thinks long term. He/she engages in various forms of graft at the expense of residents and businesses, but realizes that the illicit activities must stop short of driving wealth out of the city. That is, the stationary bandit realizes that businesses are mobile and can leave for more favorable conditions. Los Angeles, for example, has eighty-eight cities in close proximity that compete fiercely to attract businesses to enhance their tax base.

The stationary bandit, while acting dishonestly, will also engage in economic development and other investment activities to ensure that businesses and their accompanying wealth do not leave. This may entail some revenue extraction from businesses, but it usually also includes agreements that, in exchange for the graft, might allow the business to by-pass regulatory requirements or other bureaucratic hurdles—in other words, allow the business to operate more profitably.

The rover bandit, by contrast, fixates on siphoning money from the city, its residents, and businesses with no regard for the future impact of his/her actions.

It could be argued that Rizzo initially operated from a stationary bandit perspective. Early in his tenure he restructured bonds, invested in infrastructure, improved police and graffiti abatement response time, and made measurable improvements in municipal services—all while engaging in arbitrary payment schemes to extract money from businesses. But he seemed to abandon this perspective when he brought Spaccia on and they began conspiring to increase their salaries and build up their retirement payouts. In essence, they became short-term or rover bandits. Rizzo and Spaccia had planned to retire on June 30, 2008, and be long gone before the money ran out and residents began to figure out why.[41]

But the two let this end-date pass without bailing out. Was it greed that extended their original termination date? Or did they fear exposure because of the potentially explosive failures looming in the corrupt fiscal systems they designed? Indeed, Rizzo's ability to extract revenue from residents and businesses became increasingly limited. More and more his administration began to resemble a house of cards. Bell's shaky foundation was about to crumble.

From 2006 to 2010, the municipal property tax rate had doubled, giving Bell the second-highest rate of the county's eighty-eight cities.[42] Rizzo's shakedowns of businesses drove many of them from the city—and the impact of the exodus can still be felt today. Former City Administrator Willmore said that so many businesses left town that the city's sales tax in 2015 was half of it was a decade earlier.[43]

Another tactic, large and unnecessary capital projects, is often used municipal graft because such projects are easier to skim from. This is certainly what happened in Bell. Seven years after $70 million in bonds was issued for Bell's Sports Complex, there was almost nothing to show for it. But issuance of the bond provided short-term cash for Rizzo and the Councilmembers to hide their salaries, pensions, and other spending. The contract required Bell to make biannual interest payments and to pay off the principal, $35 million, by November 2010. Bell could do neither. By August 2010, the city's bond rating fell to junk status.[44]

Rizzo also extracted revenue by targeting the city's poor and otherwise vulnerable residents by misusing code enforcement, and setting quotas for police stops, citations, and impounding of cars. Knowing that as many as a third of the residents of Bell and surrounding communities were not in the United States legally, he exhorted the police to target immigrant populations for police stops and impounding of cars. Police were told to specifically target cars and trucks carrying lawn maintenance or painting materials, figuring that the occupants or their family members might not be legal residents. Few challenged the citations and impounds. At the height of this activity, police were impounding up to eight vehicles a day. The cost to recover an impounded car was triple that of surrounding cities, including Los Angeles.[45]

Overall, Rizzo's scheming led to a form of collective corruption in Bell. City employees and consultants, various branches of government, and the attorneys, auditors, and bondholders who should have supported checks and balances all became complicit.[46] Everyone seemed to be getting something. It became easy to look the other way.

Some scholars have argued that the council-manager form of government is ill suited for dealing with municipalities like Bell that contain large immigrant populations.[47] Research does show that residents in council-manager municipalities are less likely to vote in city elections than residents in mayor-council cities.[48] [49]

Voting is clearly the key to removing unethical or unresponsive leaders. Indeed, corruption tends to shrink as the level of democracy rises. As noted above, even after the Bell scandal broke, only 30 percent of registered voters turned out for the council recall election, and only 18 percent and 15 percent of registered voters respectively participated in the 2013 and 2015 elections.[50] However, there are other forms of civic participation available besides voting.

For example, attendance at council meetings increased significantly. During Rizzo's tenure, only six or seven people usually attended. After the scandal broke, some meetings drew an audience of seven hundred.[51] This level of attendance was likely encouraged by the fact that the council began holding meetings in the evenings and live-streaming them on the city's website. Citizens can now also log on to watch previous meetings.

Other scholars have argued that less important than a city's political structure is the ethics of its leaders. Under the right circumstances, these scholars say, corruption can take root in either a council-manager or strong-mayor form. Public administration scholar H. George Frederickson, for example, notes that instances of both political (elected) and administrative (appointed or civil service) corruption have occurred in local governments.[52]

The issue, of course, affects much more than just municipal governments. In general, many bureaucracies have failed to encourage ethical behavior, and have even created barriers to doing the right thing.[53] So how can organizations seek to promote ethical conduct? Typically, they create organizational ethical policies or guidelines and encourage adherence to various professional organizations' codes of ethics; they provide guidance and preventive measures by offering ethics training; and they install enforcement mechanisms.

It is generally accepted that governments should not only have rule-based or compliance-based structures, because these can tempt employees to operate on the edge of misconduct or adhere to only minimal standards. Instead, governments should promote ethical awareness and a set of behaviors employees should conform to or aspire to.

These standards should arise from both on a deontological and a teleological perspective. The former mandates standards that are universally applied—such as to place the public interest over personal interest, follow the rule of law, be fair and efficient, and avoid conflicts of interest. The teleological perspective is concerned with outcomes, or the consequences of a decision—such as maximizing the benefits to the greatest number of citizens. While using one perspective over another can create problems, employing them together can create a good balance of ethical behaviors to guide public employees and officials. [54] [55]

There were obviously serious breakdowns of ethical standards in Bell. Rizzo—quite apart from his lack of ethical leadership—actively created a culture of corruption in the City. There was no evidence of any policies or guidelines on ethics available to employees; it was reported that Rizzo discouraged employees from attending national conferences, where they could be exposed to various codes of ethics. Further, his lack of tolerance for dissent and his retribution against those who challenged him created a chilling environment for those wanting to do the right thing.

But while there seemed to be no ethics training available to employees, a comprehensive ethics training session was provided to the council by Tom Brown, with Rizzo and Spaccia in attendance. In fact, the prosecution used the fact of this training as evidence that Rizzo, Spaccia, and the council knew they were doing wrong.

Perhaps more of an applied framework, or the practitioner-philosopher approach used by the Center for Business Ethics at Bentley College, would have resonated more with councilmembers, employees, and contractors. The following six simple questions were incorporated into their training programs:

1. *Is it right?* (based on the deontological theory of moral rights)
2. *Is it fair?* (based on the deontological theory of justice)
3. *Who gets hurt?* (based on the utilitarian notion of the greatest good for the greatest number of people)
4. *Would you be comfortable if the details of your decision were reported on the front page of your local newspaper?* (based on the universalist principle of disclosure)
5. *What would you tell your child to do?* (based on the deontological principle of reversibility)
6. *How does it smell?* (based on the "gut principle," that—using ethical theory or not—we usually have a sense of whether something "feels" right). [56]

The boundaries between the two traditional forms of municipal government are blurring, which may be a good thing. Council-manager forms can incorporate district voting to increase minority representation; strong-mayor forms can incorporate a professionally trained administrator. Still, basic questions remain: Is dishonesty in local government institutional? Are there aspects of government and politics that inevitably lead to corruption, regardless of who is in power?

Perhaps we should look more closely at what might contribute to corruption in council-manager governments, the dominant municipal form in the United States. Long-term city managers can become entrenched and vulnerable to the same corrupting influences as those who occupy elected positions. While term limits have reduced the longevity of some elected offices, term limits for local officials are not as popular as they are for state or federal officials.[57]

The role of the city manager/city administrator and his/her relationship to the elected council is key. With elected officials terming out in staggered terms, a politically astute city manager can ensure his or her long-term survival. Increasingly, a complementarity relationship between elected and appointed officials is emerging that focuses on reciprocal influence and overlapping responsibilities.[58] Obviously, corrupt or unethical people elected or appointed to public office corrupt local government. And those determined to be corrupt will not be swayed by any amount of ethical training. It follows that the best way to achieve good governance is to elect or hire people to positions of public trust that are honest and conduct themselves in ethical ways.

Still, individuals holding power will always face temptations to abuse it, so strong check-and balance systems are essential. Elected boards should exercise primary oversight by careful selection and evaluations of city managers. Regular legal reviews and audits are essential, with the attorneys and auditors reporting to the council instead of the city manager. Other important elements go beyond structure and encompass transparency, and engagement by residents, civic groups, and businesses.

While the levels of checks and balances vary across cities, the astonishing thing about the Bell scandal is that all the systems failed at the same time—or were virtually non-existent when needed most. Engaged citizens, community organizations, unions, the news media—none countered the growing centralization of power in Rizzo's hands. State and professional organizations—including the L.A. District Attorney's Office, the California Political Practices Commission, CALPERS, and the ICMA—failed to detect any hint of wrongdoing, even when Bell employees and citizens reached out to them.

Even when a traditional check-and-balance system is in place and working, city managers/administrator can wield a good deal of power and influence. He/she must continually balance the interests of the city as a whole with the agendas of his/her bosses, the elected officials. Managers can get caught up in board politics and risk incurring the displeasure of a majority—

a sure recipe for unemployment. On the other hand, many elected officials quickly realize that they must work well with the individual who directly controls city staff and resources. Not doing so could place a board member in danger of not fulfilling campaign promises or of being seen as unresponsive to his/her constituents. A city manager with good communication skills can find ways to make this balance happen, and enjoy strong support from the elected body.

When there is little turnover of elected officials and their city managers, problems can arise. Over time, these relationships can develop into a closed and comfortable system that is difficult for outsiders, including residents, to penetrate. This can nurture a culture in which wrongdoing flourishes.

One area that could be more transparent is city manager compensation. While most cities post their collective bargaining agreements on their websites, rarely can citizens find the city manager's contract provisions there. Even rarer is a full accounting of the manager's total compensation.

A city manager can often receive generous benefits unavailable to other staff, in addition to his/her salary. Contracts often have provisions for additional retirement benefits, such as the purchasing of years of service pension credits; covering the manager's share of costs for retirement and /or supplemental retirement plans; additional vacation and sick leave over and beyond what employees accrue; allowances for housing, car, and telephone; travel and conference provisions; and termination clauses that either pay severance or ongoing salary for a set period of time.

Further, such compensation often has little correlation with a city's manager's years on the job or the size of his/her community.

Another valuable check and balance, therefore, would be more robust and independent public evaluations of the city's top executive. The 360-degree review, an assessment by individuals both inside and outside of the organization, is one such approach. The 360 evaluation does not rely solely on the assessment of the supervisor, in this case the council, and can more accurately capture how the city manager is performing from multiple perspectives— including his/her direct line reports, lower-level employees, colleagues in other agencies, and the community. Having the results of the 360 evaluation done in a public hearing with comments from employees and citizens can assure that not only is the city manager's performance on track but also that the direction of the city government is meeting the community's needs.

Then there are the news media. "The press is, in fact, the last hope for the flow of information necessary for democratic governance, and the press is being systematically eroded and weakened, especially in its capacity to cover local government," noted Terry Cooper, Professor at the USC School of Policy, Planning, and Development.[59] The disappearance of local news media was one of the most important systemic breakdowns that allowed the corruption in Bell to escalate undetected.

With the rapid decline of print journalism and shrinking budgets for reporters, news media coverage of Bell's government was cursory at best and nonexistent at worst. Reporters assigned to cover the city were also responsible for more than a dozen other municipalities, preventing them from regularly attending council meetings. The demise of smaller regional papers has left the *Los Angeles Times* to cover eighty-eight municipalities and ten million citizens; meanwhile, the newspaper's metro-area staff is less than half the size it was in 2000. [60]

Reporters would occasionally call in to Bell meetings for summaries of important matters, but this was rare. The two *Los Angeles Times* reporters credited with exposing the corruption only stumbled upon the scandal because of a story they were doing on the city's interactions with Maywood. The absence of local news media left Bell's uninformed citizens woefully unprepared to take on City Hall.

This dilemma is part of a national trend in which the traditional print news media are becoming increasingly obsolete and being replaced by citizen bloggers in a "new media ecosystem." The idea is that small news outlets and blogs will work with traditional news media outlets to monitor local governments, but that certainly didn't happen in Bell. In any case, Internet blogs would not reach the many households lacking an Internet connection.

Another lens through which to view the corruption in Bell is the notion of geographic contagion. In the past few decades, the southeastern Los Angeles county cities of South Gate, Bell, Cudahy, Maywood, Vernon, Huntington Park, and Lynwood, and two water districts—Maywood Water Company and Central Basin Municipal Water District—have been embroiled in corruption scandals. [61] Is there a "culture of corruption" in this area? Research has found that corruption can be contagious among neighboring countries, driven primarily by factors such as trade, tourism, and immigration. [62] It is also known that local governments have the ability to influence other neighboring cities with which they share a physical border. [63] The theory supporting this, the regional-diffusion model, focuses on adoption of policy innovation. But much might also be learned about the effects of corrupting influences among southeast Los Angeles county cities that share borders.

Are corrupt practices in some of the southeastern county cities spilling over into their neighbors' public operations? We know that some of the players in the Bell scandal were also involved in neighboring cities. George Cole, for one, was elected in 1984 as a reformer after the Bell poker corruption scandal and remained on the council for twenty-four years, including rotations as mayor, before retiring in 2008. He held numerous contractual relationships with many of neighboring cities though the Steelworkers' Old-timers Foundation. Former mayor and now Councilmember Nestor Valencia insists Cole was the true mastermind of the corruption in Bell because of his connections with many southeastern cities.

A few examples: Cole served on the Board of the Central Basin Water District while simultaneously running the Oldtimers and sitting on the Bell Council. He resigned his Central Basin board position in 2006 after the Los Angeles District Attorney begin investigating possible conflicts of interest—two of the three largest non-construction contracts awarded by Central Basin during the previous five years went to the Oldtimers Foundation. Yet even after resigning from the board, Cole's influence remained. In 2007 the board appointed a close friend of Cole's who had worked for the Oldtimers to fill the vacancy.[64] In 1995, while heading the Oldtimers Foundation, Cole was involved in attempts to secure a bingo hall in South Gate to help fund the foundation.[65] In 2010, the California Attorney General found that the Old-timers Foundation failed to disclose its service contracts with Bell, Hunting-ton Park, other southeastern cities and the Central Basin Water district.[66]

Some urban planners have recommended merging some of these cities into one larger governmental entity to achieve a larger tax base, economies of scale, and stronger oversight.[67] Combining police, fire, and other city services might also deliver services more efficiently, and better position the region for economic development and regional planning.[68] As noted above, the Bell scandal broke when reporters were examining a proposal being discussed to form a regional police force by combining the forces of Bell, Maywood, and other small cities. This is an idea worth pursuing. Public safety costs for local governments are devouring larger and larger portions of municipal revenues, while the need for every city, particularly smaller ones, to have its own police and fire departments is questionable.

Similarly, some have suggested that there are simply too many local governments in California for the public to be able to track. The total includes are fifty-eight counties, nearly five hundred cities, more than one thousand school districts and upwards of 4,500 special districts.[69] It may in fact be time to rethink how municipal services are being delivered. The number of complex, large-scale, cross-boundary problems is on the rise, and traditional city governments are often ill-equipped to deal with them. Regional governance structures and shared services may be better suited to tackle these issues—while also providing the kind of additional oversight so sorely lacking in Bell.[70]

But proposals for the consolidation or disincorporation of some southeastern Gateway cities have their fair share of critics. Notably, suggesting that the mostly Latino and working class cities in Los Angeles County cannot govern themselves—while more affluent cities should retain their autonomy—can make talk of consolidation challenging.

Yet in the end, debates over governmental structures and regional arrangements, while important, somehow fail to satisfy. The central, fundamental question remains: How could this happen? How could such blatant corruption—a veritable caricature of sleaze—thrive on such an enormous scale in a town located just a few miles away from the nation's second-largest city?

Certainly, as noted above, events in Bell were influenced by several broad trends that were—and are—well beyond residents' ability to stop. There were the years of economic decline; the deep demographic "churn" that worked against the emergence of a stable, engaged populace; the large influx of undocumented residents; the decline of media oversight; the willingness of a few professionals such as attorneys and auditors to look the other way; and a seeming lack of interest in Bell's affairs from county and state authorities. Together, they planted a fertile field for a man like Robert Rizzo.

If such factors indeed did help set the stage, all that was then needed was someone with the right credentials and the wrong motives to come along, and a small group of weak and greedy colleagues to provide cover and back-up. Bell had both. Unfortunately, bad motives, willing cronies, and vulnerable populations are not in short supply, in L.A. County or elsewhere. That's why the story of Bell, California, should serve not only as a case study, but also as a warning.

NOTES

1. James Madison, "Federalist No. 51: The Structure of the Government Must Furnish the Proper Checks and Balances Between the Different Departments," *New York Packet* (New York, NY), Feb. 6, 1788.

2. Gottlieb, J., Vives, R., & Leonard, J. "Bell Leaders Hauled Off in Cuffs: Eight Are Held in Scandal the D.A. Calls 'Corruption on Steroids.'" *Los Angeles Times.* September 22, 2010. Retrieved from http://articles.latimes.com/2010/sep/22/local/la-me-bell-arrest-20100922.

3. Bell Legal Panel. Chapman University. February 19, 2015.

4. United States Census Bureau. "Urban and Rural Populations 1790 to 1990, 1990 Census of Population and Housing." *1990 Population and Housing Unit Counts: United States.* N.D. Retrieved from http://www.census.gov/population/www/censusdata/files/table-4.pdf.

5. Ibid.

6. Ibid.

7. Ibid.

8. Ibid.

9. Ibid, p. 14.

10. Judd, D. & Swanstrom, T. *City Politics: The Political Economy of Urban America.* New York: Pearson Longman, 2006. pp. 14–15.

11. Ibid, p. 47.

12. Hogen-Esch, T. "Predator State: Corruption in a Council-Manager System – The Case of Bell, California." (white paper at the City of Bell Scandal Revisited Conference, Chapman University, 2015). p. 3.

13. "Enoch L. Johnson, Ex-Boss in Jersey." *New York Times.* December 10, 1968. Retrieved from http://query.nytimes.com/gst/abstract.html?res=9E05EEDA1230EF34BC4852DFB4678383679EDE.

14. Choi, C. G., Feiock, R.C., & Bae, J. The Adoption and Abandonment of Council-Manager Government. *Public Administration Review, 73*(5), pp. 727–736. 2013.

15. Frederickson, H. G. & Meek, J. W. Presentation. "Searching for Virtue in the City: Bell and Her Sisters." (white paper at the City of Bell Scandal Revisited Conference, Chapman University, 2015).

16. Ammons, D. N. "City Manager and City Administrator Role Similarities and Differences: Perceptions Among Persons Who have Served as Both." *The American Review of Public Administration, 38*(1), pp. 24–40. 2008.

17. Carr. J. B. "What Have We Learned about the Performance of Council-Manager Government? A Review and Synthesis of the Research." *Public Administration Review, 75*(5), pp. 673–689. 2015.

18. Terry, L. "Professionalism over Politics in the Shift to Council-Manager Government." *More Than Mayor or Manager: Campaigns to Change Form of Government in America's Large Cities*, edited by James H. Svara and Douglas J. Watson. Washington DC: Georgetown University Press, 2010. p. 225.

19. ICMA Municipal Yearbook. "Most Prevalent Form of Local Government in Specific Population Ranges (2013): Council-Manager (CM) vs. Mayor-Council (MC)." 2013.

20. Choi, Feiock, & Bae, The Adoption.

21. Frederickson, H. G., Johnson, G. A., & Wood, C. H. *The Adapted City: Institutional Dynamics and Structural Change.* New York: M.E. Sharpe, 2004. p. 7.

22. Trounstine, J. *Political Monopolies in American Cities.* Chicago: University of Chicago Press, 2008. p. 217.

23. Ibid, p. 2.

24. Wikipedia. "Bell, California." Last Modified July 27, 2015. Retrieved from https://en.wikipedia.org/wiki/Bell,_California.

25. People v. Hernandez, Jacobo, Mirabel, Cole, Bello, & Artiga. BA376025. Preliminary Hearing. February 14, 2011. p. 85.

26. Hogen-Esch, Predator.

27. Aleshire, D. & Taylor, A. "Corruption on Steroids: The Bell Scandal from the Legal Perspective." (white paper at the City of Bell Scandal Revisited Conference, Chapman University, 2015).

28. James Corcoran, interview with author, February 12, 2015, p. 19.

29. Doug Willmore, interview with author, February 12, 2015.

30. Ibid.

31. U.S. Federal Communications Commission. "Newspapers." *Part One: The Media Landscape, Section One: Commercial Media.* N.D. pp. 33–57. Retrieved from https://transition.fcc.gov/osp/inc-report/INoC-1-Newspapers.pdf.

32. People v. Hernandez, Jacobo, Mirabel, Cole, Bello, & Artiga. BA376025. Preliminary Hearing. February 7, 2011.

33. McNary, S. "Legacy of Bell's Corruption Case: High Tax Rates, New Civic Engagement." *89.3 KPCC Southern California Public Radio.* January 18, 2013. Retrieved from http://www.scpr.org/blogs/politics/2013/01/18/12088/legacy-bells-corruption-bust-high-tax-rates-new-ci/.

34. Gottlieb, J. "Bell: A Total Breakdown." (white paper at the City of Bell Scandal Revisited Conference, Chapman University, 2015).

35. Pringle, P., Knoll, C., & Murphy, K. "Rizzo's Horse Had Come In." *Los Angeles Times.* August 22, 2010. Retrieved from http://www.pulitzer.org/archives/9205.

36. Gottlieb, Bell: A Total.

37. Gottlieb, J. "Judge Refuses to Dismiss Charges Against Ex-Bell Council Members." *Los Angeles Times.* December 2, 2011. Retrieved from http://articles.latimes.com/2011/dec/02/local/la-me-12-02-bell-dismiss-20111202.

38. Knoll, C. & Mather, K. "Former Bell Second-in-Command Gets 11 Years in Prison for Corruption." *Los Angeles Times.* April 10, 2014. Retrieved from http://www.latimes.com/local/la-me-spaccia-sentencing-20140411-story.html.

39. Aleshire & Taylor, Corruption.

40. McGuire, M. & Olson, M. "The Economics of Autocracy and Majority Rule: The Invisible Hand and the Use of Force." *Journal of Economic Literature*, 34,1996, pp. 72–96.

41. People v. Spaccia. BA 382701, BA376026. Spaccia's Trial. November 18, 2013.

42. Christiansen, K. & Esquivel, P. "Bell Property Tax Rate Second-Highest in L.A. County." *Los Angeles Times.* July 30, 2010. Retrieved from http://articles.latimes.com/2010/jul/30/local/la-me-bell-taxes-new-20100730.

43. Willmore, interview.

44. Christensen, K. & Gold, S. "Bell's Bonds Downgraded to Junk Status." *Los Angeles Times.* August 11, 2010. Retrieved from http://articles.latimes.com/2010/aug/11/local/la-me-bell-ratings-20100811.

45. Corcoran, interview.

46. Byrne, T. P. "Ethical Dilemmas in a California City: Lessons in Leadership, Transparency, and Accountability." *California Journal of Politics and Society, 6*(4), pp. 577-598. 2014.

47. Hogen-Esch, Predator.

48. Hajnal, Z. L. & Lewis, P. G. "Municipal Institutions and Voter Turnout in Local Elections." *Urban Affairs Review, 38* (5), pp. 645–668. 2003.

49. Wood, C. "Voter Turnout in City Elections." *Urban Affairs Review, 38* (5), pp. 209-231. 2002.

50. Los Angeles County Registrar-Recorder/County Clerk. "March 03, 2015 – Consolidated Elections: Final Official Election Returns." March, 10, 2015. Retrieved from http://rrcc.co.la.ca.us/elect/15032316/rr2316p01.htm#3754.

51. Vo, T. "Keeping City Hall Accountable: Reflections on the Bell Scandal." *Voice of OC.* February 20, 2015. Retrieved from http://voiceofoc.org/2015/02/keeping-city-hall-accountable-reflections-on-the-bell-scandal.

52. Frederickson & Meek, Presentation.

53. Cooper, T. Big Questions in Administrative Ethics: A Need for Focused, Collaborative Effort. *Public Administration Review*, 64 (4), pp. 395–417. 2004.

54. Svara, J. H. "The Ethics Primer for Public Administrators in Government and Nonprofit Organizations." Sudbury, MA: Jones and Bartlett, 2007.

55. Benavides. A., Dicke, L., & Maleckaire, V. "Creating Public Value Sector Pedestals and Examining Falls from Grace: Examining ICMA Ethical Sanctions." *International Journal of Public Administration, 35(11), 2012*, pp. 749–759.

56. Bowditch, J. Buono, A., & Stewart, M. A *Primer on Organizational Behavior*, 7th Edition, John Wiley & Sons, 2008, p. 4.

57. Petracca, M. & O'Brien, K. "Municipal Term Limits In Orange County, California." *National Civic Review*, 83 (2), 2007, pp. 87–94.

58. Demir, T. & Reddick, C. "Understanding Shared Roles in Policy and Administration: An Empirical Study of Council-Manager Relations." *Public Administration Review*, (72) 4, 2012, pp. 526–536.

59. Lytal, C. "SPPD Panel Examines Lessons from Bell Scandal." *USC News.* October 26, 2010. Retrieved from http://news.usc.edu/29733/SPPD-Panel-Examines-Lessons-from-Bell-Scandal/.

60. U.S. Federal Communications Commission, Newspapers.

61. Walton, A. "Why is Public Corruption Endemic in Southeast Los Angeles County." 89.3 KPCC. May, 20, 2014. Retrieved from http://www.scpr.org/blogs/politics/2014/05/20/16648/why-is-public-corruption-endemic-in-southeast-los/.

62. Quaz, R., Langley, S. & Tlii, A. "Corruption Contagion in South Asia and East Asia: An Econometric Study. *International Journal of Developing Societies*, 2 (3), 2013, pp. 87–95.

63. Berry, F. S., & Berry, W. D. "State Lottery Adoptions as Policy Innovations: An Event History Analysis." *American Political Science Review*, 84, 1990. pp.395–416.

64. Allen, S., Becerra, H. & McGreevy, P. "Water District Gives Millions in Contracts to Politically Connected Recipients." *Los Angeles Times.* June, 3, 2011. Retrieved from http://articles.latimes.com/2011/jun/03/local/la-me-central-basin-20110603/2.

65. "Southeast/Long Beach: No Bingo." *Los Angeles Times.* September, 28, 1995. Retrieved from http://articles.latimes.com/1995-09-28/local/me-50777_1_bingo-parlor.

66. McGreevy, P. "Charity Run By Ex-Bell Mayor Didn't Disclose Government Contracts, Attorney General Says". *Los Angeles Times.* August, 21, 2010. Retrieved from http://articles.latimes.com/2010/aug/21/local/la-me-bell-oldtimers-2010082.

002 002 0

67. Flores, A. "Agency Takes a Look at Southeast Cities' Governance." *Los Angeles Times.* Retrieved from http://articles.latimes.com/2013/apr/08/local/la-me-southeast-cities-20130408.

68. Reilly, T, & Tekniepe, R. J. "Collaborative Regional Networked Systems." In Balutis, A., and Buss, T. (editors), *American Governance 3.0: Rebooting the Public Square.* Armonk, NY: M.E. Sharpe Publishing, 2011.

69. Matthews, J. "Bell and Sacramento." (white paper at the City of Bell Scandal Revisited Conference, Chapman University, 2015).

70. Laslo, D. & Judd, D. "Building Civic Capacity Through an Elastic State: The Case of St. Louis." *Review of Policy Research,* 23 (6), 2006. pp. 1235–1255.

Bibliography

"5 Convicted Bell Leaders Sue Former City Attorney." *CBS LA.* March 7, 2014. Retrieved from http://losangeles.cbslocal.com/2014/03/07/5-convicted-bell-leaders-sue-former-city-attorney/.

"AB 23 Assembly Floor Analysis." June 9, 2011.

Abdulrahim, R. "Activist Raises Profile of Bell's Lebanese Community." *Los Angeles Times.* September 10, 2010. Retrieved from http://articles.latimes.com/2010/sep/08/local/la-me-bell-lebanese-20100908.

Adams, R. Settlement Agreement and Release of Claims. April 11, 2014.

Adams, R. Testimony. November 6, 2013.

Adams v. Bell. BC489331. Deposition of Randy Adams. May 1, 2013.

Adams v. Bell. BC489331. Notice of Order Approving Dismissal of Actions and Court's Retention of Jurisdiction of Actions Pursuant to Code of Civil Procedure Section 664.6. May 22, 2014.

Agostoni, K. "Former El Segundo's Manager's Firing Leads to Messy Lawsuit." *Daily Breeze News.* March 23, 2013. http://www.dailybreeze.com/general-news/20130323/former-el-segundo-managers-firing-leads-to-messy-lawsuit.

Albright, C. "Declaration of Clifton Wade Albright." December 14, 2012.

Albright, C. "Paid Invoice History By Vendor January 1, 2005-September 30, 2010." October 4, 2010.

Albright, C. Testimony. November 4, 2013.

Albright, Yee & Schmit, LLP. v. City of South Gate. BC297983, BC311748, BS090172. Case No. 1220031340. Settlement Agreement and Mutual Release. February 22, 2007.

Albright, Yee & Schmit, LLP. v. Henry Gonzales, et al. BC297983, BC311748, BS090172. Settlement, Vacating 2/13/07 Post-Arbitration Hearing, and OSC Hearing for May 25, 2007 at 8:30 am. February 8, 2007.

Albright, Yee & Schmit, LLP. v. Henry Gonzales, et al. BC297983. Case Summary of Court Case, Superior Court of California, County of Los Angeles. 2007.

Aleshire & Wynder, LLP. "Anthony R. Taylor." N.D. Retrieved from http://www.awattorneys.com/our-team/attorneys/anthony-r-taylor#.

Aleshire, D. "Bell City Attorney Report on Legal Fees." November 12, 2013.

Aleshire, D. "Bell Staff Report RE: Report on Status of Litigation: Conclusion of FY 2011-2012." November 7, 2012.

Aleshire, D. "City of Bell Agenda Report RE: Attorney Report on Client No-Pay Arrangement." November 11, 2013.

Aleshire, D. In discussion with the author. N.D.

Aleshire, D. "Report on the Status of Litigation FY 2011-2012." N.D.

Aleshire, D. "Report on the Status of Litigation Sept 2011-June 2013." N.D.

Aleshire, D. & Taylor, A. "City of Irvine Great Park Audit: Report of Special Counsel." March 24, 2015.

Aleshire, D. & Taylor, A. Corruption on Steroids: The Bell Scandal from the Legal Perspective. (white paper at the City of Bell Scandal Revisited Conference, Chapman University, 2015).

Allen, S., Becerra, H. & McGreevy, P. "Water District Gives Millions in Contracts to Politically Connected Recipients" *Los Angeles Times*. June, 3, 2011. Retrieved from http://articles.latimes.com/2011/jun/03/local/la-me-central-basin-20110603/.

Ammons, D.N. City Manager and City Administrator Role Similarities and Differences: Perceptions Among Persons Who have Served as Both. *The American Review of Public Administration, 38*(1). pp. 24–40. 2008.

Amundsen, I. *Political Corruption: An Introduction to the Issues*. Bergen: Chr. Michelsen Institute (CMI Working Paper WP, 1999).

"Angela Spaccia Drops Lawsuit Against Former Boss, Ex-Bell City Manager Robert Rizzo." *City News Service.* January 24, 2014. Retrieved from http://www.dailynews.com/general-news/20140124/angela-spaccia-drops-lawsuit-against-former-boss-ex-bell-city-manager-robert-rizzo.

Assem. Bill 23, 2011-2012 Reg. Sess (Cal. 2011).

Assem. Bill 93, 2011-2012 Reg. Sess (Cal. 2011).

Assem. Bill 900, 2009-2010 Reg. Sess (Cal. 2010).

Assem. Bill 1344, 2011-2012 Reg. Sess (Cal. 2011).

Audi, T. "In One City, an Islamic Center Unifies." *The Wall Street Journal*. September 20, 2010. Retrieved from http://www.wsj.com/articles/SB10001424052748704644404575482001778588866.

B013634. Robert Rizzo's Cover Letter. June 24, 1993.

Barboza, T. "New Bell City Council Sworn in Amid Promises to Rebound from Corruption Scandal." *Los Angeles Times*. April 7, 2011. Retrieved from http://latimes-blogs.latimes.com/lanow/2011/04/city-council-sworn-in-bell.html.

Barnes, M. "Rancho Palos Verdes Hires City Manager Who Helped Repair Scandal-Plagued Bell." *Daily Breeze News*. January 29, 2015. http://www.dailybreeze.com/government-and-politics/20150129/rancho-palos-verdes-hires-city-manager-who-helped-repair-scandal-plagued-bell.

Barnes, W. "Audit Findings in the City of Bell by the Office of State Controller." N.D.

Barrows, H.D. "Don Antonio Maria Lugo; A Picturesque Character of California." *Annual Publication of the Historical Society of Southern California*. (Los Angeles: University of California Press on behalf of the Historical Society of Southern California, Vol. 3, No. 4, 1896). pp. 28–29. Retrieved from http://www.jstor.org/stable/41167598.

"BASTA Attorney David Aleshire Explains The Recall Process & Timing, 8-25-10." N.D. Retrieved from https://www.youtube.com/watch?v=k4ES4CpC-MY.

"BASTA Co-Founder Speaks on Corruption." November 8, 2011. Retrieved from https://www.youtube.com/watch?v=EUQ5Wc5wMqg.

Beale, J.H. *A Selection of Cases on Municipal Corporations.* Cambridge: Harvard University Press, 1911.

Becerra, H. "Law Firm Agrees to Pay $2 Million to South Gate." *Los Angeles Times*. March 23, 2005. Retrieved from http://articles.latimes.com/2005/mar/23/local/me-southgate23.

Becerra, H. "South Gate Chases Legal Firms." *Los Angeles Times*. January 23, 2005.Retrieved from http://articles.latimes.com/2005/jan/23/local/me-southgate23.

Becerra, H. & Pringle, P. "Bell's Business Ties to Officials Probed." *Los Angeles Times*. July 31, 2010. Retrieved from http://articles.latimes.com/2010/jul/31/local/la-me-07-31-bell-properties-20100731.

Becerra, H. & Vives, R. "Authorities Probe Alleged Misconduct in Maywood City Offices." *Los Angeles Times.* February 18, 2010. Retrieved from latimesblogs.latimes.com/lanow/2010/02/authorities-probe-alleged-misconduct-among-maywood-officials.html.

Becerra, H. & Vives, R. "Bell Councilman an Accidental Hero by Staying Clear of Corruption Scandal." *Los Angeles Times.* October 13, 2010. http://articles.latimes.com/print/2010/oct/13/local/la-me-bell-councilman-20101009.

"Bell City Council Meeting Postponed." July 23, 2010. Retrieved from https://www.youtube.com/watch?v=7hYCWy2ueO0.

"Bell City Council Sues Eric Eggena for Damages in Excess of $2 Million." *Latino California.* October 1, 2012. Retrieved from http://latinocalifornia.com/home/2012/10/bell-city-council-sues-eric-eggena-for-damages-in-excess-of-2-million/.

"Bell Election: Newly Elected Pledge to Sweep Out City Hall; Interim Administrator Likely to be Fired [Updated]." *Los Angeles Times.* March 9, 2011. Retrieved from http://latimesblogs.latimes.com/lanow/2011/03/bell-rizzo-fire-carrillo-casso-police-disband-corruption.html.

Bell Legal Panel. Chapman University. February 19, 2015.

"Bell: Manager Intends to Quit." *Los Angeles Times.* December 10, 1987.

"BELL: Mirabal to Rejoin City Council." *Los Angeles Times.* April 4, 1993.

"Bell Officials Arrested." September 21, 2010. Retrieved from https://www.youtube.com/watch?v=x1Zj5MjFFo0.

"Bell Trial: After 10 Days, Jurors Say They Hope to 'Speed Up'." *Los Angeles Times.* March 7, 2013. Retrieved from http://latimesblogs.latimes.com/lanow/2013/03/bell-trial-after-10-days-jurors-say-they-hope-to-speed-up.html.

"Bell Residents Club Meeting 8-19-10." August 27, 2010. Retrieved from https://www.youtube.com/watch?v=j513gO_oKqM.

Bello, V. Letter to James Fontenette, LA County DA Investigator. May 6, 2009.

Bello, V. Letter to LA DA David Demerjian. June 17, 2009.

Benavides. A., Dicke, L., & Maleckaire, V. "Creating Public Value Sector Pedestals and Examining Falls from Grace: Examining ICMA Ethical Sanctions." *International Journal of Public Administration, 35*(11), 2012, pp. 749–759.

Bentham, Jeremy. "On Publicity". The Works of Jeremy Bentham, Vol. 2, part 2. 1839. Retrieved from http://oll.libertyfund.org/titles/1921.

Berg, M. H. "Bell City OKs Rizzo as Administrative Head." *Los Angeles Times.* August 15, 1993.

Berman, E. M. & West, J. P. "Managing ethics to improve performance and build trust." *Public Integrity Annual*, 1997, pp. 23–31.

Berry, F. S., & Berry, W. D. "State Lottery Adoptions as Policy Innovations: An Event History Analysis." *American Political Science Review*, 84, 1990. pp. 395–416.

Best Lawyers. "James W. Spertus." N.D. Retrieved from https://www.bestlawyers.com/lawyers/james-w-spertus/128574/.

Biederman, P. "Schools Trade Land to Bell for $25 Million in Future Taxes." *Los Angeles Times*. October 4, 1987, SE1, SE3.

Board of Supervisors of the City of Los Angeles. "Resolution of the Board of Supervisors of the City of Los Angeles Reciting the Fact of the City of Bell's March 8, 2011 General Municipal Election, Special Recall Election and Special Election to Fill a Vacancy, Declaring the Results of the Election and Such other Matters as Required by Law." April 5, 2011.

Boyer, E. J. "Steelworkers' Lament: Odes for a Lost Love: In Memory of 'Lady Beth'." *Los Angeles Times*. May 6, 1985.

Bowditch, J. Buono, A., & Stewart, M. A *Primer on Organizational Behavior*, 7th Edition, John Wiley & Sons, 2008.

Brandeis, Louis D. *Other People's Money and How the Bankers Use It.* New York: Frederick A. Stokes Company, 1914.

Broder, K. "Fired Bell Official Joins Parade of Ex-Officials Suing the City." *All Gov California.* August 31, 2012. Retrieved from http://www.allgov.com/USA/CA/news/where-is-the-money-going/fired-bell-official-joins-parade-of-ex-officials-suing-the-city-120831?news=845169.

Brown & White LLP. "RE: Retainer Agreement for Representation by Brown & White LLP." August 10, 2006.

Brown Act. "A Pocket Guide to Open Meeting Laws in California: The Brown Act." December 3, 2003. Retrieved from http://www.thefirstamendment.org/Brown-Act-Brochure-DEC-03.pdf.

Brown, T. "Paid Invoice History By Vendor January 1, 2007-December 31, 2010." August 17, 2011.

Brown White & Newhouse LLP and City of Bell. "Mutual General Release Agreement." August 26, 2014.

Bruder, J. "Are Dying Newspapers too Big to Fail? Can Online Start-Ups Stop the Gap?" *Alaska Dispatch News.* December 8, 2012. Retrieved from http://www.adn.com/article/are-dying-newspapers-too-big-fail-can-online-start-ups-stop-gap.

Burns, M. "Bell Reforms Aimed at Poker Club Corruption." *Los Angeles Times.* January 3, 1985.

Burns, M. "Council Wary It May Be Illegal: Bell Casino Requests Adding Asian Games." *Los Angeles Times.* January 10, 1985.

Burns, M. "Indicted City Manager Becomes Central Issue in Bell Campaign." *Los Angeles Times.* March 18, 1984.

Burns, M. "Indicted City Official Placed on Sick Leave in Bell." *Los Angeles Times.* April 26, 1984.

Burns, M. "New Bell Councilman Calls for Administrator's Ouster." *Los Angeles Times.* April 19, 1984.

Burns, M. "Springsteen Strikes Chord With Steelworkers." *Los Angeles Times.* October 28, 1984.

Byrne, T. P. "Ethical Dilemmas in a California City: Lessons in Leadership, Transparency, and Accountability." *California Journal of Politics and Society, 6*(4). 2014.

CA. Const. art.II §§ 13-19.

CA. Const. art. V § 13.

CA. Const. art. XIII (D) § 4.

CA. Government Code § 995.

CA. Government Code § 995.2.

CA. Government Code § 995.8.

CA. Government Code § 1770(h).

CA. RTC § 96.3(b).

Cain, L. P. & E. J. Rotella. Urbanization, sanitation, and mortality in the Progressive era, 1899-1929, working paper. 1990.

California Lawyer. "California Lawyer Attorneys of the Year." March 2015. Retrieved from https://ww2.callawyer.com/Clstory.cfm?eid=939885& wteid=939885_California_Lawyer_Attorneys_of_the_Year.

California Public Employees' Retirement System Board of Administration. "Pier'Angela paccia Compensation Review. OAH No. 2012020198. Proposed Decision, Attachment A." February 26, 2013.

California Public Employees' Retirement System Board of Administration. "Randy G. Adams Final Compensation Calculation. Case No. 2011-0788. Precedential Decision." March 18, 2015.

California Public Employees' Retirement System Office of Audit Services. "City of Bell Public Agency Review." November 2010.

California State Board of Equalization. "California Property Tax: An Overview." July 2015. Retrieved from http://www.boe.ca.gov/proptaxes/pdf/pub29.pdf.

California State Controller. "Audit Followup." December 10, 2010.

California State Controller. "Audit Report: Administrative and Internal Accounting Controls July 1, 2008 through June 30, 2010." September 22, 2010.

California State Controller. "Audit Report: State and Federal Expenditures July 1, 2008 through June 30, 2010." November 18, 2010.

California State Controller. "Mayer Hoffman McCann, P.C. (Irvine Office) Review Report Quality Control Report For the Firm's Audits of City of Bell and Bell Community Redevelopment Agency for the Fiscal Year Ended June 30, 2009." December 21, 2010.

California State Controller. "Quality Control Review for the Firm's Audits of City of Bell and Bell Community Redevelopment Agency for the Fiscal Year Ended June 30, 2009." December 10, 2010.

California State Controller's Office. "Controller Finds Only Modest Progress in City of Bell." May 22, 2013.

Carr. J.B. "What Have We Learned About the Performance of Council-Manager Government? A Review and Synthesis of the Research." *Public Administration Review, 75*(5). pp. 673–689. 2015.

Casso, J. & Williams, J. "Bell – What Happened and How It Happened: The Role of the New Administration and the City Attorney." *League of California Cities.* May 6, 2011. Retrieved from http://www.cacities.org/getattachment/6202b6ac-a488-4df1-9653-65a16bb3b2ae/5-2011-Spring-James-Casso-Jayne-Williams-Crisis-Ma.aspx.

"Central Los Angeles: Bell Jackpot Casino Closes After 7 Months." *Los Angeles Times.* August 18, 1985.

Center for the Advancement of Public Integrity at Columbia Law School. "The City of Bell Scandal Revisited." N.D. Retrieved from http://web.law.columbia.edu/public-integrity/city-bell-scandal-revisited.

Chiang, J. Letter to County of Los Angeles Auditor – Controller Wendy Watanabe. August 13, 2010.

Choi, C. G., Feiock, R.C., & Bae, J. "The Adoption and Abandonment of Council-Manager Government." *Public Administration Review, 73*(5), pp. 727–736. 2013.

Christensen, K. & Esquivel, P. "Bell Property Tax Rate Second-Highest in L.A. County." *Los Angeles Times.* July 30, 2010. Retrieved from http://articles.latimes.com/2010/jul/30/local/la-me-bell-taxes-new-20100730.

Christensen, K. & Gold, S. "Bell's Bonds Downgraded to Junk Status." *Los Angeles Times.* August 11, 2010. Retrieved from http://articles.latimes.com/2010/aug/11/local/la-me-bell-ratings-20100811.

Churm, S. R. "Asian Game: Good Deal or Fast Shuffle for Card Clubs?" *Los Angeles Times.* February 3, 1985.

City of Bell. "A Landmark Day in the History for the City of Bell." Press Release. March 20, 2013.

City of Bell. "A Summary of the City of Bell's Property Taxes." N.D. Retrieved from http://www.cityofbell.org/home/showdocument?id=4525.

City of Bell. "Agenda Report." 2014.

City of Bell. "Annual Budget Report." *City of Bell 2012/13 Budget.* (Bell, CA: City of Bell, 2011). A4-A6.

City of Bell. "Annual Financial Report for the Fiscal Year Ended June 30, 2011." June 28, 2013.

City of Bell. "Bell Employee Salary Information." 2015.

City of Bell. "Biography of Councilmember Nestor Enrique Valencia." N.D. Retrieved from http://www.cityofbell.org/?NavID=237.

City of Bell. "City Attorney. David Aleshire." N.D. Retrieved from http://cityofbell.org/?NavID=251.

City of Bell. "Code Enforcement." N.D. Retrieved from http://cityofbell.org/?NavID=59.

City of Bell. "Contract Services Agreement for Bond Counsel Services." March 20, 2012.

City of Bell. "First Amendment to Contract Services Agreement for Financial Advisor Services." March 6, 2012.

City of Bell. "FY2014-2015 Budget." 2014.

"City of Bell Hires a Permanent City Attorney: The Bell City Council Has Approved David Aleshire as its Permanent City Attorney." *Los Angeles Times.* June 7, 2011. Retrieved from http://latimesblogs.latimes.com/lanow/2011/06/city-of-bell-hires-a-permanent-city-attorney.html.

City of Bell. "Investments (Bonds)." N.D. Retrieved from http://cityofbell.org/?NavID=177.

City of Bell. "Minutes of the Bell City Council/Bell Community Housing Authority/Successor Agency to the Bell Community Redevelopment Agency/Bell Public Finance Authority." August 1, 2012.

City of Bell. "Minutes of the Bell City Council/Bell Community Housing Authority/Successor Agency to the Bell Community Redevelopment Agency/Bell Public Finance Authority." November 7, 2012.

City of Bell. "Minutes of the Bell City Council/Bell Community Housing Authority/Successor Agency to the Bell Community Redevelopment Agency/Bell Public Finance Authority." December 5, 2012.

City of Bell. "Regular Meeting of the Bell City Council/Bell Community Housing Authority/ Successor Agency to the Bell Community Redevelopment Agency/Bell Public Finance Authority." June 19, 2013.

City of Bell. "Regular Meeting of the Bell City Council/Bell Community Housing Authority/ Successor Agency to the Bell Community Redevelopment Agency/Bell Public Finance Authority/Planning Commission." November 13, 2013.

City of Bell. "Regular Meeting of the Bell City Council/Bell Community Housing Authority/ Successor Agency to the Bell Community Redevelopment Agency/Bell Public Finance Authority/Planning Commission." February 11, 2015.

City of Bell. "Resolution No. 2012-46: Resolution of the City Council of the City of Bell, California to Approve the Form of an Offer to Purchase and Related Documents and an Escrow Agreement and Providing For Matters Related Thereto." June 6, 2012.

City of Bell. "Resolution No. 2014-45: A Resolution Establishing a Charter Review Committee to Evaluate and Make Recommendations to the City Council of the City of Bell for Amendments to the City Charter." August 13, 2014.

City of Bell. "Resolution No. 2014-60: A Resolution of the City Council of the City of Bell, California, Calling an Election and Requesting Placement of a Ballot Measure on the General Municipal Election Ballot for the City of Bell on Tuesday March 3, 2015, to Consider an Amendment to the Bell City Charter to Revise Councilmember Candidate Residency Requirements to 30 Days, Limit Councilmember Compensation and Indemnification, Create a Citizen Planning Commission, Revise Recall Election Procedures, Eliminate the Assistant Chief Administrative Officer Position, Prohibit Financial Conflicts of Interests, and Limit the Term of City Franchises, All Consistent with State Law." October 29, 2014.

"City of Bell Salary Scandal: Jeff Gottlieb and Ruben Vives Tell How They Broke the Story." N.D. Retrieved from https://www.youtube.com/watch?v=6c_qW_HNRmU.

"The City of Bell Scandal Revisited." Conference Transcript. February 19, 2015.

City of Bell. "Special Minutes of Bell City Council." June 6, 2011.

City of Bell v. Superior Court. 220 Cal.App.4th 236 (App. 2013).

Civil Rights Division, "Investigation of the Ferguson Police Department," (report, United States Department of Justice, March 4, 2015), http://www.justice.gov/sites/default/files/opa/press-releases/attachments/2015/03/04/ferguson_police_department_report.pdf, 2.

CNN Wire Staff. "California Officials Reduce Salaries in Response to Outcry." *CNN.* July 27, 2010. Retrieved from http://www.cnn.com/2010/POLITICS/07/27/california.salaries/index.html?section=cnn_latest.

Cole, G. Campaign Flyer for Teresa Jacobo and Luis Ortega. 2009.

Committee to Elect Teresa Jacobo & Luis Artiga. Campaign Flyer. 2009.

Condrey, S (ed). *Handbook of Human Resources Management in Government.* San Francisco: Jossey-Bass, 2005.

Cooper, T. "Big Questions in Administrative Ethics: A Need for Focused, Collaborative Effort." *Public Administration Review*, 64 (4), pp. 395–417. 2004.

Cooper, T. L. *The Responsible Administrator: An Approach to Ethics for Administrative Role*, 3rd ed. San Francisco: Jossey-Bass, 2006.

Corcoran, J. Letter to James Fontenette, LA County DA Investigator. May 6, 2009.

Corcoran, J. Letter to Judge Kathleen Kennedy. January 25, 2012.

Corcoran, J. Letter to LA DA David Demerjian. November 8, 2010.

Corcoran, J. Letter to Mark Loren. May 6, 2009.

Corcoran, J. Letter to Representative Lucille Roybal-Allard. June 21, 2011.

Corcoran, J. Letter to Representative Lucille Roybal-Allard. August 22, 2011.

Corcoran, J. Letter to Thomas O'Brien. May 25, 2011.

Corcoran, J. Letter to US Attorney Andre Birotte. June 13, 2011.

Das, J. & DiRienzo, C. "Spatial Decay of corruption in Africa and the Middle East." *Economic Papers*, 31(4), 2012, pp. 508–514.

Davis, C. "Tipster in Bell Scandal Waited Months for D.A., Then Was Arrested." *Californiawatch.org.* October 11, 2010. Retrieved from http://californiawatch.org/dailyreport/tipster-bell-scandal-waited-months-da-then-was-arrested-5508.

Davis, M. "Chinatown, Revisited? The 'Internationalization' of Downtown Los Angeles." *Sex, Death and God in L.A.* Ed. David Reid. (New York: Pantheon Books, 1992) pp. 29–30.

Davis, M. "The Empty Quarter." *Sex, Death and God in L.A.* Ed. David Reid. (New York: Pantheon Books, 1992). pp. 56–71.

Decker, T. "Braun's Defense is Aggressive Defense." *Los Angeles Times.* May 12, 2001. Retrieved from http://articles.latimes.com/2001/may/12/local/me-62610.

Demerjian, D. Response Letter to Victor Bello. May 19, 2009.

Demir, T. & Reddick, C. "Understanding Shared Roles in Policy and Administration: An Empirical Study of Council-Manager Relations." *Public Administration Review, (72)* 4, 2012, pp. 526–536.

Denhardt, R. & Denhardt, J. "The New Public Service: Serving Rather Than Steering." *Public Administration Review*, 60(6), 2000, pp. 549–599.

Depangher, E. "An In-Depth Look at Public Corruption in California." *California Common Sense.* August 14, 2014. Retrieved from http://cacs.org/research/depth-look-public-corruption-california/.

Deutsch, L. "Bell Assistant City Manager Angela Spaccia Convicted in Corruption Case." *Los Angeles Daily News.* December 9, 2013. Retrieved from http://www.dailynews.com/general-news/20131209/bell-assistant-city-manager-angela-spaccia-convicted-in-corruption-case.

Dillon, J.F. *Treatise on the Law of Municipal Corporations.* Chicago: James Cockroft & Company, 1872.

Dolan, M. "Corruption Convictions Reduced for Former South Gate Official." *Los Angeles Times.* April 15, 2013. Retrieved from http://articles.latimes.com/2013/apr/15/local/la-me-ln-corruption-south-gate-20130415.

Duggan, K. Bell, California: Where our Profession is Making a Difference. *Public Management, 94*(2). pp. 20–21. 2012.

Dunstan, R. "Section V. Gambling in California." *Gambling in California.* California State Library: California Research Bureau, 1997.

Edwards, B. "Hesperia on the Hook for $80,000 of Rizzo's Pension." *Hesperia Star.* August 10, 2010. Retrieved from http://www.hesperiastar.com/article/20071103/SPORTS/311039986/0/SEARCH.

Eggena, E. Settlement Agreement and Release of Claims. December 18, 2013.

Einstein, D. & Burns, M. "Poker Scandal Key to Bell Upset." *Los Angeles Times.* April 12, 1984.

Election Fraud Investigation Unit. Letter to James Corcoran. August 25, 2010.

"Enoch L. Johnson, Ex-Boss in Jersey." *New York Times.* December 10, 1968. Retrieved from http://query.nytimes.com/gst/abstract.html?res=9E05EEDA1230EF34BC4852DFB4678383679EDE

Esquivel, P. "Bell Voters OKd Bonds for Sports Complex that Remains Unbuilt." *Los Angeles Times.* April 29, 2011. Retrieved from http://articles.latimes.com/2011/apr/29/local/la-me-bell-park-20110429.

Esquivel, P. & Gottlieb, J. "Voters in Bell Tell of Possible Fraud." *Los Angeles Times.* August 5, 2010. Retrieved from http://articles.latimes.com/2010/aug/05/local/la-me-election-fraud-bell-20100806.

Esquivel, P. & Lopez, R. "Bell Demanded Extra Fees From Some Businesses." *Los Angeles Times.* November 2, 2010. Retrieved from http://www.latimes.com/local/la-me-1102-bell-fees-20101102-m-story.html#page=1.

"Ex-Bell, Calif., Mayor Oscar Hernandez Too Uneducated to Know His Actions Were Illegal, Lawyer Says." *The Associated Press.* February 21, 2013. http://www.cbsnews.com/news/ex-bell-calif-mayor-oscar-hernandez-too-uneducated-to-know-his-actions-were-illegal-lawyer-says/.

Farr, B. "Ex-Mayor of Bell Gets 3 Years in Prison for Secret Casino Interest." *Los Angeles Times*. May 14, 1985.

"Fighting at the City of Bell Council Meeting * MUST WATCH *." August 5, 2010. Retrieved from https://www.youtube.com/watch?v=Wky-8N0X4qE.

Flores, A. "Agency Takes a Look at Southeast Cities' Governance." *Los Angeles Times*. Retrieved from http://articles.latimes.com/2013/apr/08/local/la-mesoutheast-cities-20130408.

Folkenflik, D. "How the L.A. Times Broke the Bell Corruption Story." *NPR*. September 24, 2010. Retrieved from http://www.npr.org/templates/story/story.php?storyId=130108851.

Fong, A. "The Future Looks Bright for the City of Bell." September 14, 2014. Retrieved from https://vimeo.com/105273066.

Franklin D. Roosevelt Presidential Library & Museum. "Minnewa Bell Papers, circa 1942-1962." N.D. Retrieved from http://www.fdrlibrary.marist.edu/archives/collections/franklin/index.php?p=collections/findingaid&id=73.

Frederickson, H. G. & Meek, J. W. Presentation. Searching for Virtue in the City: Bell and Her Sisters. (white paper at the City of Bell Scandal Revisited Conference, Chapman University, 2015).

Frederickson, H. G., Johnson, G. A., & Wood, C. H. *The Adapted City: Institutional Dynamics and Structural Change*. New York: M.E. Sharpe, 2004.

Fuetsch, M. & Griego, T. "Census Shows Asian, Hispanic Surge." *Los Angeles Times*. February 28, 1991.

Fund, J. "It All Starts with Vote Fraud." *The Wall Street Journal*. August 7, 2010. Retrieved from http://www.wsj.com/articles/SB10001424052748703309704575413393066886472.

Garcia, C. Building BASTA. (white paper at the City of Bell Scandal Revisited Conference, Chapman University, 2015).

Garcia, C. & Saleh, A. "Discussion of Bell Scandal at Chapman University Conference, Panel #1 – Origins & Chronology, The City of Bell Revisited. Chapman University, Wilkinson College of Arts, Humanities, and Social Sciences." February 19, 2015. Retrieved from http://ibc.chapman.edu/Mediasite/Play/aaec6c3312674b7a9151d60f8a5722cf1d.

Gateway Cities Council of Governments. "An Introduction to the Gateway Cities COG." July 2012. Retrieved from http://www.gatewaycog.org/wp-content/uploads/2012/07/An-Introduction-to-the-Gateway-Cities-COG-Rev-July- 2012.pdf. 3.

Glover, S. "Rising Star Caught in Turmoil at the LAFD." *Los Angeles Times*. February 12, 2007.

Goffard, C. "How Bell Hit Bottom." *Los Angeles Times*. December 28, 2010. Retrieved from http://www.latimes.com/local/la-me-bell-origins-20101228-story.html#page=1.

Goffard, C. & Esquival, P. "Bell Voters Cast Out the Old and Opt for the New." *Los Angeles Times*. March 9, 2011. Retrieved from http://articles.latimes.com/2011/mar/09/local/la-me-bell-elections-20110308.

Gottesman, J. "Bell's Hiring of Felon Threatens Reopening of Card Club, State Says." *Los Angeles Times*. December 15, 1993.

Gottesman, J. "Huntington Park, Maywood, Bell May Merge Some Services." *Los Angeles Times*. November 8, 1992. Retrieved from http://articles.latimes.com/1992-11-08/news/ci-546_1_huntington-park.

Gottlieb, J. "A Mountain of Lawsuits Weighs Heavily on Bell." *Los Angeles Times*. February 2, 2013. Retrieved from http://articles.latimes.com/2013/feb/02/local/la-me-bell-challenges-20130203.

Gottlieb, J. "Accused Bell Councilman Had Contacted D.A. About Misconduct in City." *Los Angeles Times*. February 6, 2013. Retrieved from http://articles.latimes.com/2013/feb/06/local/la-me-0207-bell-trial-20130207.

Gottlieb, J. "After Vowing to Cooperate, Robert Rizzo Skips His Sentencing Interview." *Los Angeles Times*. April 17, 2014. Retrieved from http://www.latimes.com/local/lanow/la-me-ln-rizzo-probation-report-20140417-story.html.

Gottlieb, J. "Audits of Bell Were 'Rubber Stamp,' State Controller Says." *Los Angeles Times*. December 22, 2010. Retrieved from http://articles.latimes.com/print/2010/dec/22/local/la-me-bell-audit-20101222.

Gottlieb, J. Bell: A Total Breakdown. (white paper at the City of Bell Scandal Revisited Conference, Chapman University, 2015).

Gottlieb, J. "Bell City Official Threatens to Cut Budget if Council Doesn't Meet." *Los Angeles Times.* February 3, 2011. Retrieved from http://articles.latimes.com/2011/feb/03/local/la-me-adv-bell-paralysis-20110202-1.

Gottlieb, J. "Bell Council Used Little-Noticed Ballot Measure to Skirt State Salary Limits." *Los Angeles Times.* July 23, 2010. Retrieved from 20130117-m-story.html.

Gottlieb, J. "Bell Corruption: Former Councilman Gets One Year in Jail." *Los Angeles Times.* July 11, 2014. Retrieved from http://www.latimes.com/local/lanow/la-me-ln-ex-bell-councilman-sentenced-corruption-20140711-story.html.

Gottlieb, J. "Bell Sues Ex-Councilman, Foundation and Construction Firm Over Contracts." *Los Angeles Times.* June 24, 2014. Retrieved from http://www.latimes.com/local/la-me-0625-bell-lawsuit-20140625-story.html.

Gottlieb, J. "Bell Sues Former Police Chief Randy Adams." *Los Angeles Times.* September 4, 2012. Retrieved from http://articles.latimes.com/2012/sep/04/local/la-me-0905-randy-adams-20120905.

Gottlieb, J. "Bell Sues Its Former City Attorney, Claiming Faulty Legal Advice." *Los Angeles Times.* July 29, 2011. Retrieved from http://latimesblogs.latimes.com/lanow/2011/07/bell-sues-its-former-city-attorney-for-faulty-legal-advice.html.

Gottlieb, J. "Corruption-Scarred Bell Finds Itself on Better Financial Footing." *Los Angeles Times.* December 22, 2013. Retrieved from http://articles.latimes.com/2013/dec/22/local/la-me-bell-settlements-20131223.

Gottlieb, J. "Ex-Bell City Attorney Unsure How His Signature Got on Contracts." *Los Angeles Times.* October 28, 2013. Retrieved from http://articles.latimes.com/2013/oct/28/local/la-me-ln-bell-city-attorney-signature-20131028.

Gottlieb, J. "Ex-Bell Official Seeks $837,000 Payout." *Los Angeles Times.* August 28, 2012. Retrieved from http://articles.latimes.com/2012/aug/28/local/la-me-bell-20120829.

Gottlieb, J. "Former Bell Administrator Robert Rizzo Pleads Guilty to Tax Charges." *Los Angeles Times.* January 14, 2014. Retrieved from http://www.latimes.com/local/la-me-0114-rizzo-20140114-story.html.

Gottlieb, J. "Former Bell Cop Who Blew Whistle on Alleged Corruption Gets Job Back." *Los Angeles Times.* August 3, 2012. Retrieved from http://latimesblogs.latimes.com/lanow/2012/08/former-bell-cop-who-blew-whistle-on-alleged-corruption-gets-job-back.html.

Gottlieb, J. "Former Bell Officials' Pensions Reduced Even Further." *Los Angeles Times.* June 18, 2012. Retrieved from http://articles.latimes.com/print/2012/jun/18/local/la-me-rizzo-20120618.

Gottlieb, J. "In Spaccia Defense, a Simple Premise: Her High Pay Wasn't a Crime." *Los Angeles Times.* November 22, 2013. Retrieved from http://www.latimes.com/local/la-me-1123-angela-spaccia-20131123-story.html.

Gottlieb, J. "Judge Questions Why Bell's Former Police Chief Isn't Facing Corruption Charges." *Los Angeles Times.* December 19, 2011. Retrieved from http://articles.latimes.com/print/2011/dec/19/local/la-me-bell-adams-20111220.

Gottlieb, J. "Judge Refuses to Dismiss Charges Against Ex-Bell Council Members." *Los Angeles Times.* December 2, 2011. Retrieved from http://articles.latimes.com/2011/dec/02/local/la-me-12-02-bell-dismiss-20111202.

Gottlieb, J. "Judge Rejects Former Bell Police Chief's Bid to Double Pensions." *Los Angeles Times.* October 23, 2012. Retrieved from http://articles.latimes.com/print/2012/oct/23/local/la-me-randy-adams-20121024.

Gottlieb, J. "Pensions For Rizzo, 40 Other Bell Employees Will Be Larger Than First Estimated." *Los Angeles Times.* September 30, 2010. Retrieved from http://articles.latimes.com/2010/sep/30/local/la-me-rizzo-pensions-20100930.

Gottlieb, J. "Robert Rizzo Gets 33-Month Prison Term for Tax Fraud." *Los Angeles Times.* April 14, 2014. Retrieved from http://articles.latimes.com/2014/apr/14/local/la-me-rizzo-prison-20140415.

Gottlieb, J. & Knoll, C. "Bell City Clerk Says: 'I Couldn't Ask Any Questions.'" *Los Angeles Times.* January 29, 2013. Retrieved from http://articles.latimes.com/2013/jan/29/local/la-me-0130-bell-trial-20130130.

Gottlieb, J. & Vives, R. "Discussion of Bell at the Los Angeles Press Club. How I Got That Story Series." *Los Angeles Press Club.* Uploaded August 29, 2010. Retrieved from https://youtu.be/6c_qW_HNRmU.

Gottlieb, J. & Vives, R. "Is a City Manager Worth $800,000?" *Los Angeles Times.* July 15, 2010. Retrieved from http://www.latimes.com/local/la-me-bell-salary 20100715,0,3275417.story#axzz30rdlU3Zb.

Gottlieb, J. & Vives, R. "'Pigs Get Fat' Email Was a Joke, Spaccia Testifies at Her Trial." *Los Angeles Times.* November 13, 2013. Retrieved from http://articles.latimes.com/2013/nov/13/local/la-me-angela-spaccia-20131114.

Gottlieb, J. & Vives, R. "Several Documents Point to Questionable Action in Bell." *Los Angeles Times.* November 15, 2013. Retrieved from latimes.com/local/la-me-angela-spaccia-20131116,0,2375241.story.

Gottlieb, J., Becerra, H., & Vives, R. "Bell Admits More Hefty City Salaries." *Los Angeles Times.* August 7, 2010. Retrieved from http://articles.latimes.com/2010/aug/07/local/la-me-bell-salaries-20100807.

Gottlieb, J., Knoll, C., & Goffard, C. "Bell's Rizzo Sentenced to 12 Years in Prison." *Los Angeles Times.* April 16, 2014. Retrieved from http://www.latimes.com/local/la-me-0417-rizzo-prison-20140417-story.html#page=1.

Gottlieb, J., Vives, R., & Leonard, J. "Bell Leaders Hauled Off in Cuffs: Eight Are Held in Scandal the D.A. Calls 'Corruption on Steroids.'" *Los Angeles Times.* September 22, 2010. Retrieved from http://articles.latimes.com/2010/sep/22/local/la-me-bell-arrest-20100922.

Gottlieb, J., Winston, R., & Vives, R. "Bell Council Was Paid For Board That Seldom Met." *Los Angeles Times.* August 25, 2010. Retrieved from http://articles.latimes.com/2010/aug/25/local/la-me-bell-meetings-20100825.

Gottlieb, J., Winston, R., & Vives, R. "Bell's Rizzo Gave $400,000 in City Loans to Two Businesses Without Council Approval." *Los Angeles Times.* September 1, 2010. Retrieved from http://articles.latimes.com/2010/sep/01/local/la-me-bell-loans-20100901-26.

Gottlieb, J., Yoshino, K., & Vives, R. "Bell Doubled Public Service Taxes and Funneled $1 Million to Rizzo, Audit Finds." *Los Angeles Times.* September 23, 2010. Retrieved from http://articles.latimes.com/print/2010/sep/23/local/la-me-bell-audit-20100923.

Grad, S. & Yoshino, K. "Bell's Robert Rizzo Pleads No Contest, To Get 10 to 12 Years in Prison." *Los Angeles Times.* October 3, 2013. Retrieved from http://articles.latimes.com/2013/oct/03/local/la-me-ln-bell-robert-rizzo-pleads-no-contest-prison-20131003.

Granda, C. "Bell Corruption Trial: Luis Artiga Acquitted on All Charges." *ABC 7 News.* March 20, 2013. Retrieved from http://abc7.com/archiver/9035318/.

Grinstein-Weiss, M., Wagner, K. & Edwards, K. "Diffusion of Policy Innovation: The Case of Individual Development Accounts (IDAs) as an Asset-Building Policy." *CSD Working Paper No. 05-08. 2005*

Guillermo Salazar, et al v. City of South Gate, et al. BC280158. Statement of Decision. January 19, 2005.

Hajnal, Z.L. & Lewis, P.G. Municipal Institutions and Voter Turnout in Local Elections. *Urban Affairs Review, 38* (5), pp. 645–668. 2003.

Hamilton, Alexander. *Federalist No. 62.* The Senate. February 27, 1788. Retrieved from http://www.constitution.org/fed/federa62.htm.

Helfand, D. "BELL: Bramble to Quit Post for Colorado Job." *Los Angeles Times.* May 2, 1993.

Heller, M. "Calif. City Can't Escape Defense Costs for Ex-Manager." *Law360.* November 28, 2012. Retrieved from http://www.law360.com/articles/397162/calif-city-can-t-escape-defense-costs-for-ex-manager.

Heller, M. "Nixon Peabody Remains in Scandal-Plagued City's Crosshairs." *Law360.* March 28, 2013. Retrieved from http://www.law360.com/articles/428320/nixon-peabody-remains-in-scandal-plagued-city-s-crosshairs.

Hernandez, M. "Ex-Bell Mayor Oscar Hernandez Sentenced in Corruption Scandal." *ABC 7 News.* July 31, 2014. http://abc7.com/news/ex-bell-mayor-oscar-hernandez-sentenced/230499/.

Hogen-Esch, T. "Failed State: Political Corruption and the Collapse of Democracy in Bell, California." *California Journal of Politics and Policy, 3*(1), pp. 1–28. 2011.

Hogen-Esch, T. "Predator State: Corruption in a Council-Manager System – The Case of Bell, California." (white paper at the City of Bell Scandal Revisited Conference, Chapman University, 2015).

Holguin, R. & Gregory, J. "Bell Corruption Case: Angela Spaccia in Hot Seat." *Abc7.com.* October 24, 2013. Retrieved from http://abc7.com/archive/9298404/.

Husted, B. "Honor Among Thieves: A Transaction-Cost Interpretation of Corruption in Third World Countries", *Business Ethics Quarterly,* 4, 1994, pp. 17–27.

ICMA Municipal Yearbook. "Most Prevalent Form of Local Government in Specific Population Ranges (2013): Council-Manager (CM) vs. Mayor-Council (MC)." 2013.

International City/County Management Association. "About: Overview." N.D. Retrieved from http://icma.org/en/icma/about/organization_overview.

"Jeff Gottlieb: Uncovering the Bell Scandal." December 13, 2012. Retrieved from https://www.youtube.com/watch?v=nsSNyyjuB2k.

Jefferson, Thomas. "10 Nov. 1798, Writings 17:385-91." In *The Writings of Thomas Jefferson*, edited by Andrew A. Lipscomb and Albert Ellery Bergh. Washington: Thomas Jefferson Memorial Association, 1905, http://press-pubs.uchicago.edu/founders/documents/v1ch8s41.html.

Johnston, M. "Accessing Vulnerabilities to Corruption. Indicators and Benchmarks of Government Performance." *Public Integrity,* 12(2), 2010, pp. 125–142.

Judd, D. & Swanstrom, T. *City Politics: The Political Economy of Urban America.* New York: Pearson Longman, 2006.

Keith, T. "5 Former Bell City Council Members Accept Plea Deal, Face Maximum 4 Years in Prison." *Los Angeles Daily News.* April 9, 2014. Retrieved from http://www.dailynews.com/government-and-politics/20140409/5-former-bell-city-council-members-accept-plea-deal-face-maximum-4-years-in-prison.

Kennedy, Robert. Attorney General, remarks before the Joint Defense Appeal of the American Jewish Committee and the Anti-Defamation League of the B'nai B'rith, Chicago, Illinois, June 21, 1961.—*A New Day: Robert F. Kennedy,* ed. Bill Adler, p. 26. 1968.

Kinchin, N. "More Than Writing on a Wall: Evaluating the Role that Code of Ethics Play in Securing Accountability of Public Sector Decision-Makers." *The Australian Journal of Public Administration,* 66(1), 2007, pp. 112–120.

Knoll, C. "Bell Residents Question City's Grass-Roots Organization." *Los Angeles Times.* September 18, 2010. Retrieved from http://articles.latimes.com/2010/sep/18/local/la-me-basta-20100918/2.

Knoll, C. "Bell's City Clerk is First to Testify in Corruption Case." *Los Angeles Times.* January 25, 2013. Retrieved from http://articles.latimes.com/2013/jan/25/local/la-me-bell-trial-20130126.

Knoll C. & Vives, R. "Bell City Clerk Testifies Signatures on Documents Were Forged." *Los Angeles Times.* January 30, 2013. Retrieved from http://articles.latimes.com/2013/jan/30/local/la-me-0131-bell-trial-20130131.

Knoll, C. "Bell's Rizzo Order to Stand Trial for Conflict of Interest, One Charge Dismissed." *Los Angeles Times.* March 16, 2011. Retrieved from http://articles.latimes.com/2011/mar/16/news/la-mem-rizzo-hearing-20110316.

Knoll, C. "Ex-Bell Council Member Gets 2 Years in Prison for Role in Pay Scandal." *Los Angeles Times.* July 25, 2014. Retrieved from http://www.latimes.com/local/lanow/la-me-ln-ex-bell-council-member-sentenced-20140725.html.

Knoll, C. "Final Bell Council Member Sentenced." *Los Angeles Times.* August 1, 2014. Retrieved from http://www.latimes.com/local/politics/la-me-0802-bell-finale-20140802-story.html.

Knoll, C. "Former Bell Councilwoman Teresa Jacobo Gets Two-Year Prison Sentence." *Los Angeles Times.* July 25, 2014. Retrieved from http://www.latimes.com/local/la-me-bell-sentence-20140726-story.html

Knoll, C. "Former Bell Mayor Gets a Year in Jail For Salary Scandal." *Los Angeles Times.* July 31, 2014. Retrieved from http://www.latimes.com/local/lanow/la-me-ln-former-bell-mayor-sentenced-20140731-story.html.

Knoll, C. "Judge Tosses California's Civil Suit Against Ex-Bell Leaders." *Los Angeles Times.* May 6, 2011. Retrieved from http://articles.latimes.com/2011/may/06/local/la-me-bell-attorney-general-20110506.

Knoll, C. & Gottlieb, J. "Bell Trial – 'Were You Robert Rizzo's Girlfriend?' DA Asks." *Los Angeles Times.* February 13, 2013. Retrieved from http://latimesblogs.latimes.com/lanow/2013/02/bell-trial-were-you-robert-rizzos-girlfriend-da-asks.html.

Knoll, C. & Mather, K. "Former Bell Second-in-Command Gets 11 Years in Prison for Corruption." *Los Angeles Times.* April 10, 2014. Retrieved from http://www.latimes.com/local/la-me-spaccia-sentencing-20140411-story.html.

Knoll, C, & Winton, R. "Fast Rise Followed By Hard Fall for Bell's Mayor." *Los Angeles Times.* November 7, 2010. Retrieved from http://articles.latimes.com/2010/nov/07/local/la-me-bell-mayor-20101107.

Knoll, C. Gottlieb, J. & Goffard, C. "Blame Flies as Bell Trial Begins." *Los Angeles Times.* January 24, 2013. Retrieved from http://articles.latimes.com/2013/jan/24/local/la-me-0125-bell-trial-20130125.

Knoll, C., Vives, R. & Winton, R. "Five of 6 Ex-Bell Council Members Found Guilty in Corruption Trial." *Los Angeles Times.* March 20, 2013. Retrieved from http://articles.latimes.com/2013/mar/20/local/la-me-bell-verdict-20130321-1.

Knoll, C., Winton, R. & Vives, R. "Bell Trial Ends in Chaos." *Los Angeles Times.* March 22, 2013. Retrieved from http://www.latimes.com/local/la-me-0322-bell-jury-20130322-story.html#page=1.

Kratzer, Michael. Personal correspondence with Thom Reilly. December 14, 2015.

Laslo, D. & Judd, D. "Building Civic Capacity Through an Elastic State: The Case of St. Louis". *Review of Policy Research, 23*(6), 2006. pp. 1235–1255.

Lee, E. Testimony. October 28, 2013.

Lee, J. & Ellis, V. "Taylor Doctors Are Accused of Prescription Violations." *Los Angeles Times.* September 8, 1990. Retrieved from http://articles.latimes.com/1990-09-08/local/me-466_1_elizabeth-taylor.

Leonard, J., Blankstein, A. & Gottlieb, J. "In E-mails, Bell Official Discussed Fat Salaries." *Los Angeles Times.* February 14, 2011. Retrieved from http://articles.latimes.com/print/2011/feb/14/local/la-me-bell-emails-20110215.

"Lessons from the City of Bell Scandal." *The Intermountain News.* April 18, 2011. Retrieved from https://vimeo.com/22573030.

Levin, C. "Ill Health Forces New CFO to Decline Job—Replacement: Transit Director Will Take Over Financial Reins of County." *Ventura County Star.* January 19, 2001.

The Library of Congress. "31st Congress, 1st Session, Chapter 50." *Statutes at Large.* 1850. pp. 452–453. Retrieved from http://memory.loc.gov/cgibin/ampage?collId=llsl&fileName=009/llsl009.db&recNum=479.

Lloyd, J. "Ex-Bell Councilman Sentenced to Home Confinement in Corruption Scandal." *NBC Los Angeles.* July 23, 2014. http://www.nbclosangeles.com/news/local/Bell-City-Corruption-Scandal-George-Cole-268307752.html.

Lloyd, J. & Wire Reports. "Last of Ex-Bell Officials Sentenced to Jail in Corruption Scandal." *NBC4 Los Angeles- KNBC.* August 1, 2014. Retrieved from http://www.nbclosangeles.com/news/local/Bell-City-Council-Corruption-Scandal-Victor-Bello-269596251.html.

Lopez, R. & Esquivel, P. "Bell Collected Hefty Fines in Numerous Code-Enforcement Cases." *Los Angeles Times.* December 16, 2010. Retrieved from http://www.latimes.com/local/la-me-bell-code-enforcement-20101216-story.html.

Lopez, S. "Robert Rizzo is Service Time Behind Cars." *Los Angeles Times.* January 13, 2011. Retrieved from http://articles.latimes.com/2011/jan/13/local/la-me-0113-lopez-20110113.

Lopez de Haro, A. "Judge Dismisses Allegations of Past Assistant to Ex-Bell City Manager." *City News Service.* June 28, 2013. Retrieved from http://patch.com/california/southgate-lynwood/judge-dismisses-allegations-of-assistant-to-exbell-city-manager.

"Los Angeles County Election Results." *Los Angeles Times.* November 6, 2003. Retrieved from http://articles.latimes.com/2003/nov/06/local/me-la1final6.

Los Angeles County Registrar-Recorder/County Clerk. "March 03, 2015 – Consolidated Elections: Final Official Election Returns." March, 10, 2015. Retrieved from http://rrcc.co.la.ca.us/elect/15032316/rr2316p01.htm#3754.

Lytal, C. "SPPD Panel Examines Lessons from Bell Scandal." *USC News.* October 26, 2010. Retrieved from http://news.usc.edu/29733/SPPD-Panel-Examines-Lessons-from-Bell-Scandal/.

MacBride, M. "Councilman: Robert Rizzo Ran City of Bell." *ABC 7 News.* February 9, 2001. Retrieved from http://abc7.com/archive/7948142/.

Madison, James . "Federalist No. 51: The Structure of the Government Must Furnish the Proper Checks and Balances Between the Different Departments." *New York Packet.* New York, NY, Feb. 6, 1788.

Maddus, G. "D.A. Steve Cooley Under Pressure from City of Bell Police Union to Fully Investigate Ex-Chief Randy Adams." *LA Weekly.* September 27, 2010. Retrieved from http://www.laweekly.com/news/da-steve-cooley-under-pressure-from-city-of-bell-police-union-to-fully-investigate-ex-chief-randy-adams-2390716.

"Mapping L.A.: Southeast." *Los Angeles Times.* N.D. Retrieved from http://maps.latimes.com/neighborhoods/region/southeast/.

Marois, M. "California City With $800,000 Manager Gets Rating Cut by Fitch." *Bloomberg.com.* August 17, 2010. Retrieved from http://www.bloomberg.com/news/articles/2010-08-17/california-city-with-800-000-manager-has-ratings-lowered-to-junk-by-fitch.

Marosi, R. "Clients Have Changed, but Needs Haven't." *Los Angeles Times.* September 9, 2001. Retrieved from http://articles.latimes.com/2001/sep/09/local/me-43904.

Martinez, A. "Angela Spaccia, Former Ventura Employee Embroiled in Bell Pay Scandal, Maintains Innocence." *Ventura County Star.* February 6, 2013. Retrieved from http://www.vcstar.com/news/former-ventura-employee-embroiled-in-bell-pay.

Martinez, M. "Former Bell, California, Administrator Sues City for His $11,000 Monthly Salary." *CNN.* November 1, 2011. Retrieved from http://www.cnn.com/2011/11/01/us/california-bell-lawsuit/.

Mather, K. & Vives, R. "Pleas Close a Chapter in Bell Corruption Scandal." *Los Angeles Times.* April 9, 2014. Retrieved from http://www.latimes.com/local/la-me-bell-council-20140410-story.html.

Matthews, J. Bell and Sacramento. (white paper at the City of Bell Scandal Revisited Conference, Chapman University, 2015).

McGrath, M. "Lessons of Bell, California." *National Civic Review, 102*(1), pp. 51–54. 2013.

McGreevy, P. "Charity Run By Ex-Bell Mayor Didn't Disclose Government Contracts, Attorney General Says". *Los Angeles Times.* August, 21, 2010. Retrieved from http://articles.latimes.com/2010/aug/21/local/la-me-bell-oldtimers-20100821.

McGreevy, P. "Former Bell Mayor Steps Down from Charity that Does Work for the City." *Los Angeles Times.* September 8, 2010. Retrieved from http://articles.latimes.com/2010/sep/08/local/la-me-oldtimers-20100908.

McGroarty, S. *History of Los Angeles County* (Chicago and New York: The American Historical Society, Inc., 1923). pp. 159–176.

McGuire, M. & Olson, M. "The Economics of Autocracy and Majority Rule: The Invisible Hand and the Use of Force," *Journal of Economic Literature*, 34, 1996, pp. 72–96.

McNary, S. "Legacy of Bell's Corruption Case: High Tax Rates, New Civic Engagement." *89.3 KPCC Southern California Public Radio.* January 18, 2013. Retrieved from http://www.scpr.org/blogs/politics/2013/01/18/12088/legacy-bells-corruption-bust-high-tax-rates-new-ci/.

Menes, R. "Corruption in Cities: Graft and Politics in American Cities at the Turn of the Twentieth Century. National Bureau of Economic Research Working Paper Series, 9990. http://www.nber.org/papers/w9900. 2003.

Moodian, M. "Unity Through Crisis: How a Latino and Lebanese American Coalition Helped Save Democracy in the City of Bell." (white paper at the City of Bell

Mooney, C. & Lee, M. "Legislating Morality in the American States." *American Journal of Political Science,* 39, 1995, pp. 599–627.

Nappi, R. "Provider of Hope Finds New Hope." *The Spokesman-Review.* March 1, 1997.

National League of Cities. "Local Government Authority." N.D. Retrieved from http://www.nlc.org/build-skills-and-networks/resources/cities-101/city-powers/local-government-authority.

"Nestor Valencia, Mayor, City of Bell." May 13, 2014. Retrieved from https://www.youtube.com/watch?v=EeP4gdcGdi0.

"New Financial Officer Quits." *Ventura County Star.* January 21, 2001.

Nordyke, P. "Hesperia's City Manager Uses Pomp, Practicality to Set Pace for New Town." *Public Management, 71*(12), p. 28. 1989. Retrieved from http://search.proquest.com/docview/204162893?accountid=13758.

Notice of Entry of Order for Restitution to the City of Bell from Defendant Victor Bello, December 16, 2014.

"Officials: Bell City Corruption Ran Deep." September 22, 2010. Retrieved from https://www.youtube.com/watch?v=X1CHFYnBj10.

Office of the Attorney General, State of California. "Opinion of Bill Lockyer and Clayton Roche Concerning Authority to Set Compensation for Elected Official." January 24, 2001.

O'Neill, A. "Harland Braun is Unfazed by His Clients' Fame." *CNN.* October 4, 2010. Retrieved from http://www.cnn.com/2010/CRIME/10/04/celebrity.lawyer.braun/.

Orzeck, K. "Ex-Calif. Official Gets Nearly 12 Yrs. For Corruption." *Law360.* April 10, 2014. Retrieved from http://www.law360.com/articles/527227/ex-calif-city-official-gets-nearly-12-yrs-for-corruption.

Overend, W. "Official Says Colleague Sexually Harassed Her." *Los Angeles Times.* June 8, 1989. ProQuest Historical Newspapers.

Palmeri, C. "California Official's $800,000 Salary in City of 38,000 Triggers Protests." *Bloomberg News.* July 10, 2010. Retrieved from http://www.bloomberg.com/news/2010-07-20/california-official-s-800-000-salary-in-city-of-38-000-triggers-protests.html.

Pamer, M. "Jury Finds Angela Spaccia Guilty of Multiple Counts in Bell Corruption Trial." *KTLA5.* December 9, 2013. Retrieved from http://ktla.com/2013/12/09/verdict-reached-in-corruption-trial-of-ex-bell-administrator-angela-spaccia/.

Patil, Pratibha Devisingh. "Speech by her excellency the President of India Shrimati Pratibha Devisingh Patil on the eve of demitting office of the president." Speech on eve of leaving office at the end of presidential term, New Delhi, India, July 24, 2012. http://pratibhapatil.nic.in/sp240712.html.

"Pay Scandal, Resignation Deflate City Council in Bell, California." *CNN.* October 5, 2010. Retrieved from http://www.cnn.com/2010/CRIME/10/05/california.bell.council/.

"Paying Too Much? Comparing Property Tax Rates for L.A. County Cities. [2010]." *Los Angeles Times.* N.D. Retrieved from http://www.latimes.com/local/la-me-city-property-tax-table-htmlstory.html.

People ex rel Brown v. Rizzo, Spaccia, Adams, Hernandez, Jacobo, Cole, Bello, and Mirabal. BC445497. Attorney General's Motion for Appointment of a Monitor for the City of Bell and Supporting Filings. November 17, 2010.

People ex rel Brown v. Rizzo, Spaccia, Adams, Hernandez, Jacobo, Cole, Bello, and Mirabal. BC445497. First Amended Complaint. November 15, 2010.

People ex rel Brown v. Rizzo, Spaccia, Adams, Hernandez, Jacobo, Cole, Bello, and Mirabal. BC445497. Order on Demurrers and Motions to Strike Directed to First Amended Complaint. May 2, 2011.

People ex rel Harris v. Rizzo. 214 Cal.App.4th 921 (App. 2013).

People ex rel Harris v. Spaccia, Hernandez, Jacobo, Cole, Bello, and Mirabal. BC445497. Second Amended Complaint. N.D.

People v. Bello. BA376025. People's Sentencing Memorandum. July 25, 2014.

People v. Bello. BA376025-05. Sentencing Minutes. August 1, 2014.

People v. Cole. BA376025. Notice of Entry of Order for Restitution to the City of Bell from Defendant George Wendell Cole, Jr. December 16, 2014.

People v. Cole. BA376025. People's Sentencing Memorandum. July 23, 2014.

People v. Cole. BA376025-04. Sentencing Minutes. July 23, 2014.

People v. Hernandez. BA376025. People's Sentencing Memorandum. July 24, 2014.

People v. Hernandez. BA376025-01. Sentencing Minutes. July 31, 2014.

People v. Hernandez. BA376025-05. Sentencing Minutes. August 1, 2014.

People v. Hernandez. BA376025. Notice of Entry of Order for Restitution to the City of Bell from Defendant Oscar Hernandez, December 16, 2014.

People v. Hernandez. BA376025. Supplemental Sentencing Brief of Defendant Oscar Hernandez July 23, 2014.

People v. Hernandez, Jacobo, Mirabel, Cole, Bello, & Artiga. BA376025. Preliminary Hearing. February 7, 2011.

People v. Hernandez, Jacobo, Mirabel, Cole, Bello, & Artiga. BA376025. Preliminary Hearing. February 9, 2011.

People v. Hernandez, Jacobo, Mirabel, Cole, Bello, & Artiga. BA376025. Preliminary Hearing. February 14, 2011.

People v. Hernandez, Jacobo, Mirabel, Cole, Bello, & Artiga. BA376025. Preliminary Hearing. February 15, 2011.

People v. Hernandez, Jacobo, Mirabel, Cole, Bello, & Artiga. BA376025. Testimony of Maria Grimaldo. S.C. CA 2011.

People v. Jacobo. BA376025. People's Sentencing Memorandum. July 21, 2014.

People v. Jacobo. BA376025-02. Sentencing Minutes. July 25, 2014.

People v. Jacobo. BA376025. Notice of Entry of Order for Restitution to the City of Bell from Defendant Theresa Jacobo. December 16, 2014.

People v. Mirabal. BA376025. People's Sentencing Memorandum. July 7, 2014.

People v. Mirabal. BA376025-03. Sentencing Minutes. July 11, 2014.

People v. Rizzo. BA376026, BA377197, BA382701. Deposition. April 16, 2014.

People v. Rizzo. BA276026, BA377197, BA382701. Plea Minutes. October 3, 2013.

People v. Rizzo. BA276026, BA377197, BA382701. Sentencing Minutes. April 16, 2014.

People v. Rizzo. BC445497. Videotaped deposition of Robert Rizzo. December 15, 2011.

People v. Rizzo. BC445497. Videotaped deposition of Robert Rizzo. May 14, 2014.

People v. Rizzo. BA276026, BA377197, BA382701. Notice of Entry of Order for Restitution to the City of Bell from Defendant Robert Rizzo. April, 16, 2014.

People v. Rizzo, Spaccia. BA376026, BA77197, BA382701. Consolidated Criminal Compliant. September 12, 2013.

People v. Rizzo, Spaccia. BA382701. Criminal Indictment. March 29, 2011.

People v. Rizzo, Spaccia, Artiga, and Hernandez. BA376026. Amended Felony Complaint. February 7, 2011.

People v. Rizzo, Spaccia, Artiga, and Hernandez. BA376026. Preliminary Hearing. February 22, 2011.

People v. Rizzo, Spaccia, Artiga, and Hernandez. BA376026. Preliminary Hearing. February 28, 2011.

People v. Rizzo, Spaccia, Artiga, and Hernandez. BA376026. Preliminary Hearing. March 1, 2011.

People v. Rizzo, Spaccia, Artiga, and Hernandez. BA376026. Preliminary Hearing. March 4, 2011.

People v. Rizzo, Spaccia, Artiga, and Hernandez. BA376026. Preliminary Hearing. March 7, 2011.

People v. Rizzo, Spaccia, Artiga, and Hernandez. BA376026. Preliminary Hearing. March 10, 2011.

People v. Rizzo, Spaccia, Artiga, and Hernandez. BA376026. Testimony of Lourdes Garcia. S.C. CA 2011.

People v. Rizzo, Spaccia, Artiga, and Hernandez. BA376026. Testimony of Roger Ramirez. S.C. CA 2011.

People v. Spaccia. BA376026, BA382701. Sentencing Memorandum. January 22, 2014.

People v. Spaccia. BA376026, BA382701. Sentencing Minutes. April 10, 2014.

People v. Spaccia. BA376026. Defense's Exhibits EE to ZZ. N.D.

People v. Spaccia. BA376026. People's Exhibits 1 to 71. N.D.

People v. Spaccia. BA376026. People's Exhibits 72 to 100. N.D.

People v. Spaccia. BA376026. People's Exhibits 101 to 156. N.D.

People v. Spaccia. BA376026. People's Exhibits 157 to 184. N.D.

People v. Spaccia. BA376026. People's Exhibits 201 to 209. N.D.

People v. Spaccia. BA 382701, BA376026. Spaccia's Trial. November 6, 2013.

People v. Spaccia. BA 382701, BA376026. Spaccia's Trial. November 14, 2013.

People v. Spaccia. BA 382701, BA376026. Spaccia's Trial. November 15, 2013.

People v. Spaccia. BA 382701, BA376026. Spaccia's Trial. November 18, 2013.

People v. Spaccia. BA376026, BA382701. Notice of Entry of Order for Restitution to the City of Bell from Defendant Pier'Angela Spaccia. April 10, 2014.

Petracca, M. & O'Brien, K. "Municipal Term Limits In Orange County, California." *National Civic Review, 83*(2), 2007, pp. 87–94.

Priest, W. Letter to David Demerjian, Los Angeles County District Attorney's Office RE: Response by City of Bell to Letter Inquiring About Setting of City Councilmember Salaries. June 23, 2010.

Pringle, P. "Injury Cited By Ex-Bell Police Chief In Disability Pension Claim Didn't Prevent Him from Exercising." *Los Angeles Times.* October 5, 2010. Retrieved from http://articles.latimes.com/2010/oct/05/local/la-me-randy-adams-20101005.

Pringle, P., Knoll, C., & Murphy, K. "Rizzo's Horse Had Come In." *Los Angeles Times.* August 22, 2010. Retrieved from http://www.pulitzer.org/archives/9205.

"Protests in Bell: City Residents Say 'Enough!'" July 27, 2010. Retrieved from https://www.youtube.com/watch?v=v1effEnDisrM.

Quaz, R., Langley, S. & Tlii, A. "Corruption Contagion in South Asia and East Asia: An Econometric Study. *International Journal of Developing Societies,* 2 (3), 2013, pp. 87–95.

Quintana, A. "Argument Against Measure C." N.D. Retrieved from http://www.cityofbell.org/home/showdocument?id=5732.

Quintana, A. Press Release. September 27, 2013.

Rainey, J. "On the Media: How Many More Bells Are Out There?" *Los Angeles Times.* July 21, 2010. Retrieved from http://articles.latimes.com/2010/jul/21/entertainment/la-et-ontheme-dia-20100721.

Ravindhran, S. "Voter Fraud Alleged in Troubled City of Bell." *ABC7 Los Angeles KABC.* July 27, 2010. Retrieved from http://abc7.com/archive/7578966/.

Reid, T. "SEC Closes Investigation into Bell, Calif. Bond Debt." *Reuters.* February 24, 2015. Retrieved from http://www.reuters.com/article/2015/02/24/usa-municipals-bell-idUSL1N0VY3EF20150224.

Reilly, T, & Tekniepe, R.J. "Collaborative Regional Networked Systems." In Balutis, A., and Buss, T. (editors), *American Governance 3.0: Rebooting the Public Square.* Armonk, NY: M.E. Sharpe Publishing, 2011.

Rizzo, R. & Lee, E. Email Exchange RE: Police Chief Contract. July 9-10, 2009.

Rizzo, R. Letter to City of Bell Mayor Ray Johnson RE: Chief Administrative Officer Recruitment. June 24, 1993.

Rizzo v. Bell. BC472566. Complaint for Damages. October 31, 2011.

Rizzo v. Bell. BC472566. Superior Court of California County of Los Angeles – Case Summary. July 5, 2015. Retrieved from http://www.lacourt.org/casesummary/ui/casesummary.aspx?.

Rizzo v. ICMA Retirement Corporation, et al. CV 12-02690-RGK (VBKx). Order.

"Robert Rizzo Sentenced to 33 Months in Prison for Tax Evasion." *Abc7.com.* April 14, 2014. Retrieved from http://abc7.com/archive/9503371/.

Rodgers, J. Rebuilding Bell, California: Review and Recommendations for Continued Improvement of Accountability, Oversight, and Transparency. (white paper at the City of Bell Scandal Revisited Conference, Chapman University, 2015).

Rogers, J. "Ex-Officials Convicted in California Corruption Case." *The Big Story.* March 20, 2013. Retrieved from http://bigstory.ap.org/article/verdicts-reached-bell-calif-corruption-case.

Rogers, J. "Voters in Troubled California City Bring New Day." *Huffington Post.* March 9, 2011. Retrieved from http://www.huffingtonpost.com/huff-wires/20110309/us-bell-salaries-recall/.

Rogers, J. "Voters in Troubled California City Bring New Day." *The Washington Post.* March 9, 2011. Retrieved from http://www.washingtonpost.com/wp-dyn/content/article/2011/03/09/AR2011030900219.html.

Romero, D. "Robert Rizzo Sues City of Bell for $1.5 Million." *LA Weekly.* November 11, 2013. Retrieved from http://www.laweekly.com/news/robert-rizzo-sues-city-of-bell-for-15-million-2388051.

Saavedra, T. "Building Inspectors Took Bribes, Left New House Unlivable, Suit Says." *The Orange County Register.* February 12, 2010. Retrieved from http://www.ocregister.com/taxdollars/strong-477324-wink-building.html.

Saavedra, T. "Yorba Linda Case Linked to Bell Figure." *The Orange County Register.* September 30, 2010. Retrieved form http://www.ocregister.com/taxdollars/strong-477694-city-winks.html.

Seattle Times Staff. "Ex-Official in Bell, Calif., Scandal Has Auburn Farm." *Seattle Times.* September 22, 2010. Retrieved from http://www.seattletimes.com/seattle-news/ex-official-in-bell-calif-scandal-has-auburn-farm/.

Sforza, T. Baby Bells. (white paper at the City of Bell Scandal Revisited Conference, Chapman University, 2015).

"SH City Attorney Working Pro Bono to Help Bell Citizens Recall Their Controversial Officials." *Signal Tribune.* November 10, 2010. Retrieved from http://www.signaltribunenewspaper.com/?p=8410.

"Southeast/Long Beacg: No Bingo". *Los Angeles Times.* September, 28, 1995. Retrieved from http://articles.latimes.com/1995-09-28/local/me-50777_1_bingo-parlor.

Spaccia, A. Email Exchange to Alan Pennington. November 5-18, 2007.

Spaccia, A. Statement of Economic Interests Cover Page Form 700. 2005.

Spertus, J. Drawing the Line Between Crime and Mistake. (white paper at the City of Bell Scandal Revisited Conference, Chapman University, 2015).

Spertus, Landes & Umhofer, LLP. "James W. Spertus – Managing Partner." N.D. Retrieved from http://www.spertuslaw.com/attorney/james-w-spertus/.

Sprague, M. "Bell Sues Ex-Councilman, Construction Company, Foundation for $3.4 Million." *Whittier Daily News.* June 25, 2014. Retrieved from http://www.whittierdailynews.com/general-news/20140625/bell-sues-ex-councilman-construction-company-foundation-for-34-million.

State of California Department of Justice Office of the Attorney General. "Brown Sues to Recover Bell Officials' Excessive Salaries and Cut Their Pensions, And Announces Other Steps on Public Pay and Benefits." September 1, 2010. Retrieved from http://oag.ca.gov/news/press-releases/brown-sues-recover-bell-officials-excessive-salaries-and-cut-their-pensions-and.

Stream, C. "Health Reform in the States: A Model of State small group health insurance market reforms, *Political Research Quarterly* 52(3) 1999, pp. 499–526.

Sullivan, J. "'Y' Has List of Needs, A to Z Management Team Good Fit for Heavily Relied-Upon Resources." *The Spokesman-Review.* February 23, 1997.

Super Lawyers. "Harland W. Braun." N.D. Retrieved from http://profiles.superlawyers.com/california-southern/los-angeles/lawyer/harland-w-braun/2946e2d6-c0e0-4644-a040-16e25d7145d8.html.

Super Lawyers. "James W. Spertus." N.D. Retrieved from http://profiles.superlawyers.com/california-southern/los-angeles/lawyer/james-w-spertus/bd14c9fc-cadb-4fca-82cd-bc44567fa1f4.html.

Superior Court of California, County of Los Angeles. George Mirabal (Redacted). April 3, 2014.

Superior Court of California, County of Los Angeles. George Wendell Cole, Jr. (Redacted). April 3, 2014.

Superior Court of California, County of Los Angeles. Letters of Guardianship – Pier' Francesco Spaccia and Pier' Angela Spaccia. December 20, 1974.

Superior Court of California, County of Los Angeles. Oscar Cantu Hernandez (Redacted). April 3, 2014.

Superior Court of California, County of Los Angeles. Probation Officer's Report: Angela Spaccia. February 26, 2014.

Superior Court of California, County of Los Angeles. Probation Officer's Report: Robert Adrian Rizzo. March 12, 2014.

Superior Court of California, County of Los Angeles. Teresa Jacobo (Redacted). April 3, 2014.

Superior Court of California, County of Los Angeles. Victor Antonio Bello (Redacted). April 3, 2014.

Svara, J.H. "The Ethics Primer for Public Administrators in Government and Nonprofit Organizations." Sudbury, MA: Jones and Bartlett, 2007

Svara, J. "Who Are the Keepers of the Code? Articulating and Upholding Ethical Standards in the field of Public Administration." *Public Administration Review, (74)* 3, 2014, pp. 561–569.

Tarango, D. Memo to Bell Planning Chair and Commissioners Concerning Architectural Review Board Project. August 17, 2009.

Tasci, C. "Former Bell Councilman Luis Artiga's House in Chino Quiet After Verdict." *Daily Bulletin News.* March 20, 2013. Retrieved from http://www.dailybulletin.com/general-news/20130320/former-bell-councilman-luis-artigas-house-in-chino-quiet-after-verdict

Terry, L. "Professionalism over Politics in the Shift to Council-Manager Government." *More Than Mayor or Manager: Campaigns to Change Form of Government in America's Large Cities*, edited by James H. Svara and Douglas J. Watson. Washington DC: Georgetown University Press, 2010. pp. 225–244.

Trounstine, J. *Political Monopolies in American Cities.* Chicago: University of Chicago Press, 2008.

United States Census Bureau. "Urban and Rural Populations 1790 to 1990, 1990 Census Population and Housing." *1990 Population and Housing Unit Counts: United States.* N.D. Retrieved from http://www.census.gov/population/www/censusdata/files/table-4.pdf.

United States Census Bureau. "Bell California Census QuickFacts." Last Modified October 14, 2015. Retrieved from http://quickfacts.census.gov/qfd/states/06/0604870.html

United States District Court, Central District of California CR 13-878GHK. Criminal Minutes, Sentencing and Judgment for Robert A. Rizzo. April 14, 2014.

U.S. Attorney's Office. "Former Chief Administrative Officer for City of Bell Agrees to Plead Guilty to Conspiracy and Tax Charges in Plot to Avoid Income Taxes." December 12, 2013. Retrieved from https://www.fbi.gov/losangeles/press-releases/2013/former-chief-administrative-officer-for-city-of-bell-agrees-to-plead-guilty-to-conspiracy-and-tax-charges-in-plot-to-avoid-income-taxes.

U.S. District Court Central District of California criminal minutes and sentencing judgement, CR 13-878 GHK, April 14, 2014.

U.S. Federal Communications Commission. "Newspapers." *Part One: The Media Landscape, Section One: Commercial Media.* N.D. pp. 33–57. Retrieved from https://transition.fcc.gov/osp/inc-report/INoC-1-Newspapers.pdf.

Valencia, C. "Bell Club's Fiscal Health Called Better Yet Delicate." *Los Angeles Times.* January 19, 1986.

Valencia, N. "Comments at Bell Residents Club Meeting." August 19, 2010. Retrieved from https://www.youtube.com/watch?v=j513gO_oKqM.

Vives, R. "Bell Councilman Accidental Hero by Staying Clear of Corruption Scandal." *Los Angeles Times.* October 13, 2010. Retrieved from http://articles.latimes.com/print/2010/oct/13/local/la-me-bell-councilman-20101009.

Vives. R. "Bell Seeks Emergency Legislation to Certify Election Results." *Los Angeles Times.* March 16, 2011. Retrieved from http://latimesblogs.latimes.com/lanow/2011/03/bell-emergency-legislation-election-results.html.

Vives, R. & Becerra, H. "Top Public Pension Earner Sues Vernon After CALPERS Cuts His Benefit." *Los Angeles Times*. July 22, 2013. Retrieved from http://articles.latimes.com/2013/jul/22/local/la-me-highest-pension-20130723.

Vives, R. & Gottlieb, J. "3 Bell Leaders to Quit in Pay Scandal." *Los Angeles Times*. July 23, 2010. Retrieved from http://articles.latimes.com/2010/jul/23/local/la-me-bell-council-20100723.

Vives. R. & Gottlieb, J. "Bell Council Members Cut Salaries 90%; Some Will Forgo Pay." *Los Angeles Times*. July 27, 2010. Retrieved from http://articles.latimes.com/2010/jul/27/local/la-me-bell-salaries-20100727.

Vo, T. "Keeping City Hall Accountable: Reflections on the Bell Scandal." *Voice of OC*. February 20, 2015. Retrieved from http://voiceofoc.org/2015/02/keeping-city-hall-account-able-reflections-on-the-bell-scandal

Walton, A. "Why is Public Corruption Endemic in Southeast Los Angeles County." 89.3 KPCC. May 20, 2014. Retrieved from http://www.scpr.org/blogs/politics/2014/05/20/16648/why-is-public-corruption-endemic-in-southeast-los/.

Webster, K. "Bell, Calif. Pays $257,000 IRS Fine, Retains Tax Exempt Status on $35M GOs." *The Bond Buyer*. November 26, 2014. Retrieved from http://www.bondbuyer.com/news/regionalnews/bell-calif-pays-257000-irs-fine-retains-tax-exempt-status-on-35m-gos-1068302-1.html.

Wikipedia. "Bell, California." Last Modified July 27, 2015. Retrieved from https://en.wikipedia.org/wiki/Bell,_California.

Wikipedia. "John Forrest Dillon." Last Modified September 20, 2015. Retrieved from https://en.wikipedia.org/wiki/John_Forrest_Dillon.

Willmore, D. "City of Bell Agenda Report RE: November 13, 2013. Consideration of Stipulation for Settlement with Dexia Credit Local Including Limited Settlement Terms with BB& K." April 3, 2013.

Willmore, D. "City of Bell Agenda Report RE: Status Report On Recent Court of Appeal Victory Against Robert Rizzo's Claim for Legal Fees." November 13, 2013.

Willmore, D. City of Bell – Reformed and Reborn. (white paper at the City of Bell Scandal Revisited Conference, Chapman University, 2015).

Willon, P. "Lawmakers Push to Scrap Prop. 13 Tax Limits for Factories and Business." *Los Angeles Times*. June 10, 2015. Retrieved from http://www.latimes.com/local/political/la-me-pc-lawmakers-prop-13-tax-limits-20150610-story.html.

Wilson, S. "Weapons Dealer from City of Bell Ranks 10th for Most Guns Found in Mexico." *LA Weekly*. December 13, 2010. Retrieved from http://www.laweekly.com/news/weapons-dealer-from-city-of-bell-ranks-10th-for-most-guns-found-in-mexico-2397797.

Wilson, Woodrow, "The New Freedom." 1912. Retrieved from: https://www.gutenberg.org/files/14811/14811-h/14811-h.htm.

Winton, R. "Attorney General's Lawsuit Against Bell Officials Could be in Jeopardy." *Los Angeles Times*. November 5, 2010. Retrieved from http://articles.latimes.com/2010/nov/05/local/la-me-bell-ag-20101105.

Winton, R. "Lawsuit Against Bell Suggests Voter Fraud in 2009 Election." *L.A. Now*. July 27, 2010. Retrieved from http://latimesblogs.latimes.com/lanow/2010/07/bell-lawsuit-suggests-voter-fraud.html.

Winton, R., Esquivel, P. & Vives, R. "Federal Probe Targets Possible Civil Rights Violations in Bell." *Los Angeles Times*. September 10, 2010. Retrieved from http://articles.latimes.com/2010/sep/10/local/la-me-bell-feds-20100910.

Wood, C. "Voter Turnout in City Elections." *Urban Affairs Review*, *38* (5), pp. 209–231. 2002.

Woolery, E. "Great Park Audit a Cautionary Tale." *Orange County Register*. April 10, 2015.

Writ, C. "Dillon's Rule." *Virginia Town & City*, *24*(8) (1989): pp. 12–15. Retrieved from http://www.fairfaxcounty.gov/dmb/fcpos/dillon.pdf.

Index

About The Authors

Dr. Thom Reilly is director of the Morrison Institute for Public Policy and professor in the School of Public Affairs at Arizona State University. He is a former chief executive officer/county manager for Clark County, Nevada (the Las Vegas Valley), and head of the child welfare system for Nevada. Reilly received his master's and doctorate in public administration from the University of Southern California (USC) and a master's in social work from Arizona State University. He is a fellow of the National Academy of Public Administration (NAPA). His research focuses on governance issues as well as trends in public pay and benefits. He is author of the book *Rethinking Public Sector Compensation: What Ever Happened to the Public Interest?* (M.E. Sharpe, 2012).

Gregory D. Coordes received his law degree from the University of Chicago Law School and his master of public policy degree from Arizona State University. Throughout his career he has worked in government on the local, state, federal, and international levels. Gregory practiced law in New York before moving with his wife, Laura, to Arizona.